Brilliant Origami

Brilliant Origami

A Collection
of
Original Designs

David Brill

Japan Publications, Inc.

Published by Japan Publications, Inc., Tokyo and New York

Distributors:
UNITED STATES: Kodansha America, Inc., through Oxford University Press, 198 Madison Avenue, New York, N.Y. 10016. CANADA: Fitzhenry & Whiteside Ltd., 195 Allstate Parkway, Markham, Ontario, L3R 4T8. UNITED KINGDOM & EUROPEAN CONTINENT: Premier Book Marketing Ltd., 1 Gower Street, London WC1E 6HA. AUSTRALIA AND NEW ZEALAND: Bookwise International, 54 Crittenden Road, Findon, South Australia 5023. THE FAR EAST AND JAPAN: Japan Publications Trading Co., Ltd., 1-2-1, Sarugaku-cho, Chiyoda-ku, Tokyo 101.

First edition: January 1996
Second printing: October 1997

LCCC No.98-081402
ISBN 0-87040-896-8

Printed in U.S.A.

Foreword

1978: It's a sunny afternoon and John Smith is driving me back to Southampton. I sit admiring the Sussex countryside, as John proves to be an excellent guide. Naturally the conversation is about folding since we are on our way home from the British Origami Society convention in Birmingham. I ask him a question: "John, who do you consider to be the greatest living folder ?" He replies: "Dave Brill".

1994: Late one sunny afternoon I am sitting at home in Paris. Much water has flowed under the bridges of my city and I still agree with John's statement. Dave is great because he is unique. When he creates a model he can already see the finished form in his mind; he has a profound understanding of that form, and his skills as a folder are directed by it. Hence the beauty of his models - his Elephant is a perfect example. Matisse said that the hand must be submissive and obedient to the artist's intent. He also added that the servant must never be allowed to become the master...

Study Dave's models and fold them so that your fingers can appreciate this integrity.

Paperfolding is more than just a recreational pastime adopted from the Far East and intended merely to amuse our children. When one folds a piece of paper, one leaves behind a permanent trace, namely the fold. With the passing of time our joys, our sorrows, our passions and our cares are successively engraved on our faces; we call them wrinkles. Plateau, valley, mountain and depression are some of the words we use to describe our geographical surroundings. It is within the folds and contours of the brain that our ideas are born, and it is the contours of our hands that allow us to caress our loved ones. We will not dwell on the folds of the human heart; they conceal a secret part of us, hidden away within, undisclosed to others. Let us not squander that.

It is important to realize that the very act of folding paper implies a far greater understanding of man and his universe than one might at first imagine. Dave Brill is not content with a superficial view; take any model in this book and you will find it embodies everything we have mentioned.

It is a great honour for a Frog* to talk about a Roast† Beef.

Jean-Claude Correia
Founder of Mouvement Francais des Plieurs de Papier
(French Paperfolders' Association)
(translation: Edwin Corrie)

※ Frog: Frenchman
† Roast Beef: Englishman

Preface

This book has been long delayed. While my fellow origami friends and creators have been swift to make collections of their designs, I have not followed suit. This is for many reasons, and is despite many hard-to-ignore demands from those who have appreciated my work. But finally I have managed to clear my desk and set aside any excuses for not getting down to the job. I apologize deeply to those who have waited for too long and I hope that they will find their patience has been in some way rewarded.

I began my acquaintance with origami in my childhood through the innocent pages of Alfred Bestall's Rupert Annuals. As I continued to learn more designs, and to acquire new origami books, I realized that origami was for me the perfect activity. No complicated tools or equipment are required, and the raw material is the most easily obtainable: the simple sheet of paper. It was not until I made contact with the British Origami Society in the mid 1970's, meeting Martin Wall and Max Hulme, themselves already accomplished creators, that I was moved to design my own original models. A thrilling period of friendly rivalry followed where the three of us tried to out-do each other with new techniques and challenges. In any creative sphere, one is stimulated by the ideas of others, and I am the first to admit that my work is a distillation of other people's designs. I freely acknowledge my debts to my talented colleagues. However, frequently I have drawn inspiration from areas other than origami, such as architecture,geometry, art and nature. I encourage all potential origami creators not to wear blinkers! Seek your ideas everywhere.

The present richness of origami has, I believe, been accentuated by its inherent restrictions: either the established but unwritten rules such as "no cuts, no glue, no paint", or the personally adopted ones: in my case these include "economy, three dimensionality and avoidance of classic geometry." I like to draw the analogy between origami styles and the richness of cigarette advertising, which also is restricted almost to the point of censorship. Here in England the adman's ingenuity to overcome these restrictions has been taxed to its maximum, and the results are always cryptic and stimulating.

I believe my origami work provides a bridge between the styles seen in the West: analytical, highly detailed and engineered; and the Eastern approach: minimal and artistic. Thanks to the lessons learned from my painting teacher, Alan Thompson, I have tried to emphasize the form of the whole rather than home-in on details. The danger is to think that the whole subject is the sum of its parts and to fold each of these in precise representation. This approach leads to awkward designs, lacking integrity. To overcome this temptation I have learned to step back from my work periodically, or to hold it at arms length, to judge the overall effect, much as a painter will view his own work in the making.

In my work I have tried (not always successfully) to cultivate a sensitive touch, always to have respect for the paper, and never to ask it to do more than it is able.

This "touch" is a thing lacking in the work of many Western folders, whose work can be contorted and ugly. I admire those origami artists whose work is finely executed: anyone can appreciate delicacy and finesse, but sadly they are things rarely seen.

In conclusion I sincerely hope you enjoy folding the designs featured in the following pages. The work has been long and painstaking, but ultimately hugely rewarding for me.

Dave Brill

Gift Box (p.46), Box and Lid (p.54)

"Woven" Strip Dodecahedron(p.82), and Double Cubes (pp.90 and 92)

Lioness, Lion and Lion Cub (pp. 150, 159 and 163)

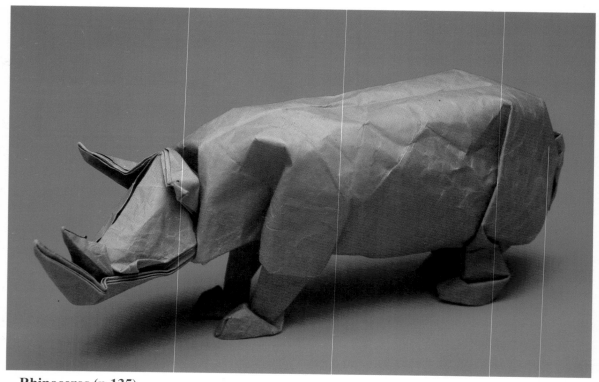

Rhinoceros (p.135)

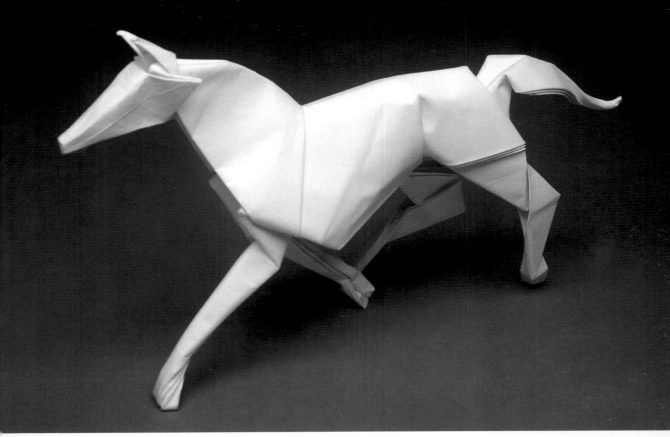

Horse (p.168)

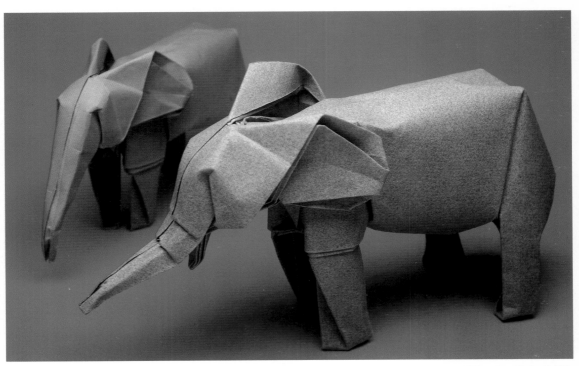

Elephant (p.140)

11

Fox Hunt (pp.123, 125 and 128)

Oxford and Cambridge Boat Race (pp.198–201)

Geppetto, Pinocchio (pp.216 and 220) and
Spelling Book (p.224)

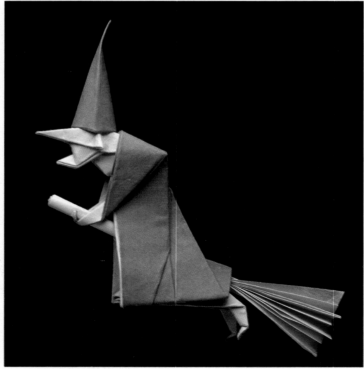

Hallowe'en Witch (p.210)

Christmas Tree Fairy (p.183)

Three Wise Men (pp.204–209)

Show Jumper (p.212)

Father Christmas, Reindeer and Sleigh (pp.193, 228 and 230)

Acknowledgments

Thanks are due to the following friends and supporters for the help and encouragement they have given me during the preparation of this book:

Humi Huzita, for putting me in touch with the publishers, and insisting that I start the work in the first place;

Kunihiko Kasahara and Tomoko Fuse, for assuring the publishers of my good intentions;

Jean-Claude Correia, for his broad viewpoint and open mind;

David Petty, for his painstaking proof-reading;

John Smith, for his critical approval of my work;

Paul Jackson, for helping me to remove my "blinkers"from time to time;

Max Hulme and Martin Wall, for their friendly and encouraging rivalry;

Neil and Hazel McAllister, for the meticulous photographic work;

Doreen Montgomery, for her advice with the complexities of the publisher's contract;

The late Iwao Yoshizaki, his successor Yukishige Takahashi, Toshihiro Kuwahara and Akiko Shibata of Japan Publications, Inc. who have demonstrated so much faith in me;

All my friends in the international origami movement who have shown appreciation for my work;

The British Origami Society which has given me so many opportunities in the origami world.

I thank you all deeply.

CONTENTS

Signs and Symbols

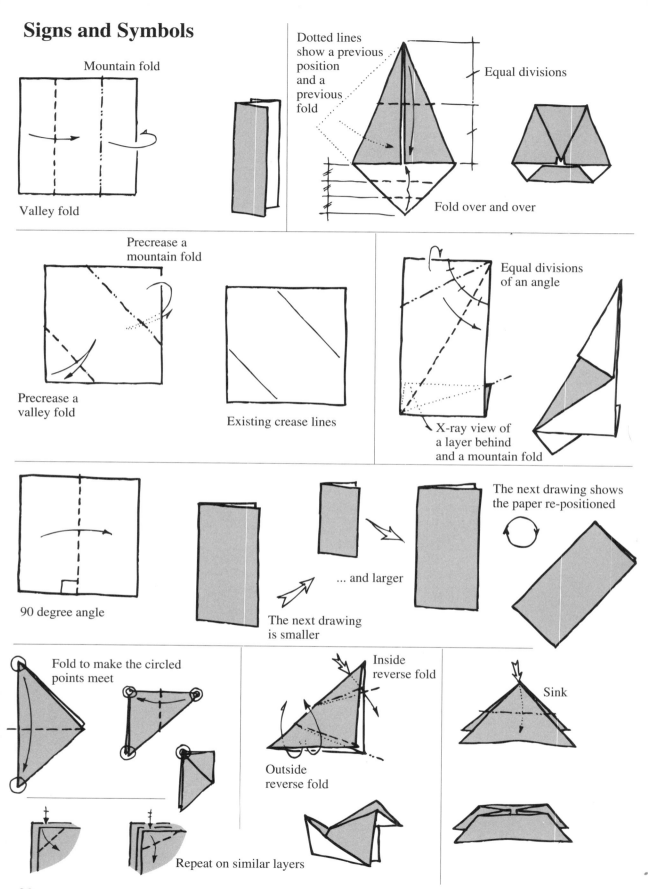

Mountain fold

Valley fold

Dotted lines show a previous position and a previous fold

Equal divisions

Fold over and over

Precrease a mountain fold

Precrease a valley fold

Existing crease lines

Equal divisions of an angle

X-ray view of a layer behind and a mountain fold

90 degree angle

The next drawing is smaller

... and larger

The next drawing shows the paper re-positioned

Fold to make the circled points meet

Repeat on similar layers

Inside reverse fold

Outside reverse fold

Sink

Symbols and Suggestions

Although the level of the work included in this book may appeal more to the experienced folder, who should be well acquainted with the standard folding symbols which are used internationally, I nevertheless feel it is appropriate to include some word of additional explanation at this point.

I believe that the symbols pioneered by Akira Yoshizawa in Japan, and continued in the West by Samuel Randlett and Robert Harbin, do offer the best means available of describing a way of folding an origami design .There must be doubts, however, about the overall effectiveness of drawings like this for the beginner, who frequently is discouraged when faced with apparently complicated diagrams and symbols.But again this is not a book that will necessarily fall within the scope of a novice paper-folder, although I hope that those new to origami may find something worth trying.

For the sake of uniformity, I have not introduced new symbols,but you may notice some slight variations to the norm.For example I have not always included the repeat symbol as it should be quite obvious in a symmetrical design that a manoeuvre has to be repeated on similar flaps, or on the layers behind.

Akira Yoshizawa's practice of folding in the air, rather than on a flat surface is an attractive principle for me. This means that you are fully in contact with the paper, and are not hindered by the apparently "comforting" surface of the table. Nevertheless,the need to have the support of a flat surface in the early stages of the folding of a large design with a sizeable sheet, will at times be essential. You'll be able to pick up the paper when it becomes more manageable in the later stages.

When folding living creatures, it's worth remembering that precision in the final stages may not always be appropriate. In fact it can be worth experimenting with handling the paper quite roughly in order to obtain a more naturalistic result. Another small point: when it's necessary to run a crease between two points, I find it easier to "squeeze in" a mountain fold. If a valley fold is attempted then invariably the points you are trying to connect are obscured.

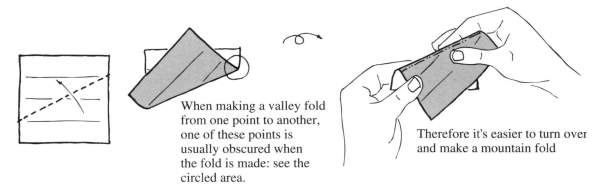

When making a valley fold from one point to another, one of these points is usually obscured when the fold is made: see the circled area.

Therefore it's easier to turn over and make a mountain fold

You should certainly be aware of all the paper types which you come across, experimenting with them to explore their folding suitabilities. Paper is all around us, and you should not feel it essential to use commercially manufactured origami paper. Types of paper for which I have a particular fondness include common brown wrapping paper which gives the impression that the finished design has been made from wood. Fabriano paper, from Italy, which comes in a variety of weights, is good for wet folding, which I'll describe later. Canson from France has similar qualities, and the available colours are brighter.

The Silver Rectangle, A size paper, and the 1:√2 proportion

There are many references in this book to "A" size paper. Although "A4" is well known internationally as the standard paper size, in the USA, paper measuring 8 1/2 x 11 inches is commonplace.

The relationship between the sides of all "A" papers is described geometrically as 1:√2. This means that the long side of the rectangle is equal to the diagonal of a square, whose side is equal to the short side of the rectangle. A useful benefit of this rectangle is that if it is folded in half, short side to short side, then the smaller rectangle obtained has the same proportion as the original, and is also in the ratio 1:√2.

Also known in the origami world as The Silver Rectangle, this paper size is useful to the practising paperfolder for many reasons. It is widely available and thus needs no advance preparation. You'll realise from the above that if you need a smaller version of the design you are working on, it's a simple matter to start from a sheet cut in half. The term Silver Rectangle has given rise to many of the titles of the constructions featuring in the *Modular Origami* section of this book, for example the Dimpled Silver Dodecahedron, and the Sunken Silver Star.

The measurements of "A" rectangles are based on metric units, the largest size in common use being A0, equivalent in area to 1 square metre. To help you make the paper size for various designs in this book, here are the measurements of each of the "A" rectangles. Remember though, that if you have an A4 sheet, you can make an A5 by simply cutting it in half.

Size		Inches	Centimetres	Size		Inches	Centimetres
A0	=	43 3/4 x 33 1/8	118.8 x 84.1	A4	=	11 3/4 x 8 1/4	29.7 x 21.0
A1	=	33 1/8 x 23 3/8	84.1 x 59.4	A5	=	8 1/4 x 5 3/4	21.0 x 14.8
A2	=	23 3/8 x 16 1/2	59.4 x 42.0	A6	=	5 3/4 x 4 1/4	14.8 x 10.5
A3	=	16 1/2 x 11 3/4	42.0 x 29.7	A7	=	4 1/4 x 2 7/8	10.5 x 7.4

To form a Silver Rectangle from a U.S. sheet measuring 8 1/2 x 11 inches, all you have to do is cut a 5/8 inch wide strip from the long side. This will not of course be an exact "A" rectangle but will have the correct proportions of 1:√2.

How to cut a Silver Rectangle from any sheet

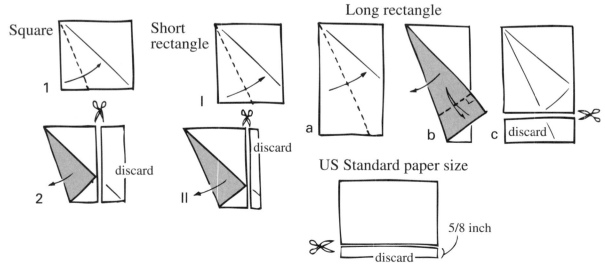

Square

Short rectangle

Long rectangle

1

2   discard

I

II   discard

a

b

c   discard

US Standard paper size

5/8 inch

discard

Toys and Working Models

Emu (p.24)

Walking Man (p.30)

Exhibitionist (p.26)

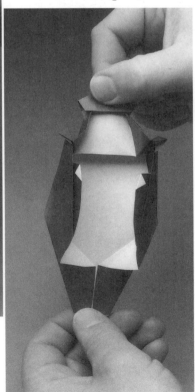

Emu

This subject is the puppet made famous by the New Zealand entertainer, Rod Hull. He uses his hand to form the face of the bird which frequently attacks and humiliates those people whom it dislikes. Although resembling a ventriloquist's dummy, Emu never talks ...

This origami version (call it a Crocodile if you prefer), uses an action mechanism used previously by Randlett, Momotani and Jackson.

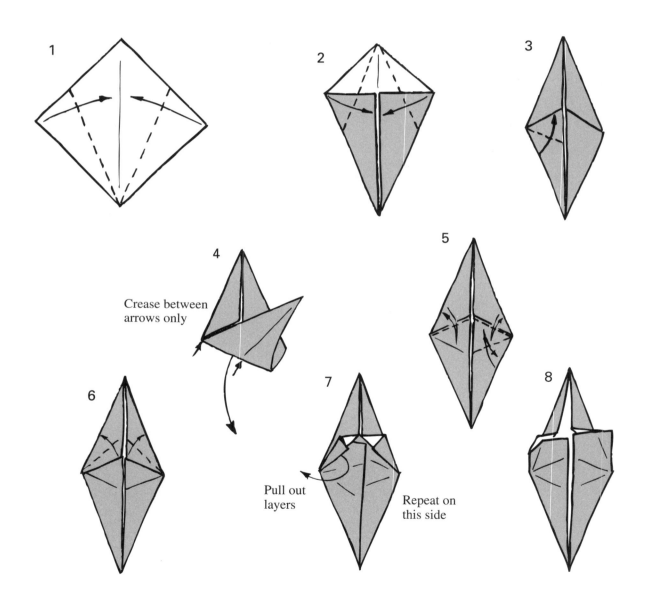

1

2

3

4

Crease between arrows only

5

6

7

Pull out layers

Repeat on this side

8

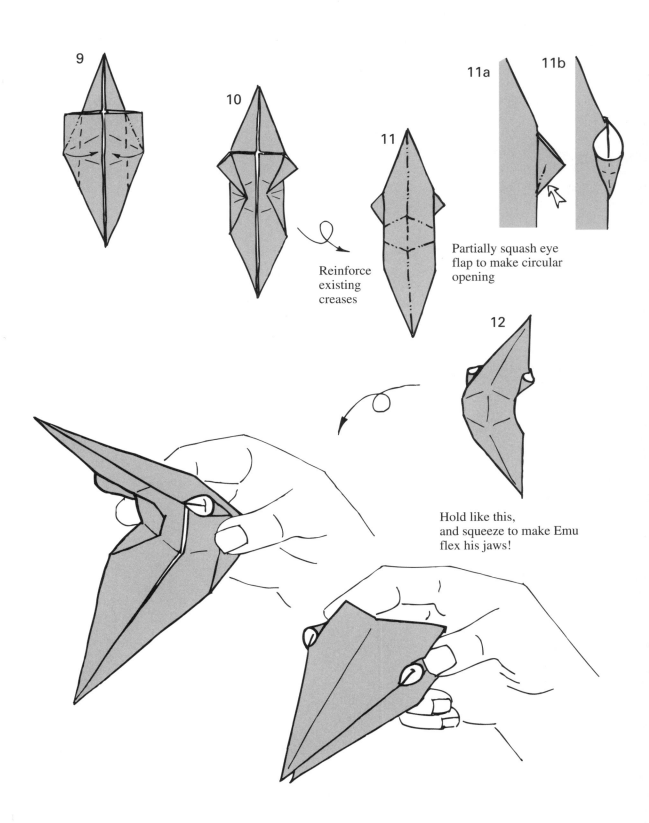

9

10

11

Reinforce existing creases

11a   **11b**

Partially squash eye flap to make circular opening

12

Hold like this, and squeeze to make Emu flex his jaws!

Exhibitionist

Also known as a "Flasher", this design was influenced by the human figure designs of Eric Kenneway. The action is not so smooth, and may need a little breaking in. You may be tempted to add a message inside the man, to be revealed when he flashes: "Nothing much to see in here"... or "I just had a flash of inspiration."

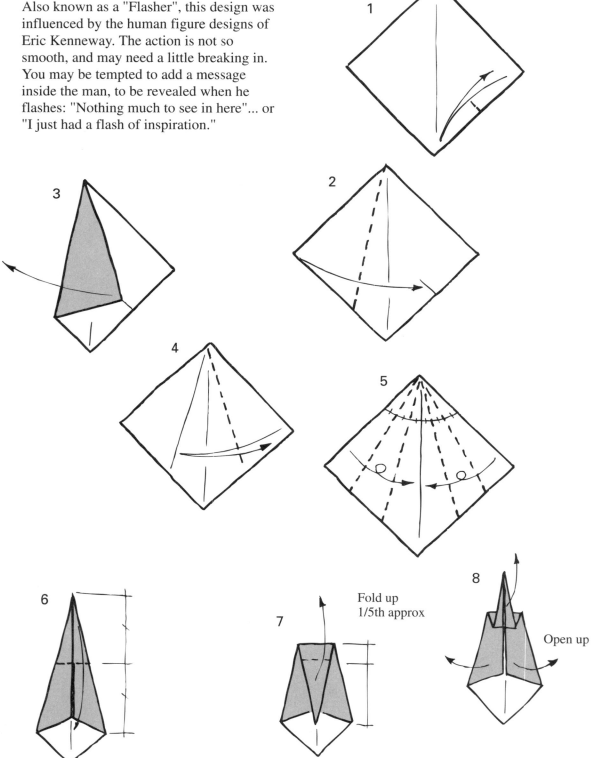

1

2

3

4

5

6

7

Fold up
1/5th approx

8

Open up

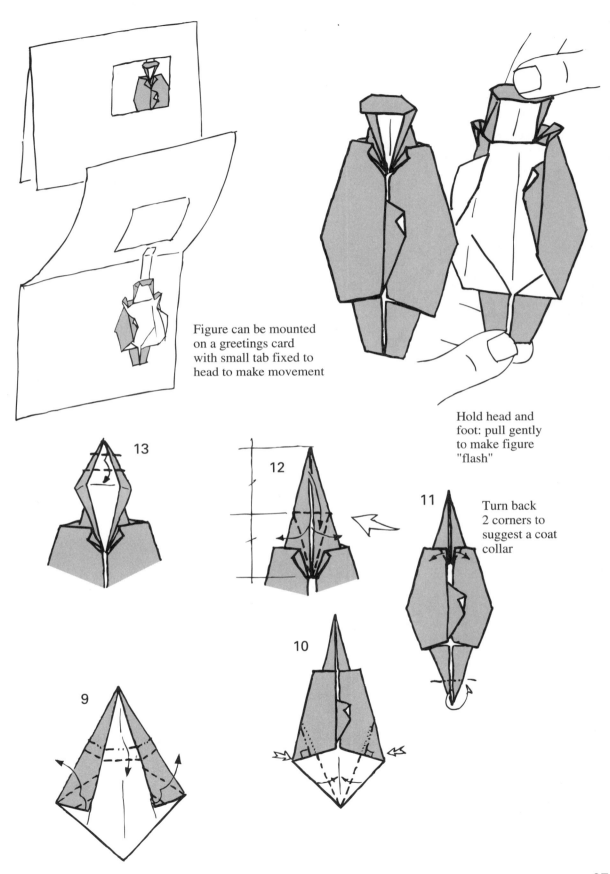

Figure can be mounted
on a greetings card
with small tab fixed to
head to make movement

Hold head and
foot: pull gently
to make figure
"flash"

13

12

11

Turn back
2 corners to
suggest a coat
collar

10

9

A creation which dates back to 1975, this book still remains one of my favourites, and I fold it frequently as a gift.

It has, I believe, inspired many other books by creators worldwide, some maybe more elegant in concept than this, but I am pleased to have given others food for thought.

Book

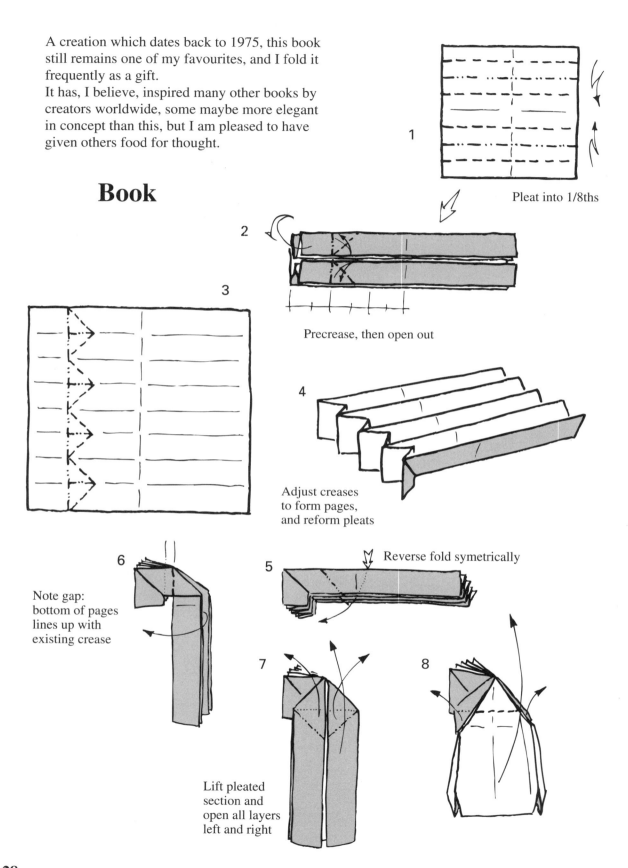

1

Pleat into 1/8ths

2

Precrease, then open out

3

4

Adjust creases
to form pages,
and reform pleats

Reverse fold symetrically

5

6

Note gap:
bottom of pages
lines up with
existing crease

7

Lift pleated
section and
open all layers
left and right

8

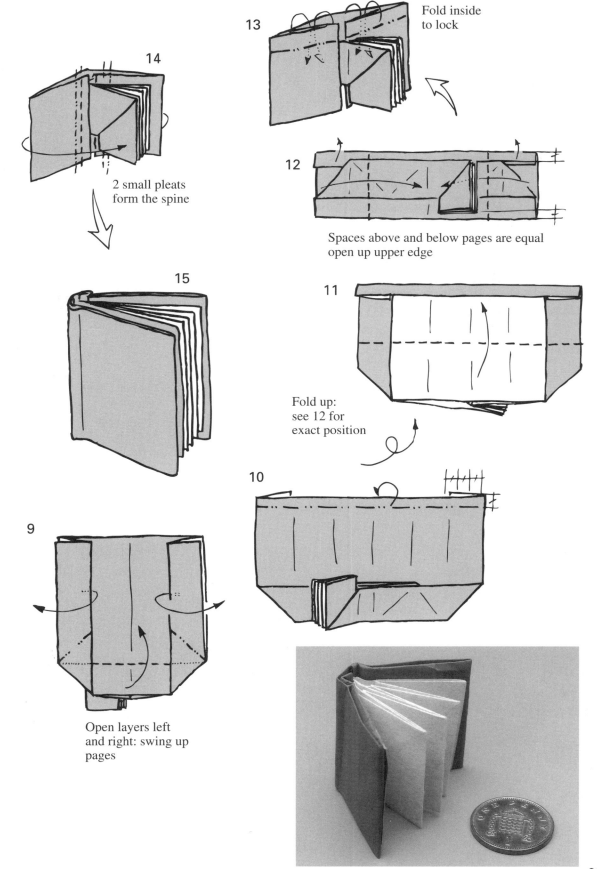

13 Fold inside
to lock

14

2 small pleats
form the spine

12 Spaces above and below pages are equal
open up upper edge

15

11 Fold up:
see 12 for
exact position

10

9

Open layers left
and right: swing up
pages

29

The idea of using two half-bird bases came from Alice Gray in various designs appearing in Robert Harbin's last paperback, *Origami 4*. I had previously tried human figures which were bulky and ill-proportioned. This 2-piece idea may raise a purist's eybrow, but the proportion of the figure is good and justifies the liberty. In any case I later made a 1-piece variation, but this is thicker and is less well proportioned.

The action method I found by accident. Try a game of football with a small waterbomb!

Walking Man: 2 piece version

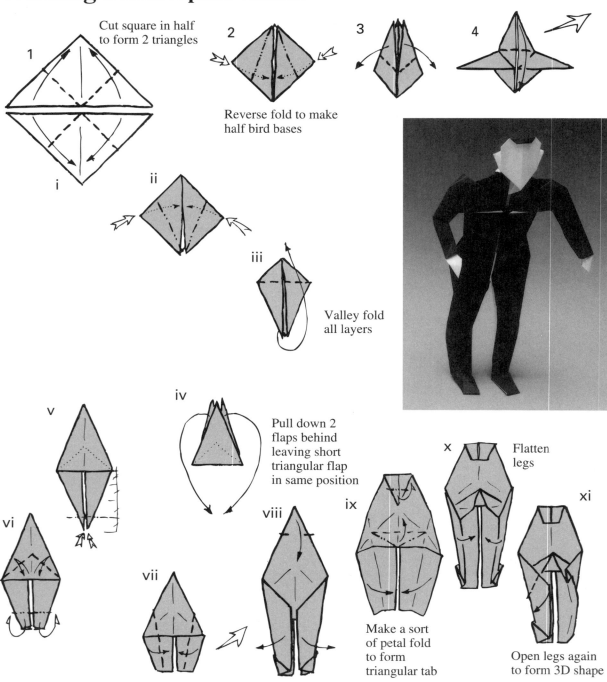

1 Cut square in half to form 2 triangles

2 Reverse fold to make half bird bases

iii Valley fold all layers

iv Pull down 2 flaps behind leaving short triangular flap in same position

ix Make a sort of petal fold to form triangular tab

x Flatten legs

xi Open legs again to form 3D shape

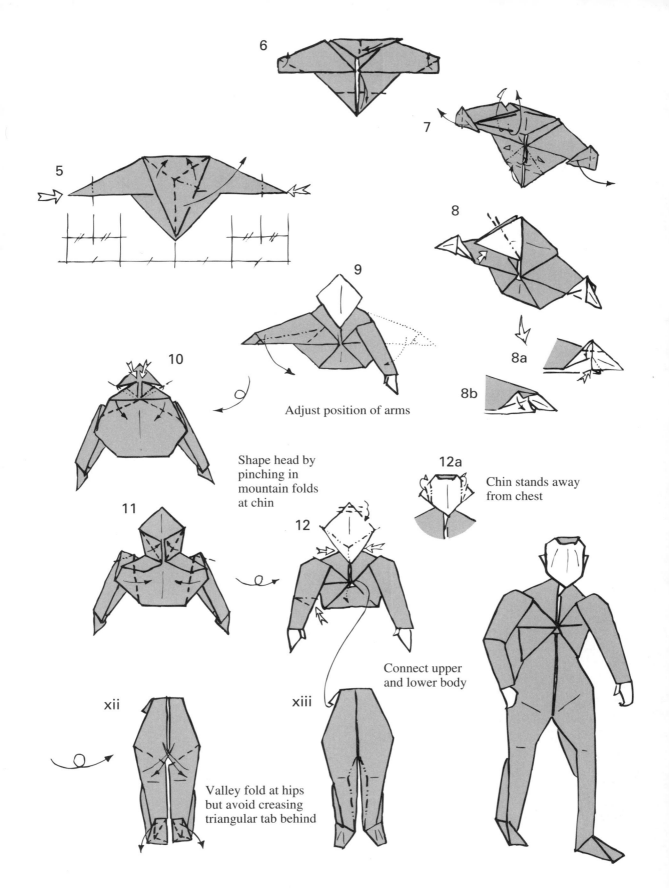

6

7

5

8

8a

8b

9

Adjust position of arms

10

Shape head by
pinching in
mountain folds
at chin

12a

Chin stands away
from chest

11

12

Connect upper
and lower body

xii

xiii

Valley fold at hips
but avoid creasing
triangular tab behind

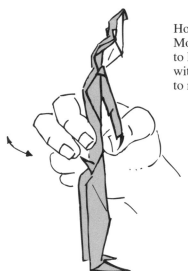

Hold like this:
Move triangular tab
to left and right
with middle finger
to make man walk

Single piece version

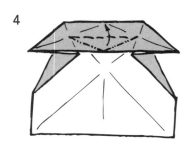

5

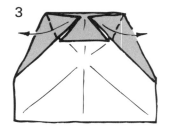

4

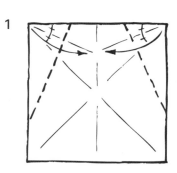

1

3

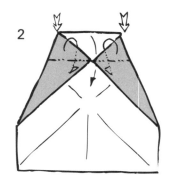

2

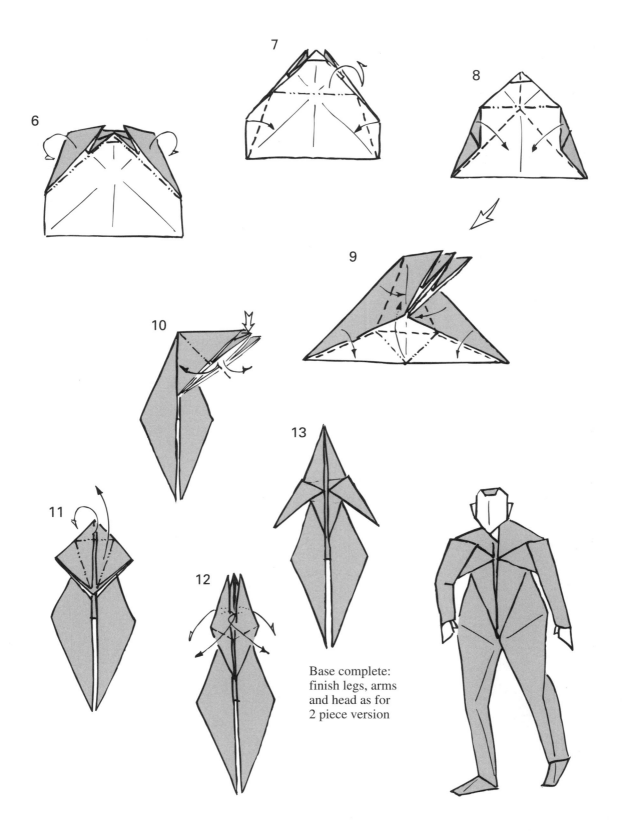

6

7

8

9

10

11

12

13

Base complete:
finish legs, arms
and head as for
2 piece version

Spectacles

Influenced by a spectacles design of Yoshihide Momotani, this design was created to complete a disguise theme I wanted for a demonstration. The rectangle needs to be about 8 x 16 inches (40 x 20 cms) to be wearable. Try drawing eyes on the lenses.

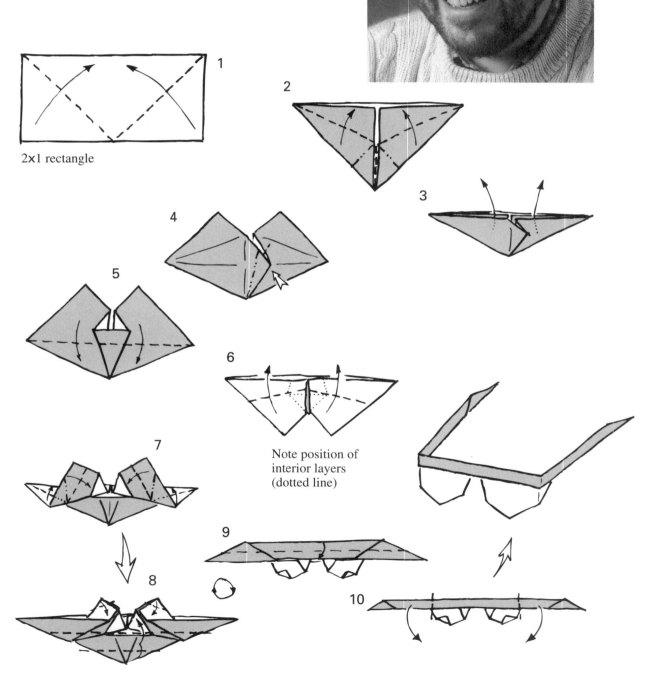

1

2×1 rectangle

2

3

4

5

6

Note position of interior layers (dotted line)

7

8

9

10

Talking Fox

A design which emerged from a doodle. The basic fold in step 7 is a stimulating shape to me, and I first saw it effectively used by Czech folder, Ivo Zuber, in a "Snow White and Seven Dwarves" scene. Try using a small thickish square to obtain the necessary snap to the action.

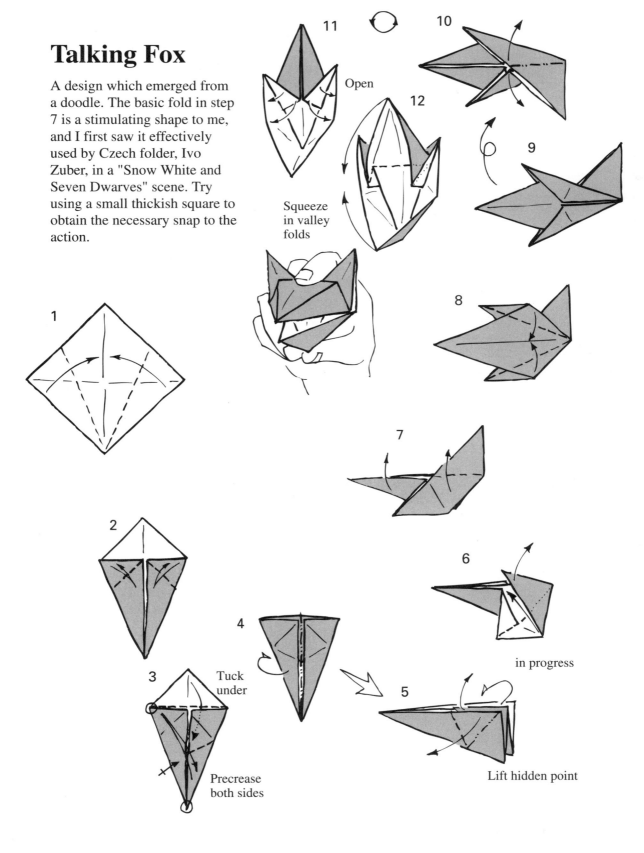

11

Open

10

12

9

Squeeze
in valley
folds

8

1

7

2

6

in progress

4

3   Tuck
under

5

Precrease
both sides

Lift hidden point

The complexity of this design may come as rather a surprise after the preceding models in this chapter! It was the product of extensive trial and error as a response to a challenge issued by the *Whodunnit* column in the British Origami Society magazine in 1976.

Here a list of then unachieved subjects was published as a stimulus to potential creators. Although you may be tempted to use foil, I don't recommend it: try instead a stiffish conventional paper such as crisp brown wrapping paper.

Nut and Bolt

Bolt

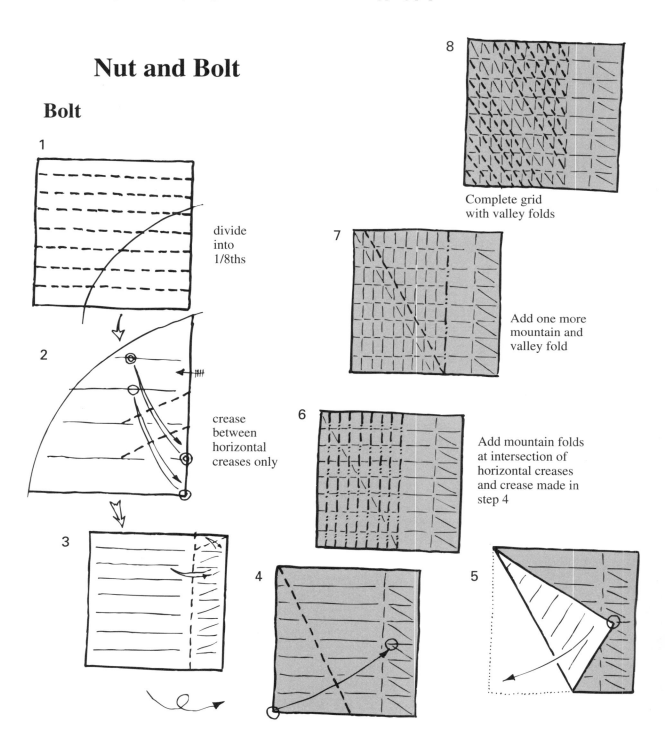

1

divide into 1/8ths

2

crease between horizontal creases only

3

4

5

6

Add mountain folds at intersection of horizontal creases and crease made in step 4

7

Add one more mountain and valley fold

8

Complete grid with valley folds

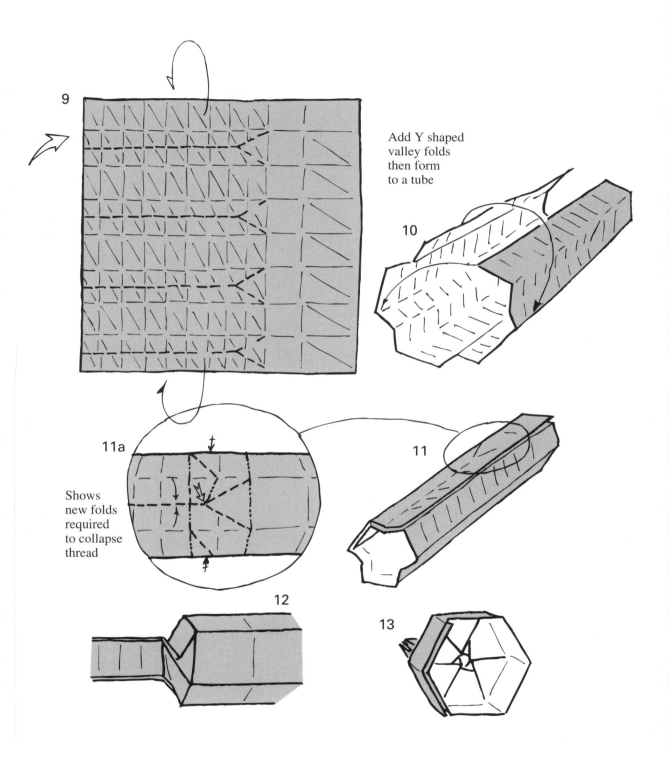

9

Add Y shaped
valley folds
then form
to a tube

10

11a

Shows
new folds
required
to collapse
thread

11

12

13

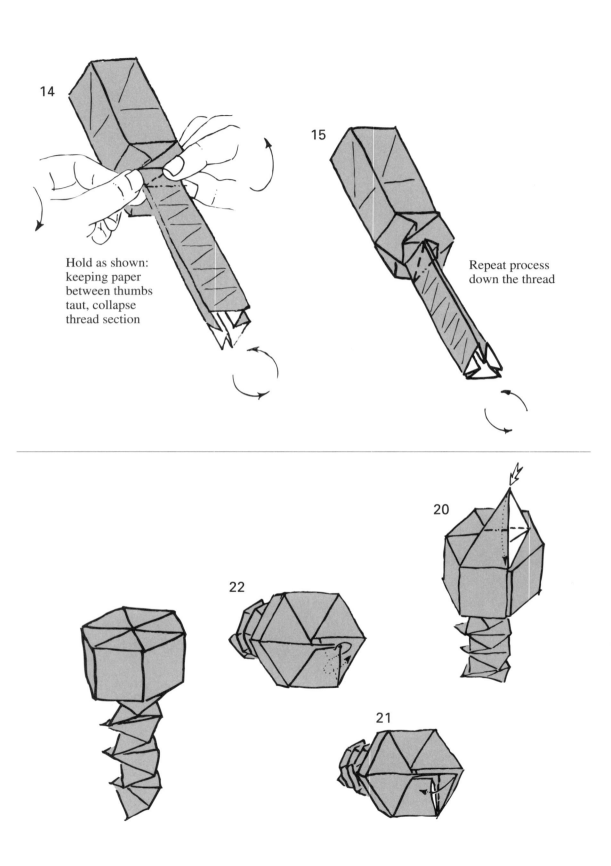

14

Hold as shown:
keeping paper
between thumbs
taut, collapse
thread section

15

Repeat process
down the thread

20

22

21

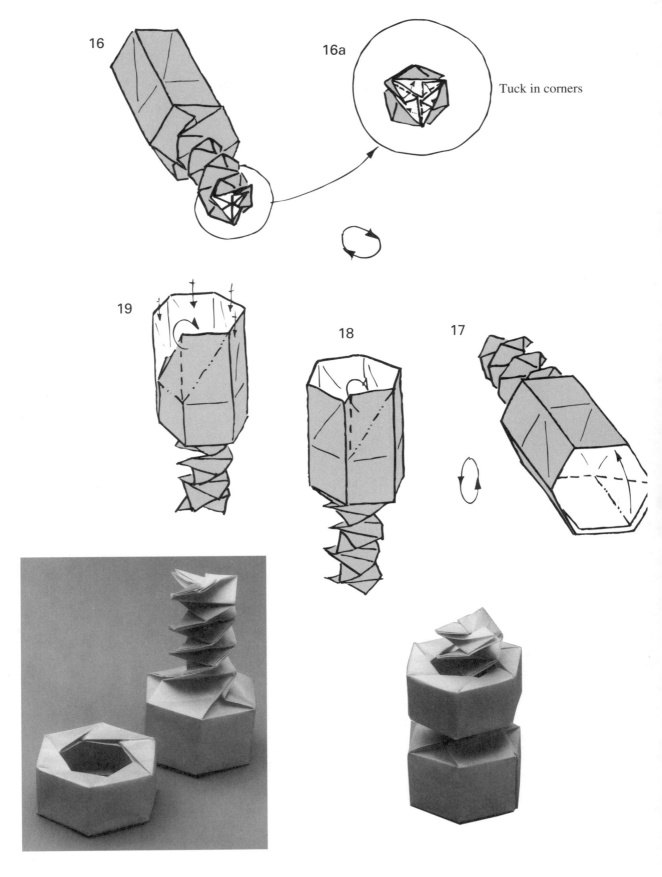

16

16a

Tuck in corners

19

18

17

39

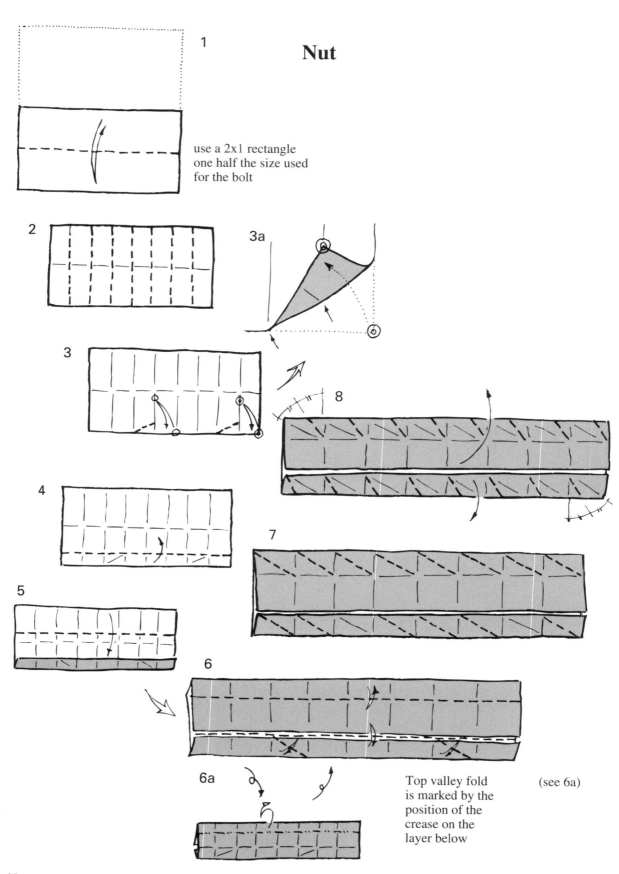

Nut

1

use a 2x1 rectangle
one half the size used
for the bolt

2

3a

3

4

5

6

6a

7

8

Top valley fold
is marked by the
position of the
crease on the
layer below

(see 6a)

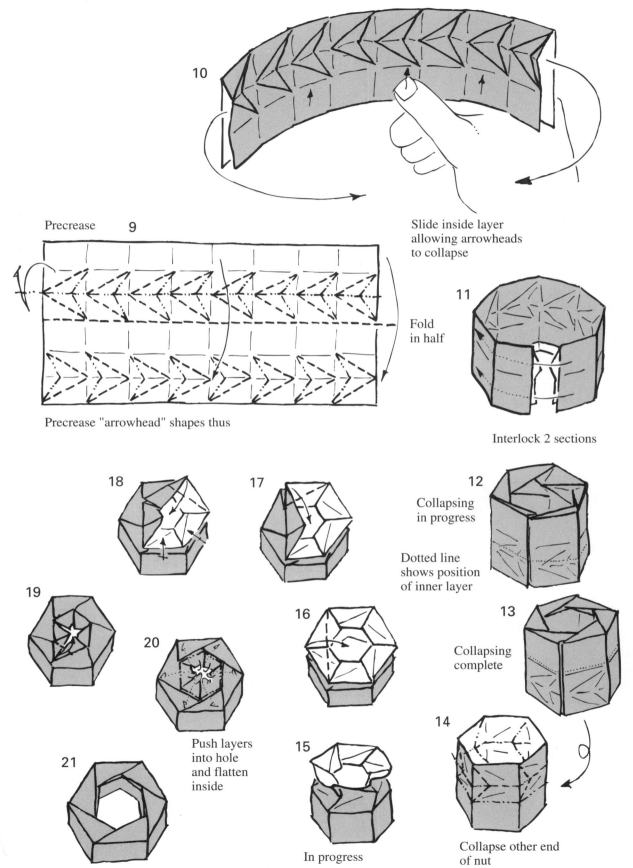

10

Slide inside layer
allowing arrowheads
to collapse

Precrease   9

Fold
in half

Precrease "arrowhead" shapes thus

11

Interlock 2 sections

18   17

12

Collapsing
in progress

Dotted line
shows position
of inner layer

19

20

16

13

Collapsing
complete

Push layers
into hole
and flatten
inside

15

14

21

In progress

Collapse other end
of nut

41

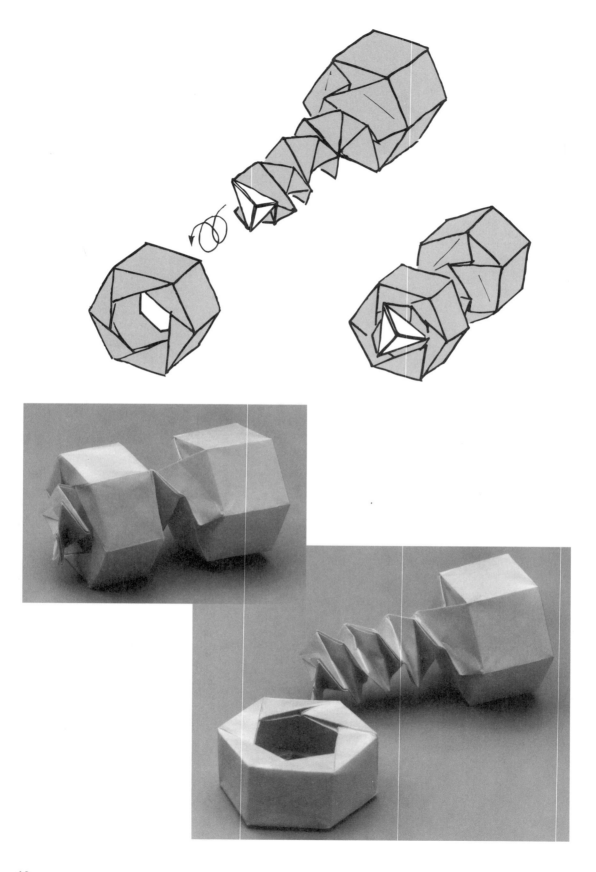

Thoughts on Diagramming

Until the preparation of this book began, I resisted the task of diagramming my work. I have used many rather pompous excuses from time to time to disguise my lack of enthusiasm for this meticulous job...

"Making a drawing fixes a design too much: it may be incomplete and I prefer to be able to return to it and improve it in the future " or "I fold for myself, not others, and I don't think that drawings are really necessary" or perhaps " For me the folding is more important than the diagramming"..."I can always lay my hands on an old folded example and work out how to recreate it, that's if I *want* to recreate it!"

It must be said, however, that there many useful bonuses which do often justify the work. It eases communication with other folders with whom you correspond, to show off your latest work: it's far easier to send a set of diagrams, than a rather fragile model that needs to be securely packaged. Frequently it sorts out an ill-defined folding sequence for you. Many times I have "completed" a design which contains a poor method: but making drawings forces you to get these compromises resolved. Remember too that if your design is good enough, then there is the possibility of the drawings being published in one of the many periodicals of origami organisations in the world today. Finally, your drawings provide a tangible record of your work for the future. Somehow a set of diagrams seem to be a much more permanent statement of your work than the actual finished model itself.

Over the last decade or so, I have been lucky to have had experience of drawing in a more conventional sense, having studied painting portraits and life drawing at evening classes. To improve drawing skills (and they are skills that can be acquired, not inborn in an individual) I recommend that you study at an art class. I have found that this is a fascinating and stimulating activity which helps my origami work: it has encouraged my sense of form and proportion which has in turn emphasized the integrity of my origami subjects. The ability to draw makes you look at the world around you in a quite new and more analytical way.

I have fervently resisted the recent fashion of making drawings by computer, which to me look very cold and lacking in sometimes appealing imperfections. I prefer the simple tools of pencil, pen and drawing board.

Finally, it is most important to give the greatest priority to the drawing of the finished design: it is this that will tempt the reader to fold your work, and therefore this drawing will demand your best efforts! I wish you the best of luck!

Boxes and Containers

There is something irresistible about a small box: it has a completeness and a simplicity of form which makes it an ideal origami subject. Tomoko Fuse has shown us that.

Not all apparently simple boxes in origami have a simple folding method, however, but the challenge of folding a box to a precise format is always intriguing. In this chapter, there are a variety of boxes and containers, some of which are practical, others which are a technical challenge, providing container and contents from a single sheet. The cigarette packet and matchbox could even be described as trompe l'oeil, and have been known to trick a smoker into accepting the offer of a smoke....

Star Container (p. 46)

This was inspired by the simple
pentagon created by David Collier.
It pointed me towards the exploration
of the A-, or Silver-rectangle in relation
to pentagonal forms; see p.22.

Pentagonal Envelope

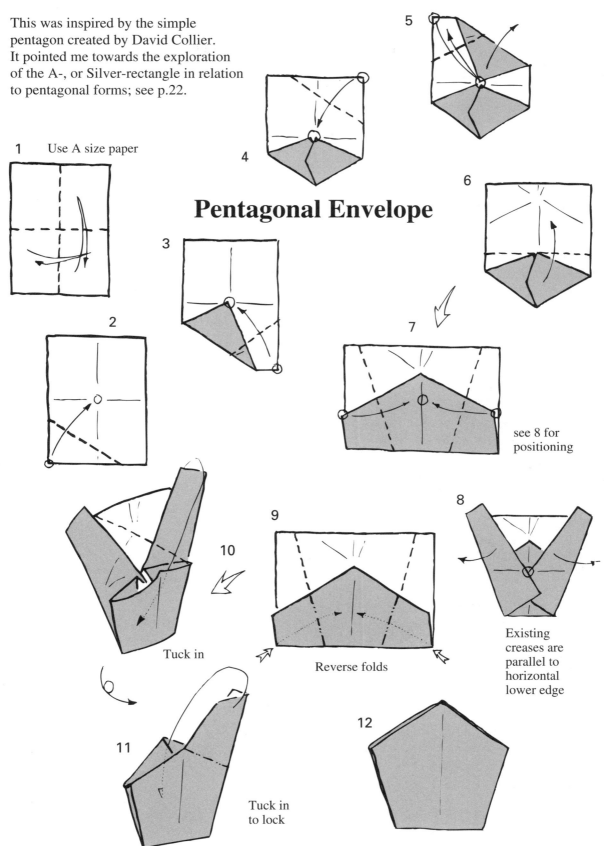

1   Use A size paper

2

3

4

5

6

7   see 8 for
    positioning

8   Existing
    creases are
    parallel to
    horizontal
    lower edge

9   Reverse folds

10

11 Tuck in
    to lock

12

Tuck in

Gift Box

Lid

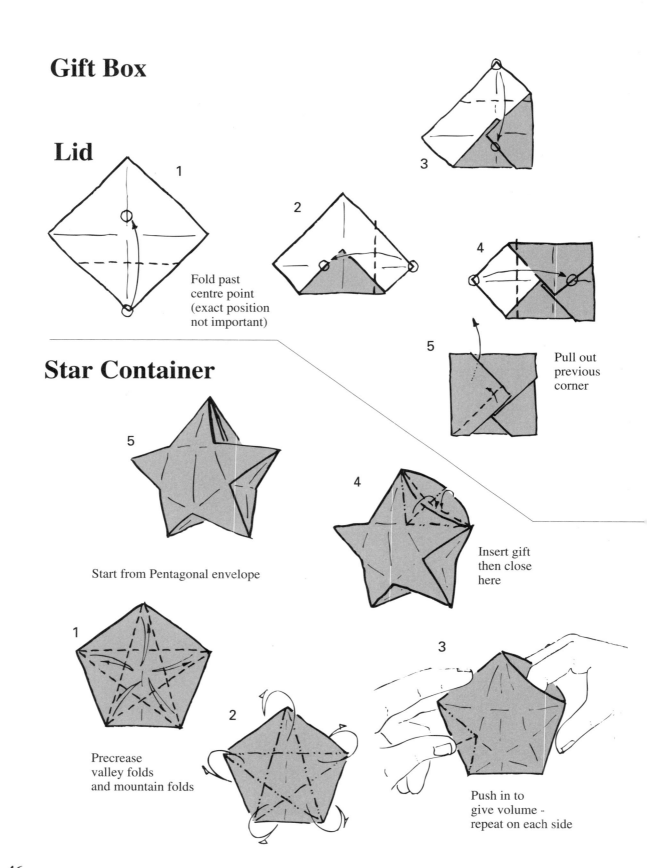

1

Fold past
centre point
(exact position
not important)

2

3

4

5

Pull out
previous
corner

Star Container

5

Start from Pentagonal envelope

4

Insert gift
then close
here

1

Precrease
valley folds
and mountain folds

2

3

Push in to
give volume -
repeat on each side

This gift box was influenced
by a blintz-form box by
Akira Yoshizawa: a relation to
the traditional masu but with
locked corners. Unlike the
excellent modular boxes of
Tomoko Fuse, the lid and
box have no direct size relationship,
and it's necessary to make the box
a little smaller than the lid.
Only trial and error
will make the results fully
satisfactory, so try again
if your first attempt was
unsuccessful.

14

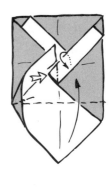

13

Tuck final edge
underneath
to make
symetrical

12

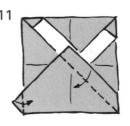

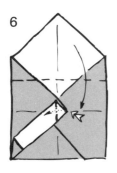

6

Reverse fold
corner at
centre

11

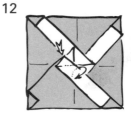

7

Repeat process in 5+6
clockwise around square

9

10

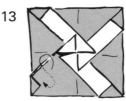

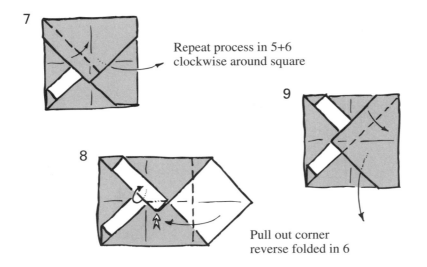

8

Pull out corner
reverse folded in 6

47

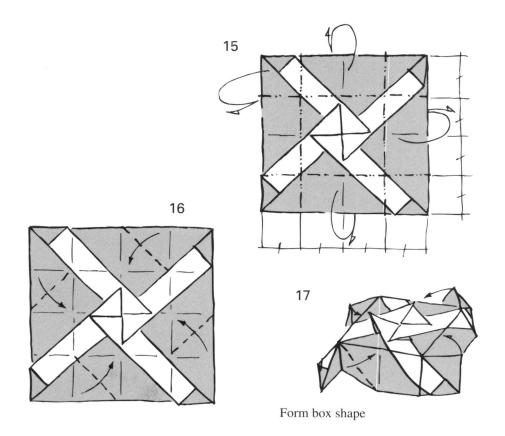

15

16

17

Form box shape

18

Valley fold
twice and tuck in

19

12

Tuck under
"blintz" edges
to lock

14

13

11

Size and proportions
of box and lid can
be varied by
positions of creases
in Lid 1 + 15
and Box 9

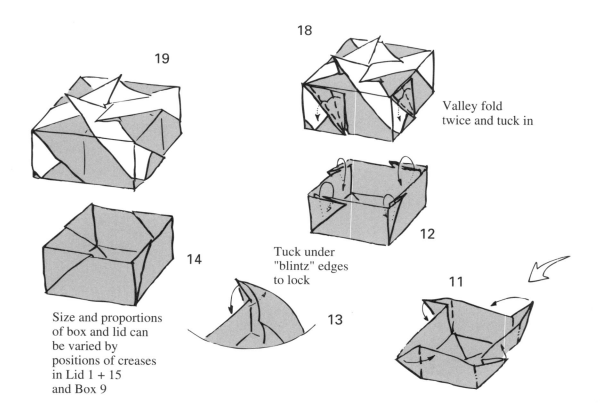

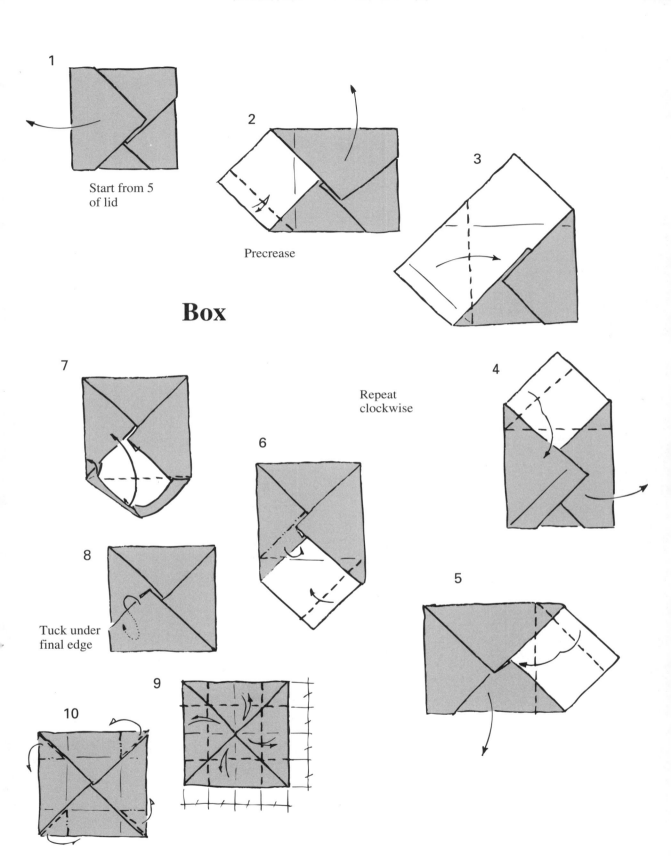

1

Start from 5
of lid

2

Precrease

3

Box

7

6

Repeat
clockwise

4

8

Tuck under
final edge

5

9

10

Bottle

The bottle was a development of an earlier triangular section bottle folded to have Pat Crawford's three-masted ship placed inside. It was requested by Eric Kenneway for his book *Origami Paperfolding for Fun,* in 1979.

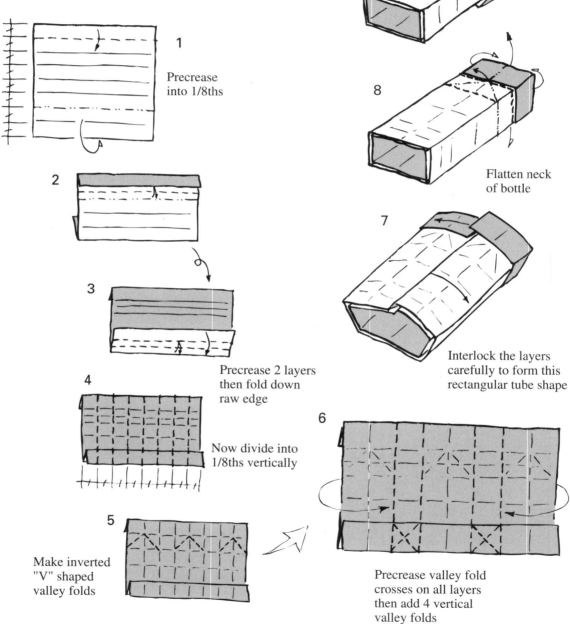

1 Precrease into 1/8ths

2

3 Precrease 2 layers then fold down raw edge

4 Now divide into 1/8ths vertically

5 Make inverted "V" shaped valley folds

6 Precrease valley fold crosses on all layers then add 4 vertical valley folds

7 Interlock the layers carefully to form this rectangular tube shape

8 Flatten neck of bottle

9

The best material
for folding the design is
non-adhesive book covering
film available from stationers.
This holds its crease reasonably
well, but needs a little practice
to get good results.

Release layers to trap
top of inverted "V" shape
which was precreased in 5

Lock layers within neck

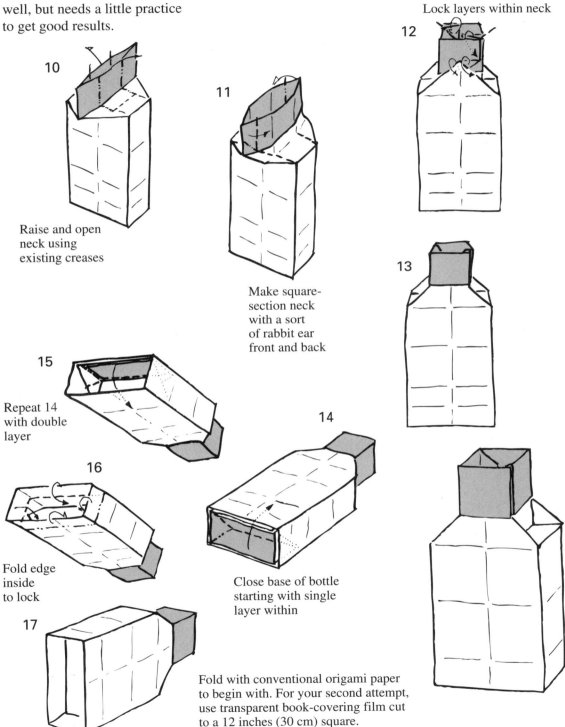

10

Raise and open
neck using
existing creases

11

Make square-
section neck
with a sort
of rabbit ear
front and back

12

13

15

Repeat 14
with double
layer

14

16

Fold edge
inside
to lock

Close base of bottle
starting with single
layer within

17

Fold with conventional origami paper
to begin with. For your second attempt,
use transparent book-covering film cut
to a 12 inches (30 cm) square.

Yacht

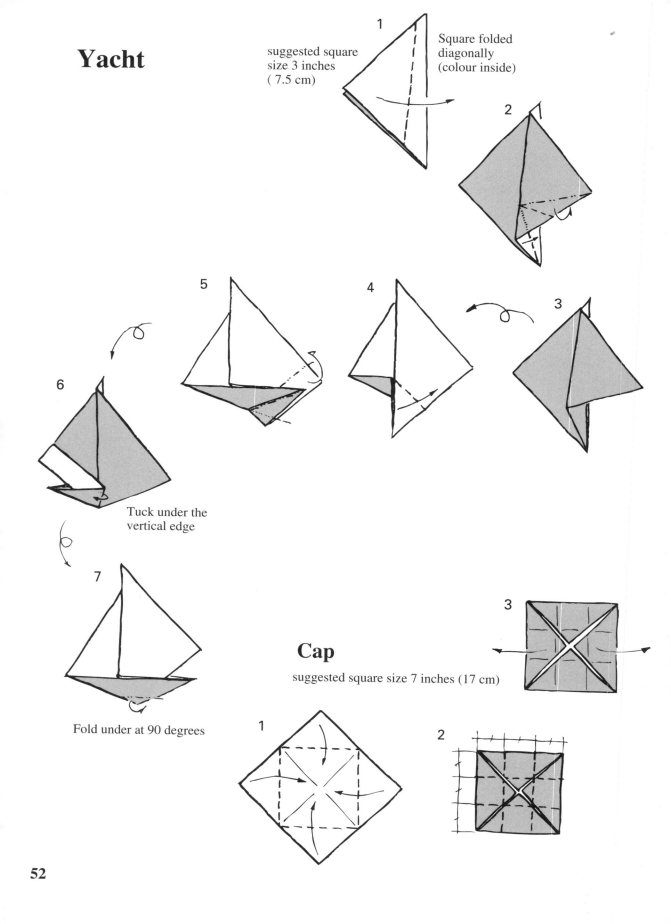

suggested square
size 3 inches
(7.5 cm)

1

Square folded
diagonally
(colour inside)

2

5

4

3

6

Tuck under the
vertical edge

7

Fold under at 90 degrees

Cap

suggested square size 7 inches (17 cm)

3

1

2

52

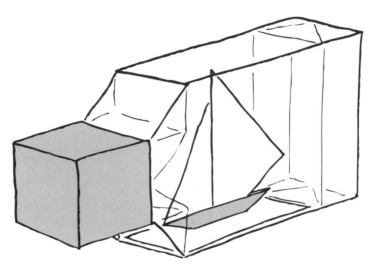

Glue the yacht to a small rectangle approximately the same size as the base of the bottle, and insert this inside the bottle before you close the bottle end. (step 14)

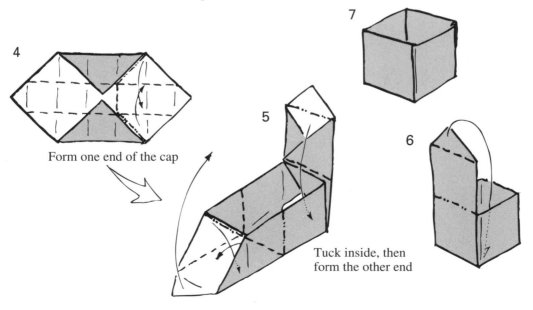

4

Form one end of the cap

5

Tuck inside, then form the other end

6

7

Box and Lid

The Box and Lid is a particular favourite and was created to hold a present for a girlfriend in 1977. It is a particular favourite of mine and I love the collapsing movement in steps 16 and 17. It was published in Kenneway's book *Origami Paperfolding for Fun* with a different folding method.

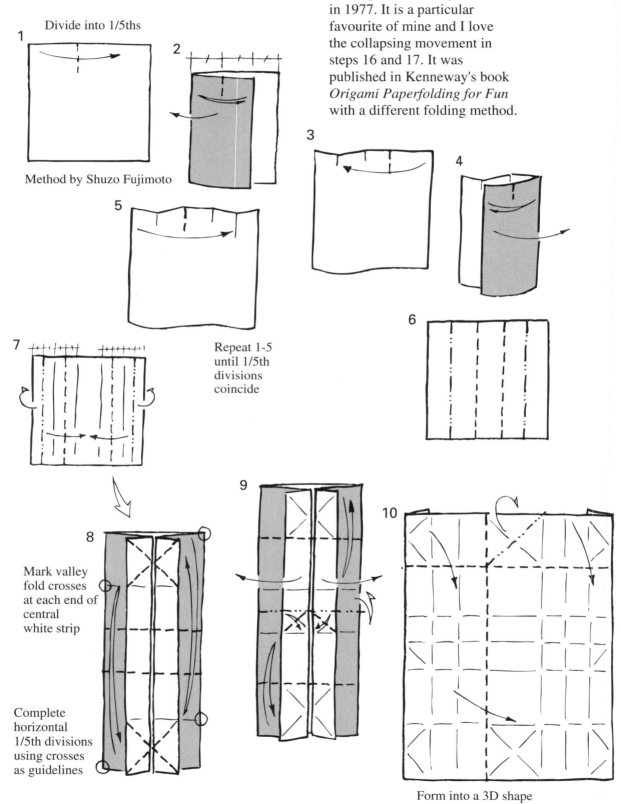

Divide into 1/5ths

1

2

Method by Shuzo Fujimoto

5

Repeat 1-5 until 1/5th divisions coincide

3

4

6

7

8

Mark valley fold crosses at each end of central white strip

Complete horizontal 1/5th divisions using crosses as guidelines

9

10

Form into a 3D shape

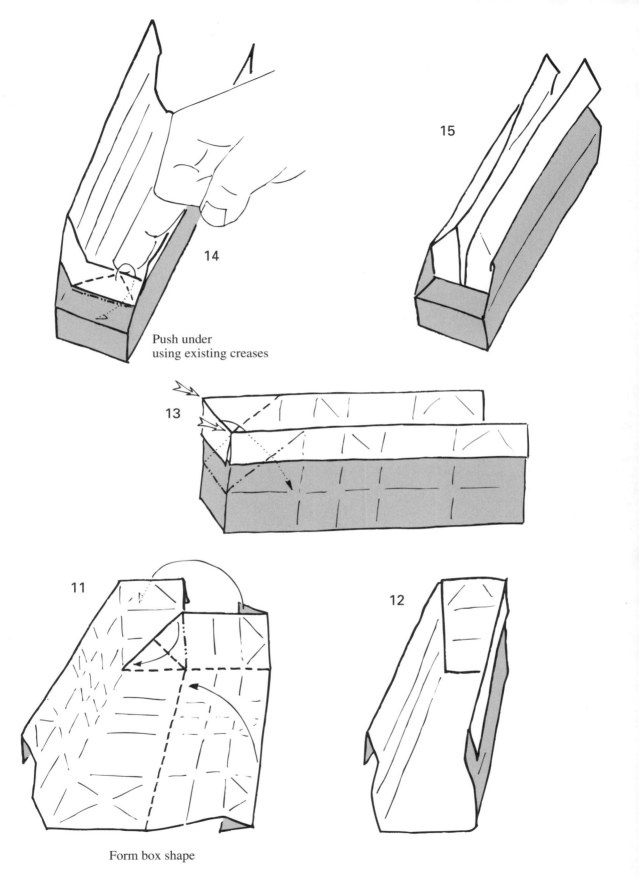

14

Push under
using existing creases

15

13

11

Form box shape

12

55

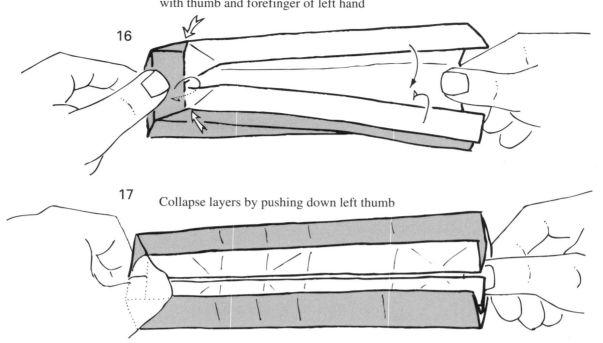

Hold hidden triangle in position
with thumb and forefinger of left hand

16

17 Collapse layers by pushing down left thumb

18

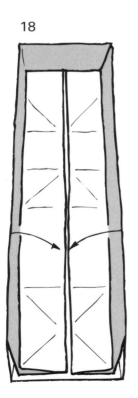

19

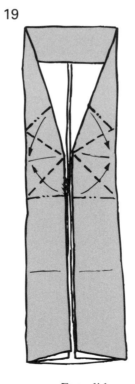

20

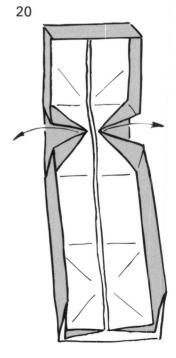

Form lid

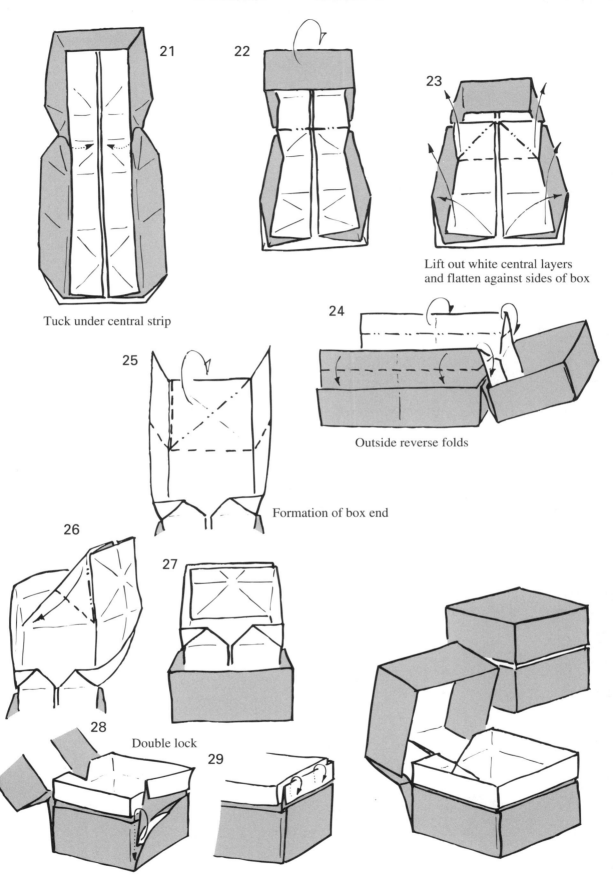

21

Tuck under central strip

22

23

Lift out white central layers
and flatten against sides of box

24

Outside reverse folds

25

Formation of box end

26

27

28

Double lock

29

57

Cigarette Packet

This cigarette packet was a
direct product of my admiration
for Max Hulme's matchbox,
which was shown to me at
my first BOS convention in 1975.

Use a 4x1 rectangle, 20x5 inches (48x12 cm) for a
finished model slightly smaller than a life-size
"packet of ten"

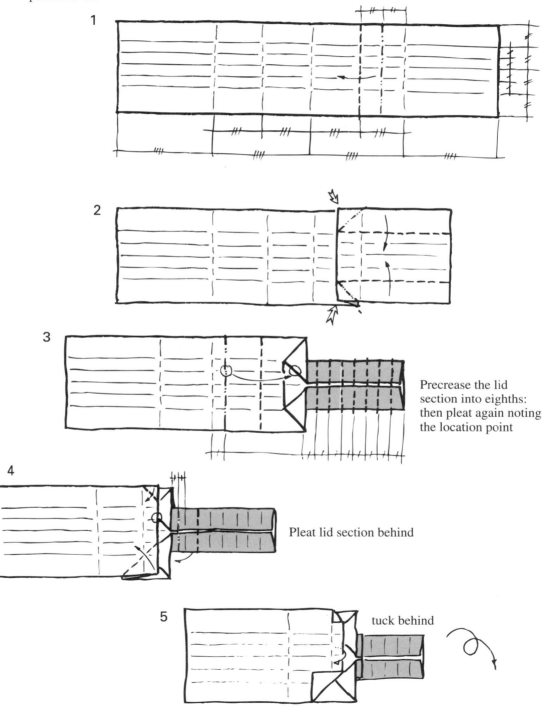

1

2

3

Precrease the lid
section into eighths:
then pleat again noting
the location point

4

Pleat lid section behind

5

tuck behind

I was immensely
proud of the design
when I first created it,
and I still enjoy folding
it today, although I no
longer tackle multi-subject
folds from a single sheet.

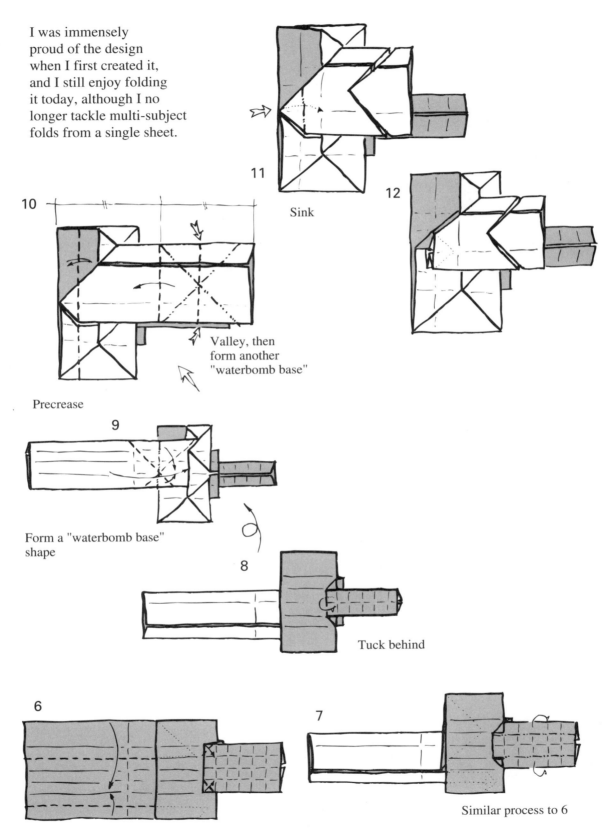

11

Sink

12

10

Valley, then
form another
"waterbomb base"

Precrease

9

Form a "waterbomb base"
shape

8

Tuck behind

6

7

Narrow allowing diagonal folds
made in 5 to rotate behind

Similar process to 6

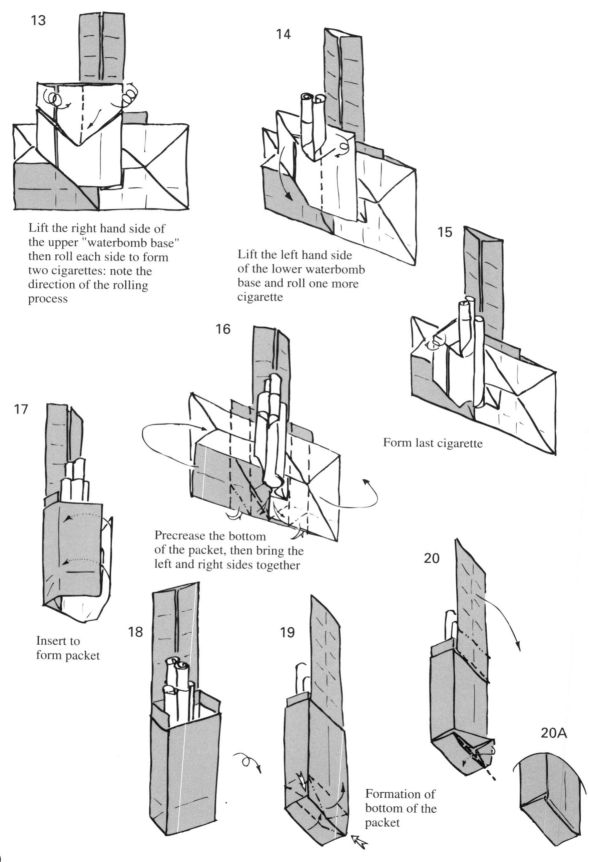

13

Lift the right hand side of
the upper "waterbomb base"
then roll each side to form
two cigarettes: note the
direction of the rolling
process

14

Lift the left hand side
of the lower waterbomb
base and roll one more
cigarette

15

Form last cigarette

16

Precrease the bottom
of the packet, then bring the
left and right sides together

17

Insert to
form packet

18

19

Formation of
bottom of the
packet

20

20A

60

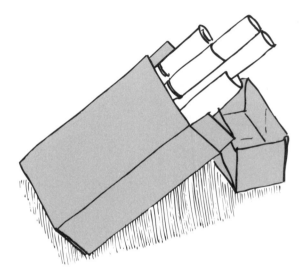

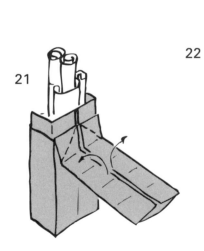

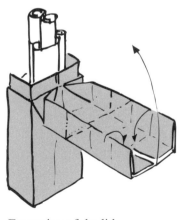

21

22

23

Formation of the lid

Matchbox

The matchbox came after the cigarette packet: like the Nut and Bolt it was in response to the BOS *Whodunnit* challenge. Many other moveable matchboxes emerged from the same stimulus, but I believe mine was the only one with authentic(?) contents!

Use a 3x1 rectangle of red paper, recommended size 12x4 inches(30x10cm)

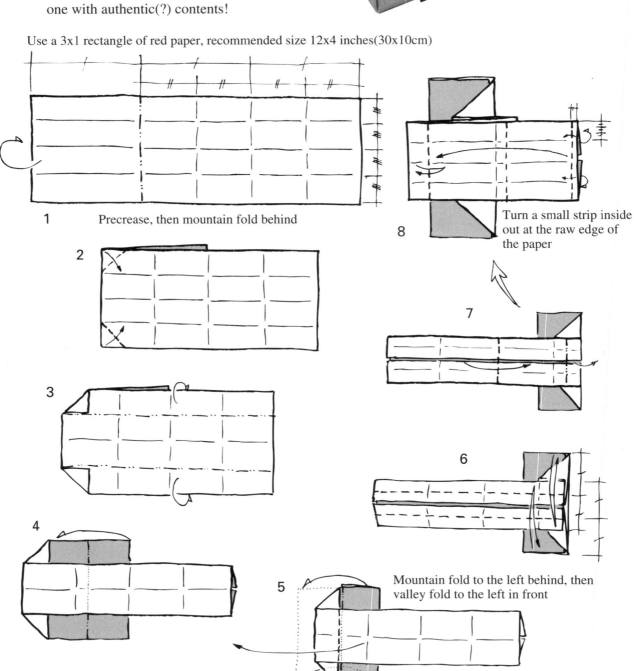

1   Precrease, then mountain fold behind

2

3

4

5

6

7

8   Turn a small strip inside out at the raw edge of the paper

Mountain fold to the left behind, then valley fold to the left in front

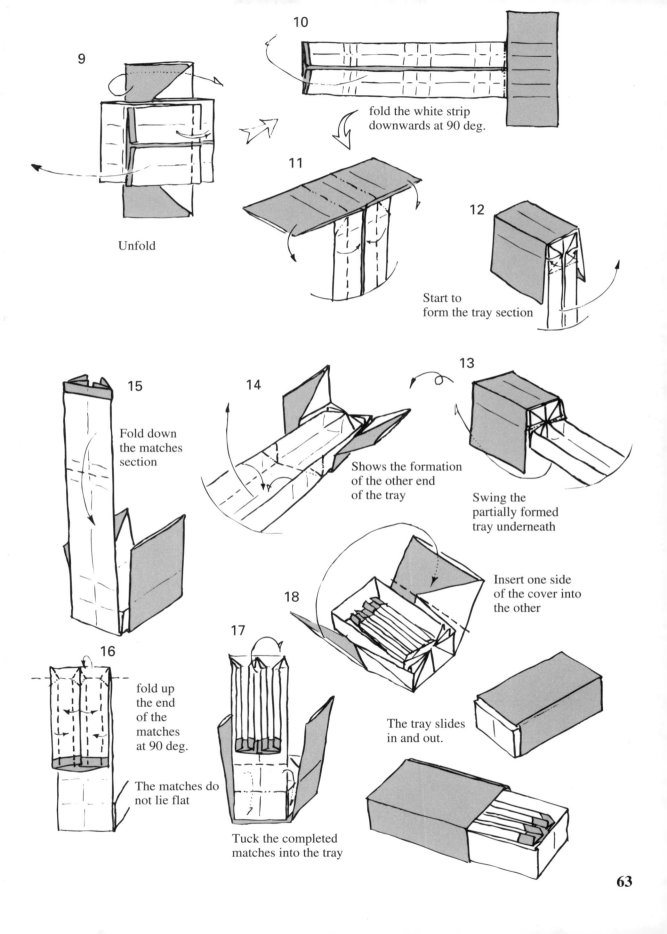

9

Unfold

10

fold the white strip
downwards at 90 deg.

11

12

Start to
form the tray section

13

Swing the
partially formed
tray underneath

14

Shows the formation
of the other end
of the tray

15

Fold down
the matches
section

16

fold up
the end
of the
matches
at 90 deg.

The matches do
not lie flat

17

Tuck the completed
matches into the tray

18

Insert one side
of the cover into
the other

The tray slides
in and out.

Money Box

The money box was originally a ballot box: it was inspired by Max Hulme's matchbox, but uses division into 1/3rds to produce the required proportions, and the slot.

Use a large square: minimum side length 10 inches (25 cm)

1   Division into 1/3rds: method by Shuzo Fujimoto

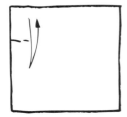

Mark only: a very approximate guess will do

2

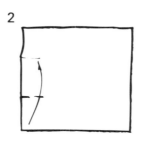

Fold to meet the first mark, then unfold

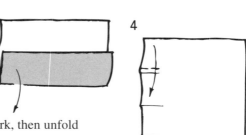

3

4

Fold to the second mark, then repeat the process in steps 123&4 until the 1/3rd divisions coincide.

6

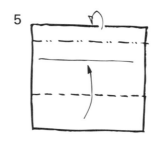

5

7

Precrease diagonals on one layer only

8

Precrease these verticals using the ends of the diagonals as reference points

9

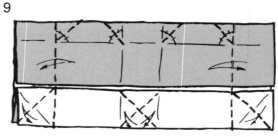

Add further verticals, then precrease further diagonals noting that the upper short diagonals are on all layers, and the lower diagonals are on the upper white layer only

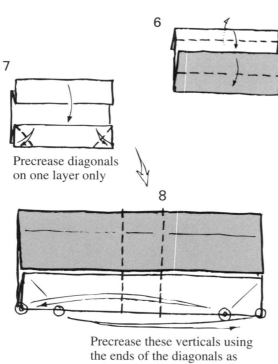

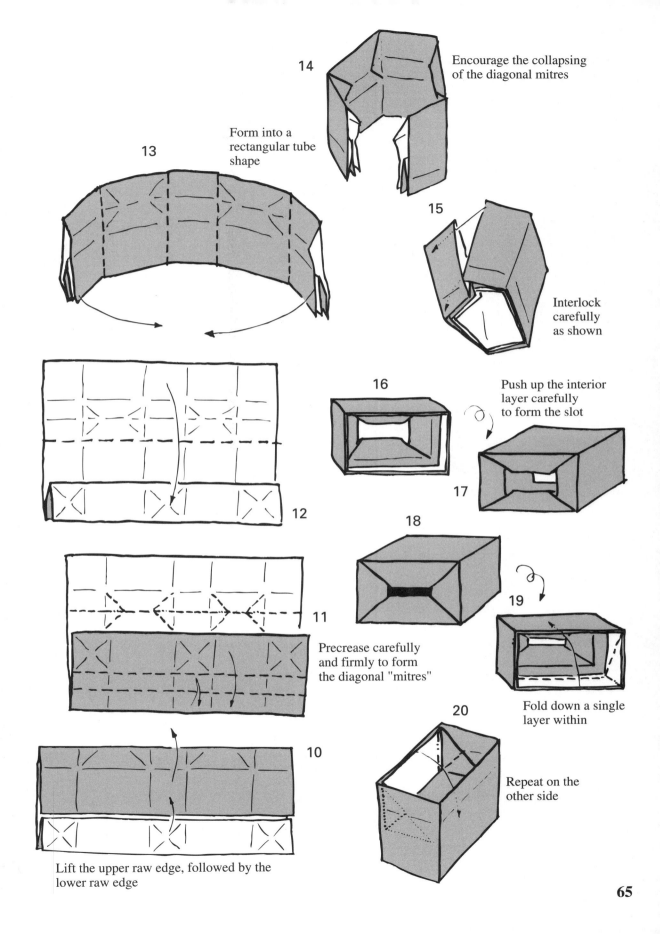

14 Encourage the collapsing of the diagonal mitres

13 Form into a rectangular tube shape

15 Interlock carefully as shown

12

16 Push up the interior layer carefully to form the slot

17

18

11 Precrease carefully and firmly to form the diagonal "mitres"

19 Fold down a single layer within

10

20 Repeat on the other side

Lift the upper raw edge, followed by the lower raw edge

21

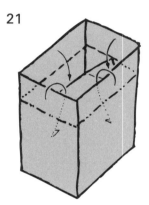

Fold edges inside
to lock the bottom
of the box

22

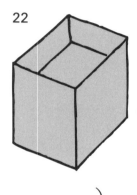

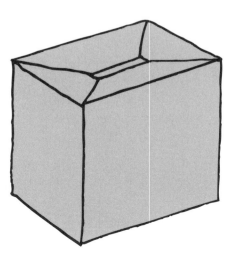

Honeymoon Box

This box was created on my honeymoon in Italy, to contain a present for my wife. It is rather complicated and bulky and needs careful folding but has some interesting movements. Fold it several times to get the best result.

Use a sheet at least 12 inches (30 cm) square Precrease into eighths, then remove one row of eighths from 2 adjacent sides

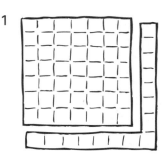

1

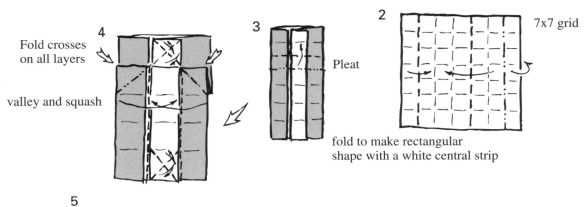

2

7x7 grid

fold to make rectangular shape with a white central strip

3

Pleat

4

Fold crosses on all layers

valley and squash

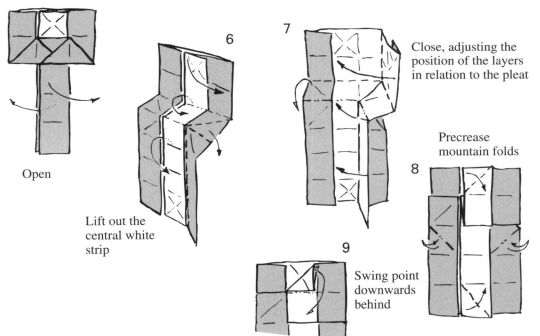

5

Open

6

Lift out the central white strip

7

Close, adjusting the position of the layers in relation to the pleat

Precrease mountain folds

8

Swing point downwards behind

9

10

Lock the point with a mountain fold

11

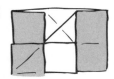

Repeat at the other end of the white strip but in mirror image

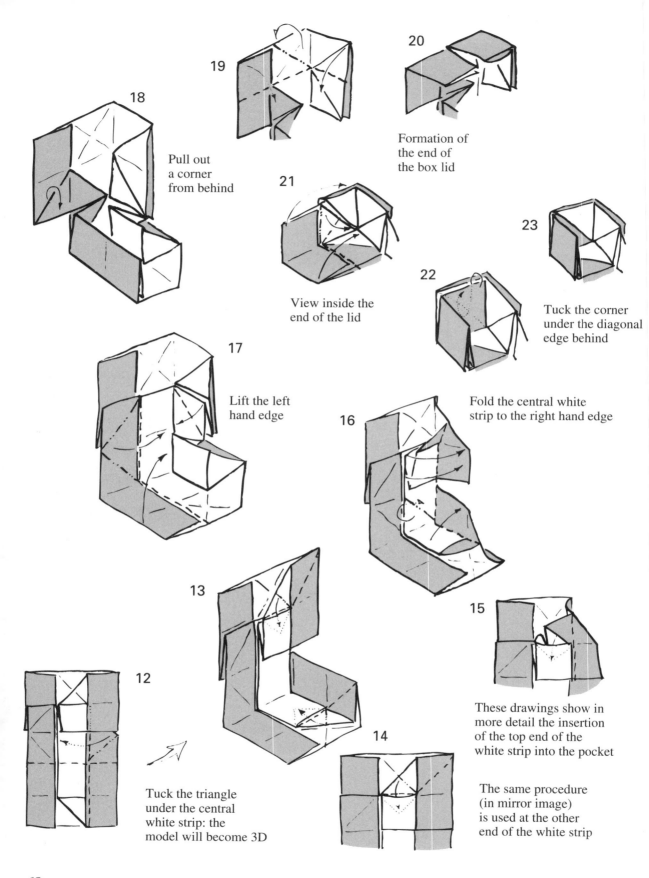

19

20

Formation of
the end of
the box lid

18

Pull out
a corner
from behind

21

View inside the
end of the lid

23

22

Tuck the corner
under the diagonal
edge behind

17

Lift the left
hand edge

Fold the central white
strip to the right hand edge

16

13

15

12

These drawings show in
more detail the insertion
of the top end of the
white strip into the pocket

Tuck the triangle
under the central
white strip: the
model will become 3D

14

The same procedure
(in mirror image)
is used at the other
end of the white strip

68

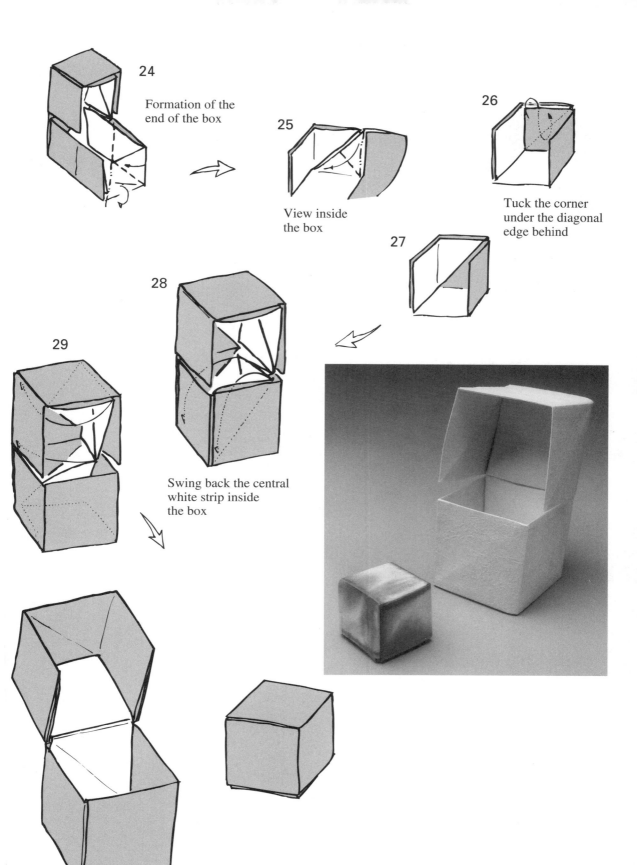

24

Formation of the
end of the box

25

View inside
the box

26

Tuck the corner
under the diagonal
edge behind

27

28

Swing back the central
white strip inside
the box

29

Modular Origami

Modular Stars & Balls

Stained Glass Balls (p. 85) and Spiky Star (p. 87)

Modular Theories

We have Tomoko Fuse to thank for the recent popularity in Modular or Unit origami. This is the construction of geometric forms from many simply folded units. The joining of the units is achieved by folding alone, and by the insertion of the flap of one unit into the pocket of the next.

Tomoko Fuse has managed to open a new door in this already established style, by creating wonderful boxes which display a neatness, a practicality, and an expression not previously seen in modular work. She has additionally shown herself to be great technician in the other areas of the style, by making elaborate polyhedrons and puzzle-like transformations from one shape to another by adding further units to the construction. A favorite design of mine is Fuse's unit Lizard, with a body which wriggles when shaken. The units are connected by such a simple method, they lock together securely, and yet are able to move smoothly, providing the movement in the body which is so effective. To me, this technique is a brilliant use of an apparently overworked and unpromising starting point.

Tomoko Fuse's Lizard

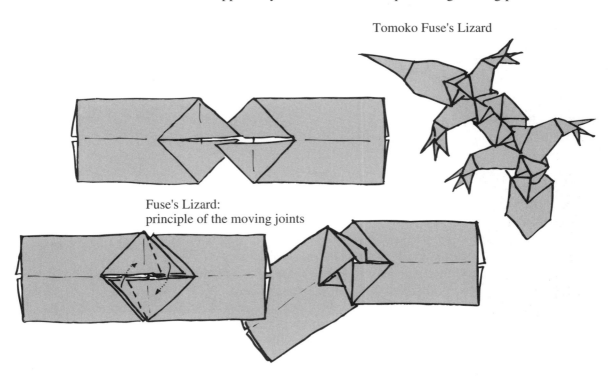

Fuse's Lizard:
principle of the moving joints

At first I was quite unattracted to the modular fashion, which seemed to me to be a form of origami "knitting'. However following experimentation with a unit based on Yoshizawa's simplest butterfly, it later became an obsession, Thinking at the time that the resulting three-sided pyramid was original, I made a range of geometric solids with it, and several variations of the unit later gave more complex star-shaped polyhedra. I later found that both Tomoko Fuse and John Smith had made similar shapes with an identical unit! This is an increasingly common occurrence, when simple shapes and geometries are being explored.The important point is surely that the design you came up with is original to you at the time, even though discovered separately by others. My own modular predilections have involved the explorations of "A" size rectangles, and their relationship (albeit approximate) with the regular pentagon. Shuzo Fujimoto and David Collier pointed me in these directions. It's worth experimenting also with knotted strips. The pentagonal knot so formed can be used to make a dodecahedron similar to those shown on page 80.

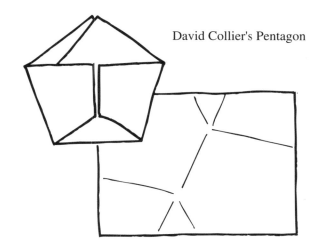

David Collier's Pentagon

Shuzo Fujimoto's Pentangle

Tomoko Fuse's work relies on color combination and decorative effect. I prefer to make constructions in plain colored paper, or using one color alone for all units. In this way the spectator is not tempted to admire decorative paper or the kaleidoscopic patterns created by many-colored constructions but will have to concentrate on the shapes of the design alone.

The Double Star Flexicube is a comparatively recent creation based on a plastic toy which has always fascinated me. You may find that a little glue is helpful here, though I have made several non-glued examples which work satisfactorily when handled carefully. Francis Ow devised a neat method of locking the units by folding alone, but I unfortunately received his suggestions after the diagrams for the design were complete.

I'd like to suggest further study of the polyhedron known as the Rhombic Dodecahedron, which to me is a shape of most pleasing proportion. H.M.Cundy and A.P.Rollett, in their book *Mathematical Models* (Oxford University Press 1961) suggest interesting ideas with a simple pyramid which can be combined to form three stellations of the Rhombic Dodecahedron as well as the figure itself. The shape of this pyramid looks easy to achieve from an "A" size rectangle, but I haven't yet succeeded in producing a satisfactory solution to build these polyhedra despite several attempts. Incidentally the first stellation of the Rhombic Dodecahedron is the same shape as the Star of the Double Star Flexicube.

The Rhombic Dodecahedron and its Three Stellations

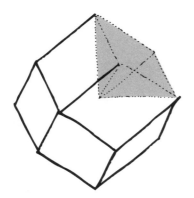

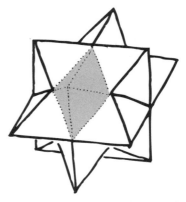

The dotted lines show the position of the pyramid which can be used to build all these polyhedra.

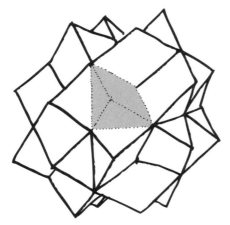

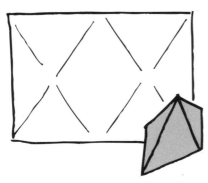

Geometry of the pyramid in relation to an A rectangle

Sunken Silver Cube and Icosahedron

A design which examines the relationship between the diagonal of the "A" rectangle and the cube. The unit used is simple to fold. The approximation in the Icosahedron development is acceptable to me, at least, although Kunihiko Kasahara has published an improvement from a slightly different rectangle with a more precise geometry.

Sunken Silver Icosahedron

Cube

(12 units needed)

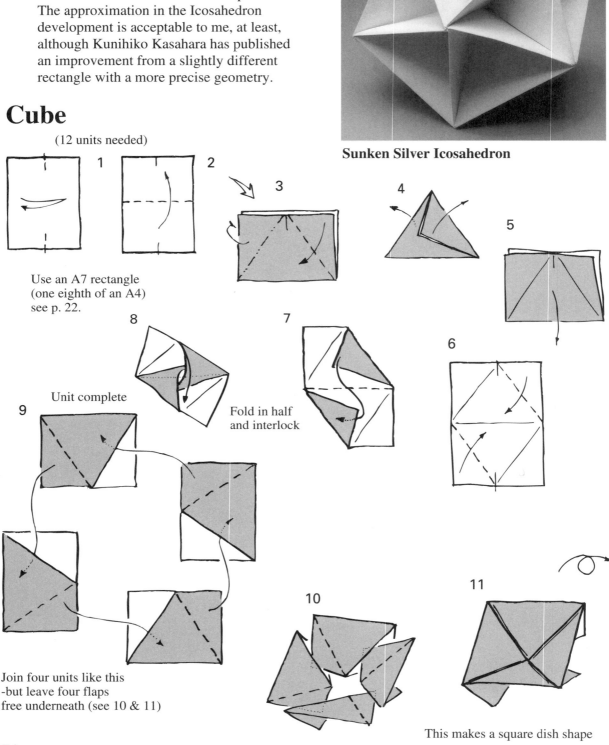

Use an A7 rectangle (one eighth of an A4) see p. 22.

Unit complete

Fold in half and interlock

Join four units like this -but leave four flaps free underneath (see 10 & 11)

This makes a square dish shape

74

Icosahedron

(30 units)

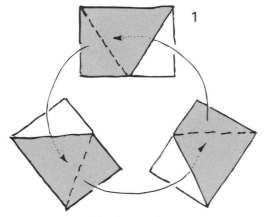

1

2

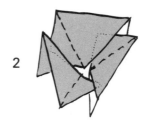

3

A triangular sunken pyramid is formed

Join three units: leave three flaps free underneath.

4

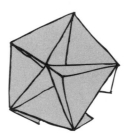

Add 7 more units to make pentagonal cluster of sunken pyramids

5

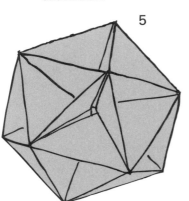

Continue building the structure in the same way, adding 20 more units to make the icosahedron.

There is a small inaccuracy in the geometry of the units which makes a small hole at the centre of the sunken pyramids. Nevertheless, the construction is quite stable.

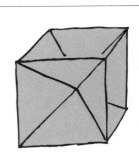

12

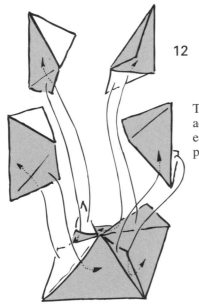

Turn the dish shape over, then add four more units inserting each flap into its appropriate pocket

13

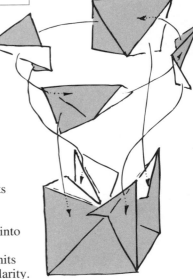

A further four units will complete the Sunken Cube. Flaps are inserted into pockets as before but diagram 13 omits some arrows for clarity.

Sunken Silver Star

This unit and the constructions are related to those shown on the previous pages. The unit has an identical triangle added which protrudes from the completed figure. In creating the design, I was influenced by a pointed star design by Tomoko Fuse. I have tried also to make another longer-pointed variation on the same theme, but the unit in this case proved bulky and the locking was less secure.

1

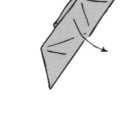

Use an A6
(A4 divided
into quarters)
see p.22.

2

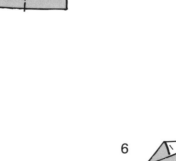

3

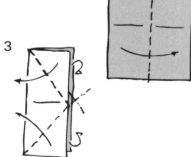

4

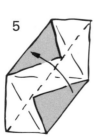

Open up
unfolding the
upper right &
lower left corners

5

6

7

8

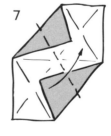

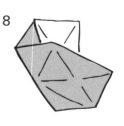

Fold in half,
lining up the
lower left &
upper right
quarter diagonals

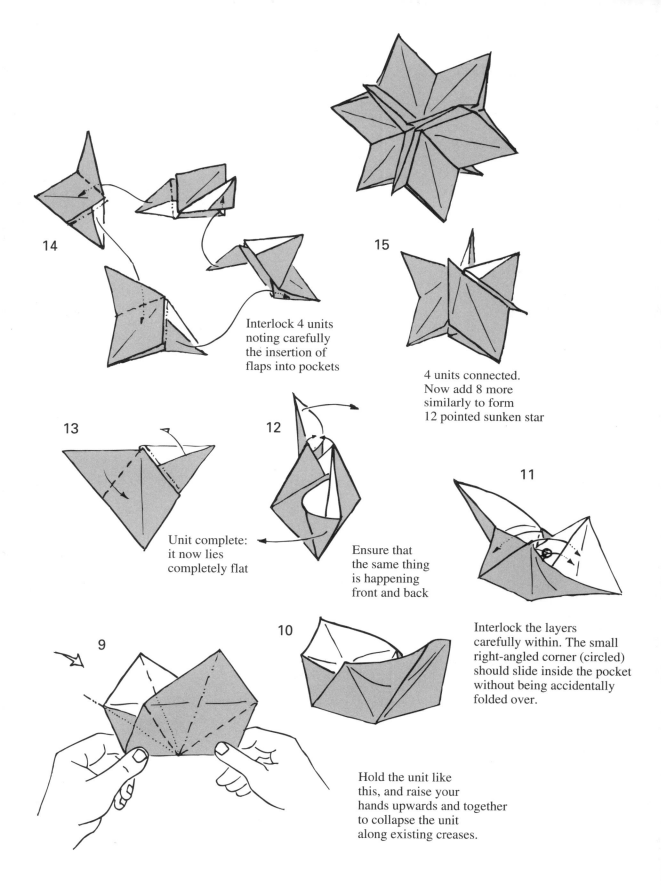

14

Interlock 4 units
noting carefully
the insertion of
flaps into pockets

15

4 units connected.
Now add 8 more
similarly to form
12 pointed sunken star

13

Unit complete:
it now lies
completely flat

12

Ensure that
the same thing
is happening
front and back

11

Interlock the layers
carefully within. The small
right-angled corner (circled)
should slide inside the pocket
without being accidentally
folded over.

10

9

Hold the unit like
this, and raise your
hands upwards and together
to collapse the unit
along existing creases.

30 Point Sunken Star

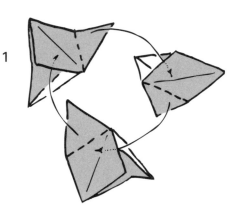

1

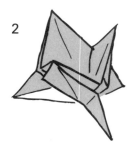

2

Triangular sunken pyramid complete.

Connect 3 units to
form triangular sunken
pyramid.
Pay attention to inserting
the flaps of each unit
into the correct pocket
of the next.
(see step 14 of the
12 point sunken star)

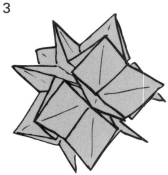

3

Add 12 more units
to form this pentagonal
shape, comprising 5 sunken
pyramids combined

Continue adding further units
to build the completed star
(30 units in all are required)

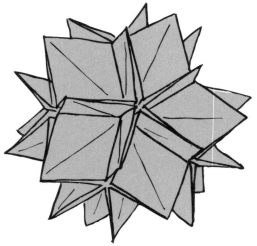

Dimpled Silver Dodecahedron

Inspired by Kunihiko Kasahara's similar design
appearing in *Origami Omnibus*. I wanted to make
the same shape from a more accessible rectangle.
I spent several hours on a train journey experimenting
with angles, throwing away many partially completed
constructions in the process. Some care is needed in the
folding to avoid bulkiness on the exposed folded edges.

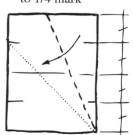

Valley to meet
imaginary line
connecting corner
to 1/4 mark

1

A6 rectangle
(one quarter of A4)
see p. 22.

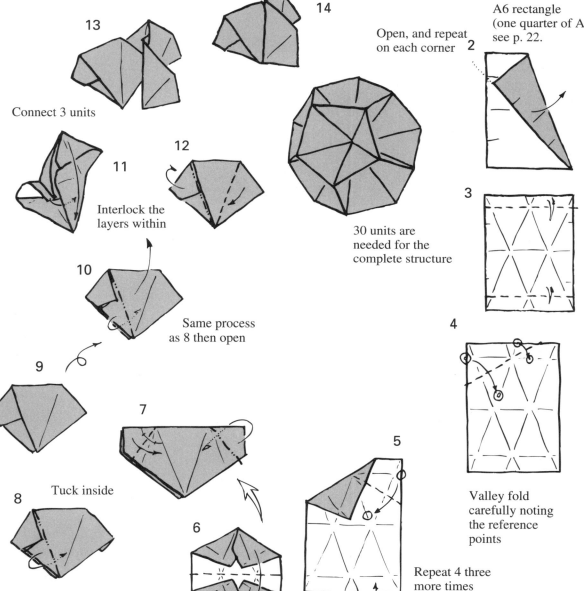

14

13

Connect 3 units

Open, and repeat
on each corner 2

11

12

Interlock the
layers within

30 units are
needed for the
complete structure

3

10

Same process
as 8 then open

4

9

7

5

8   Tuck inside

6

Valley fold
carefully noting
the reference
points

Repeat 4 three
more times

79

Silver Dodecahedra

A variation of the Pentagonal Envelope (page 45) and a simpler larger alternative were early experiments with A rectangles and pentagon-related modular designs. The smaller version was dubbed "BOTTOM" (Brill's Own Toilet Tissue Origami Module) at a BOS convention, when we found that some paper towels in the toilet were A size, and a fragile example of the construction was possible!

i

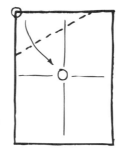

ii

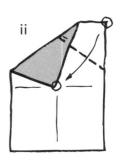

iii

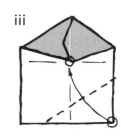

1

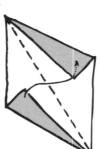

Each construction requires 12 A6 rectangles; see p.22.

10

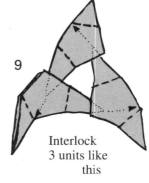

9

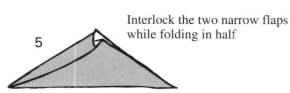

Interlock 3 units like this

2

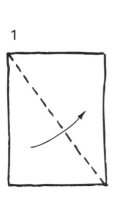

3

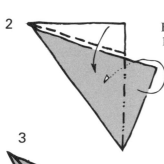

Unfold

These edges should be parallel

Fold the left hand corner to the right hand edge

7

8

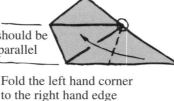

4

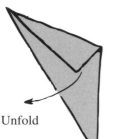

6

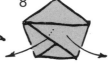

Interlock the two narrow flaps while folding in half

5

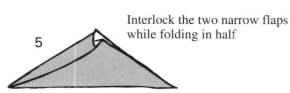

vii

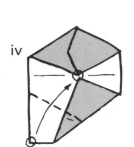

viii

similar to 7

ix

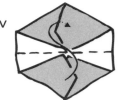

vi

x

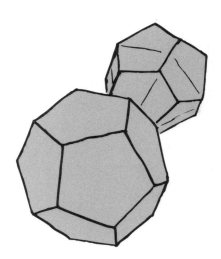

3 units connected
-complete as for the larger construction

v

iv

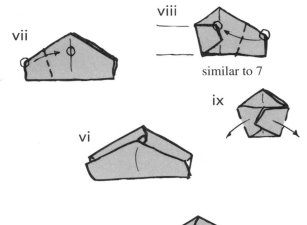

Fold in half
and interlock the layers

Connect 3 groups of
3 units.

11

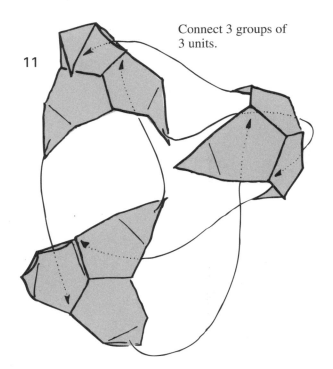

12

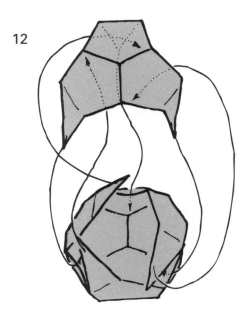

Add a final cluster of 3 units
to complete the larger dodecahedron.

"Woven" Strip Dodecahedron

This was inspired by the marvellous dodecahedron unit of Robert Neale. I was anxious that the finished design should seem to be made from woven strips, which would be an improvement on Neale's version where the units were slightly offset. Once again the A rectangle proved to be the solution to the problem with the diagonal of the rectangle playing an important part in the design process.

Starting sheet size A6; see p. 22.
Divide into thirds

1 both ways as shown

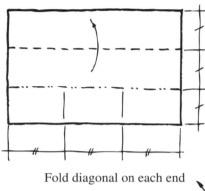

Fold diagonal on each end

2

3

4

5

Unfold the two ends

6

Unfold

8

7

Interlock three units like this

Add further units as shown, continuing with units of 6 different colours to complete the construction

30 units needed in all

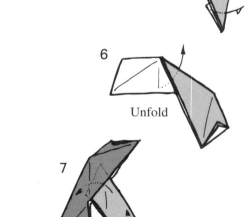

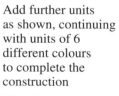

True Woven Dodecahedron

A logical development of the previous design: I realised that I could make a dodecahedron from strips which really were woven together. I am particularly pleased with the design which uses all of an A4 sheet with no waste. The finished ball is very strong.

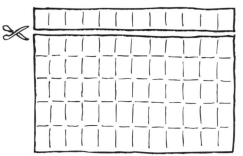

1

Use an A4 sheet; see p. 22.
Divide the short side into 1/6ths, and the long side into 1/12ths. Then cut into 6 equal strips. First cut shown here.

2

3

Fold diagonals along the strip starting and ending at the double raw corners

In the finished construction each strip is formed into a ring interlocked by inserting one end into the other, overlapping 2 divisions. The rings are not formed until step 7

Interlocking divisions

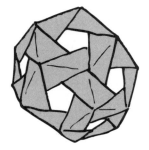

3a

4

Start by connecting 3 strips. This is made easier by using paperclips to hold them together.

7

6th strip

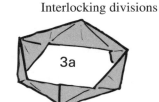

5

A fourth strip can now be added

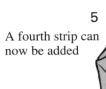

6

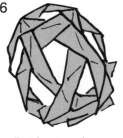

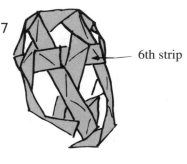

5a

Where 3 strips cross this pattern is formed

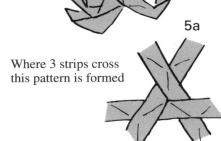

5 strips together. Note the pentagon formed at the top.

6th strip added
This should be interlocked as described above. Finish the construction by weaving the strips together as shown in 5a and interlocking the ends of each strip. Remove any paperclips you have used.

Stellated Dodecahedron

Borrowing the geometry of a well-known
method of cutting a pentagon from a square,
I found that this rather clumsy design is possible.
Some precision is required in steps 4&7 to ensure
that all the layers are folded exactly together.
The points of the star are not as sharp as I would
like.

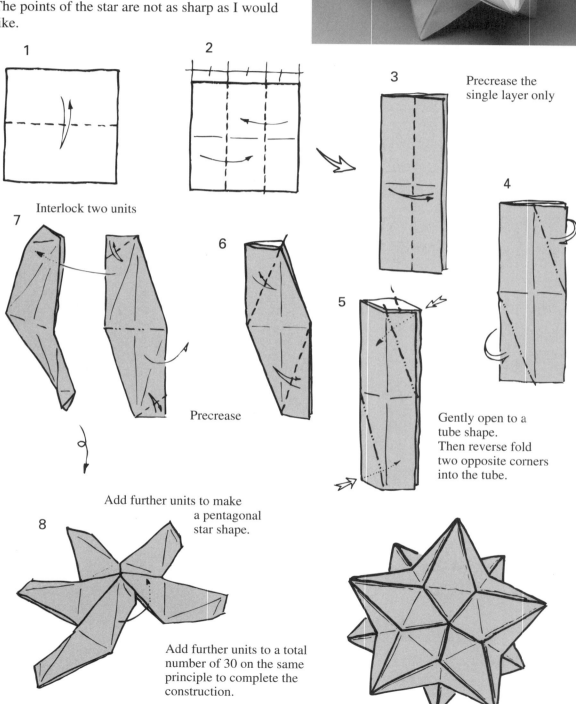

1

2

3

Precrease the
single layer only

4

Interlock two units

7

6

5

Precrease

Gently open to a
tube shape.
Then reverse fold
two opposite corners
into the tube.

Add further units to make
a pentagonal
star shape.

8

Add further units to a total
number of 30 on the same
principle to complete the
construction.

Stained Glass Balls

These designs employ similar geometry to the previous star but the coloured side of the paper is placed inside and then exposed to give the "stained-glass" impression. The units do not hold together well until the final stages of the construction.

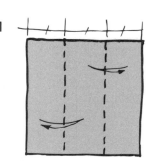

1

Divide into 1/3rds, and then 1/6ths.

2

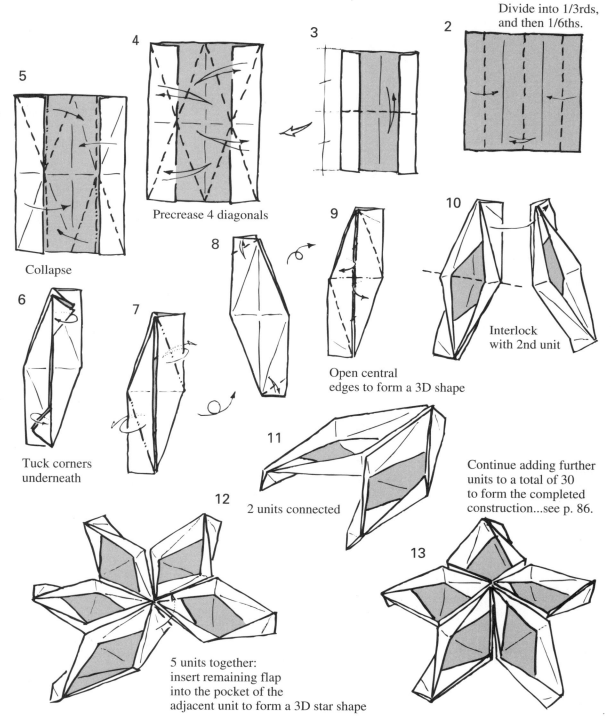

3

4

Precrease 4 diagonals

5

Collapse

6

Tuck corners underneath

7

8

9

Open central edges to form a 3D shape

10

Interlock with 2nd unit

11

2 units connected

Continue adding further units to a total of 30 to form the completed construction...see p. 86.

12

5 units together: insert remaining flap into the pocket of the adjacent unit to form a 3D star shape

13

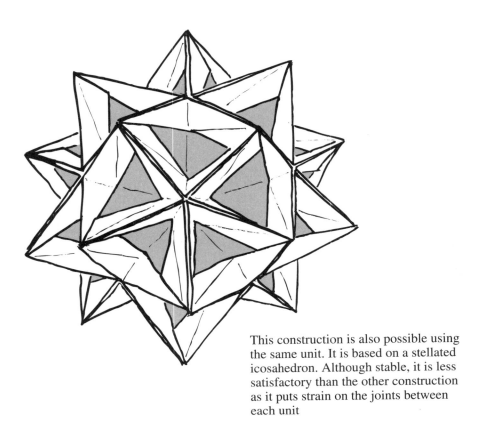

This construction is also possible using the same unit. It is based on a stellated icosahedron. Although stable, it is less satisfactory than the other construction as it puts strain on the joints between each unit

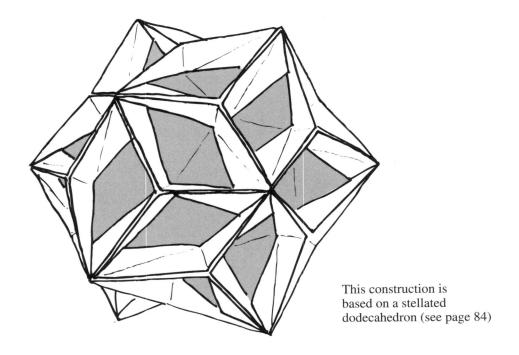

This construction is based on a stellated dodecahedron (see page 84)

Spiky Star

Start with an
A6 rectangle; see p. 22.

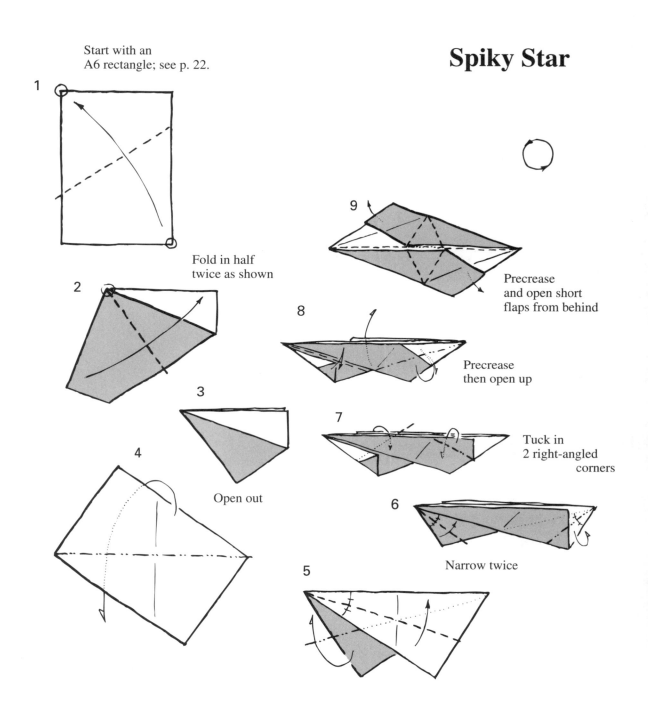

1

2 Fold in half
twice as shown

3 Open out

4

5

6 Narrow twice

7 Tuck in
2 right-angled
corners

8 Precrease
then open up

9 Precrease
and open short
flaps from behind

Using the "A" rectangle again, I wanted to make a really pointed
star. I am fond of the result, but there is a small inaccuracy in the
geometry of the unit. This is insignificant in practical terms but
offends my sense of perfection a little!

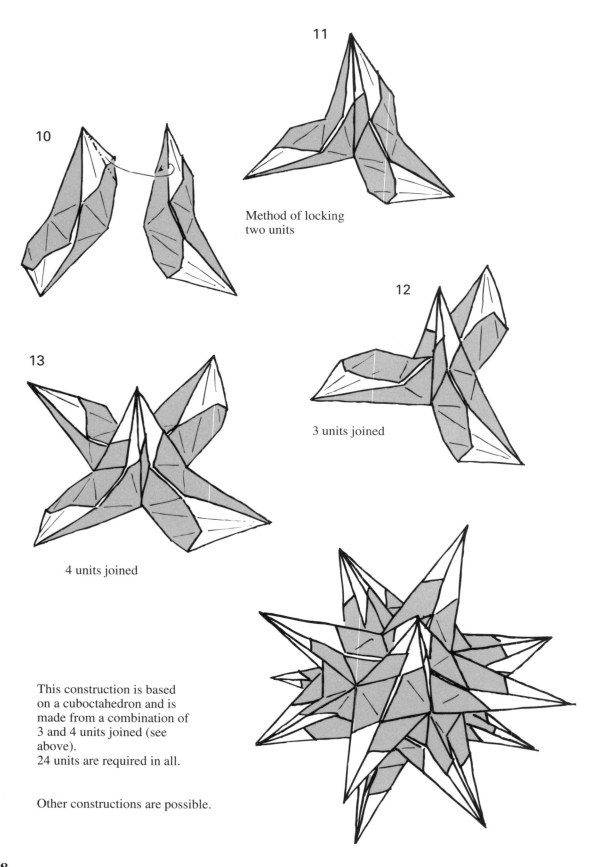

11

Method of locking
two units

10

12

3 units joined

13

4 units joined

This construction is based
on a cuboctahedron and is
made from a combination of
3 and 4 units joined (see
above).
24 units are required in all.

Other constructions are possible.

Stained Glass Ball

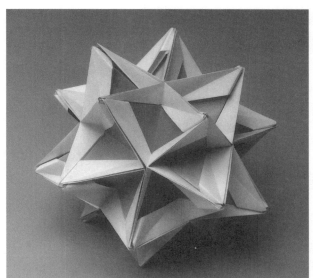

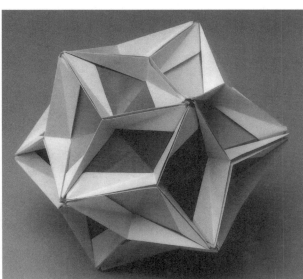

Stained Glass Ball

Spiky Star

Double Cube

I was fascinated to see this geometric shape in one of M C Escher's prints (which seem to be a constant source of inspiration for paper-folders), and I was determined to make an origami version. I also made a hollow "frame" variation, but this is not so elegant. There exists a single sheet double cube of similar appearance, by American folder Kenneth Kawamura.

16a

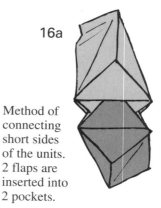

Method of connecting short sides of the units. 2 flaps are inserted into 2 pockets.

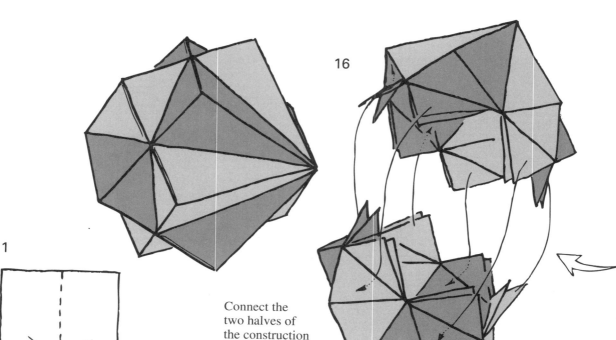

16

Connect the two halves of the construction to complete.

1

2

3 Reverse fold

4

5

6

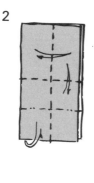

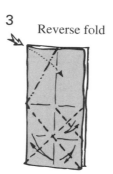

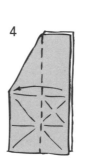

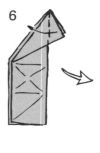

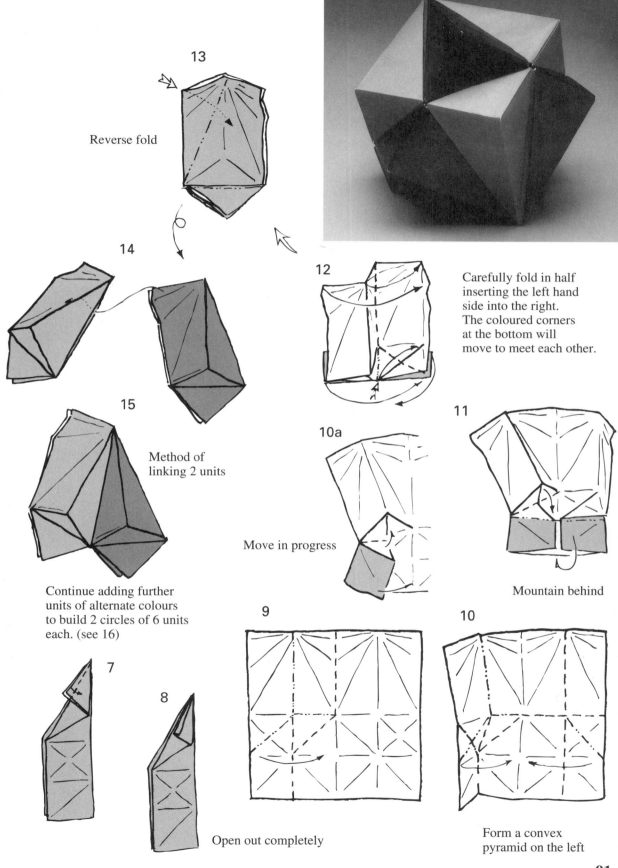

13

Reverse fold

14

15

Method of
linking 2 units

Continue adding further
units of alternate colours
to build 2 circles of 6 units
each. (see 16)

12

Carefully fold in half
inserting the left hand
side into the right.
The coloured corners
at the bottom will
move to meet each other.

11

10a

Move in progress

Mountain behind

9

7

8

Open out completely

10

Form a convex
pyramid on the left

Venetian Double Cube

So-called because this variation of the Double Cube emerged during a hot, mosquito-filled, sleepless night in Venice, where I spent a brief holiday in 1985. Curiously 4 different modules are required, unlike the simpler design which makes use of 12 identical units.

iv

1

i

Cut 6 more rectangles of a contrasting colour. Note the position of the existing crease.

ii

iii

Use this method to out 3x2 rectangles from a square: discard the narrow strip at the bottom

2

6 rectangles like this are required. Note the position of the existing crease

7

3

8

6

4

9

5

Open out completely

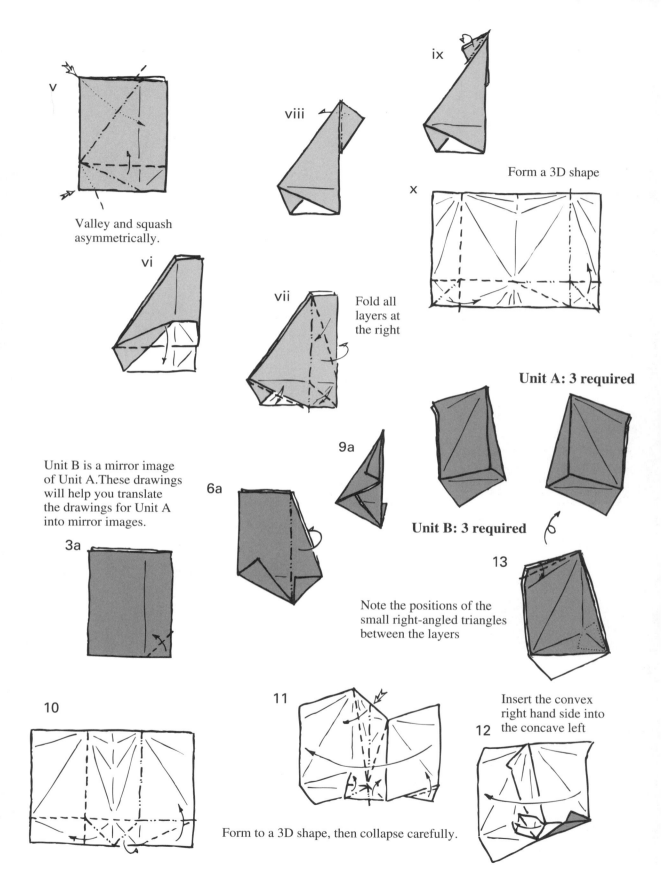

v

Valley and squash asymmetrically.

vi

vii

Fold all layers at the right

viii

ix

Form a 3D shape

x

Unit A: 3 required

Unit B: 3 required

Unit B is a mirror image of Unit A. These drawings will help you translate the drawings for Unit A into mirror images.

3a

6a

9a

Note the positions of the small right-angled triangles between the layers

13

10

11

Form to a 3D shape, then collapse carefully.

Insert the convex right hand side into the concave left

12

93

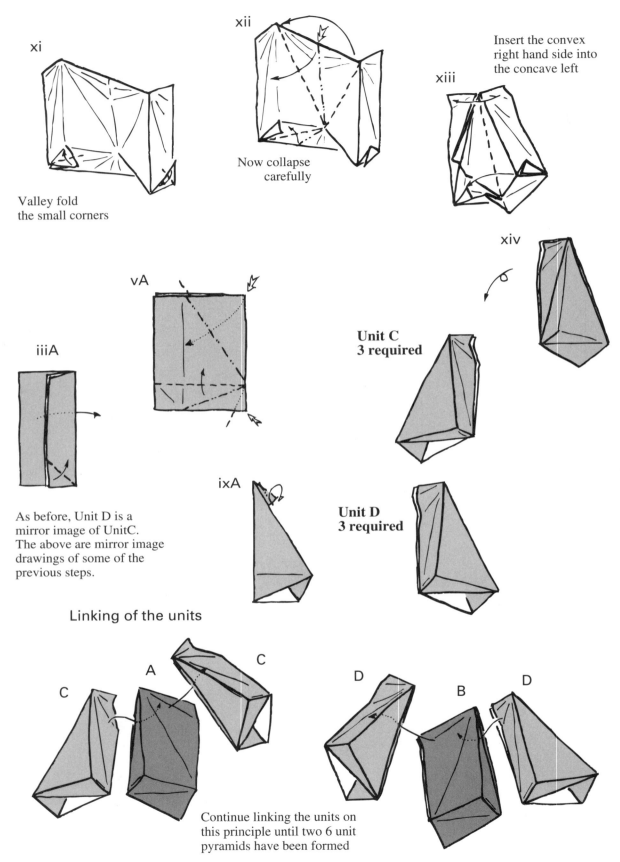

xi

Valley fold
the small corners

xii

Now collapse
carefully

Insert the convex
right hand side into
the concave left

xiii

xiv

vA

iiiA

As before, Unit D is a
mirror image of UnitC.
The above are mirror image
drawings of some of the
previous steps.

**Unit C
3 required**

ixA

**Unit D
3 required**

Linking of the units

C

A

C

D

B

D

Continue linking the units on
this principle until two 6 unit
pyramids have been formed

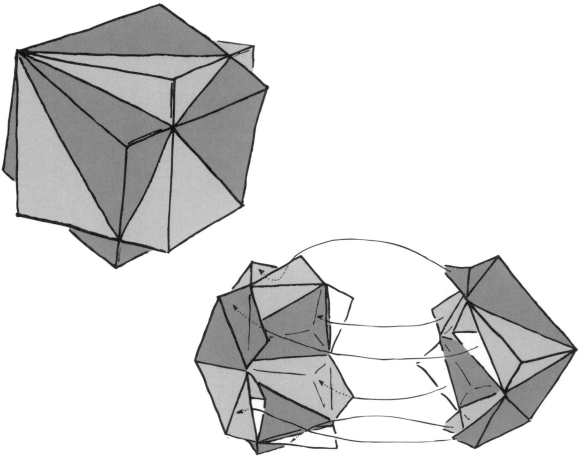

Connect the two pyramids like this:
inside flaps are inserted into inside pockets,
and outside flaps are inserted into outside pockets

Waterbombic Dodecahedron

The title of this design stems from the similarity
of the faceted pyramids to a conventional waterbomb base. The stimulus for the construction was
a dimpled ball, creator unknown, collected by
Lewis Simon. This was made from strips with curved
scored creases, linked together with cuts and slots.
I was tempted to reproduce it without the slots, but was
unable to reproduce the curved folds satisfactorily.
The final design used straight lines rather than curves.
The final locking pushing-in manouevres provide a good
climax to the folding sequence.

Use an A4 rectangle cut
in half lengthwise.
3 strips like this are needed.

1

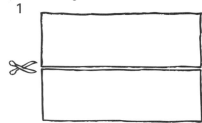

2

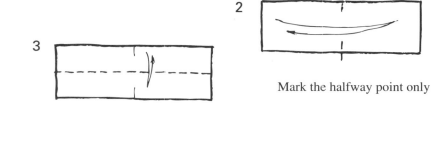

Mark the halfway point only

3

4

5

Adjust the position
of the ring and form
a new valley fold

9

6

8

Mark a square
then valley fold

7

Tuck in to
form a ring

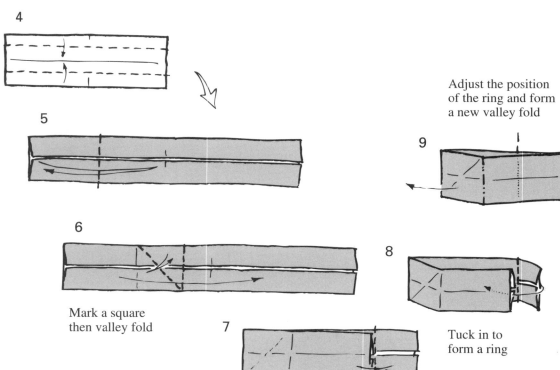

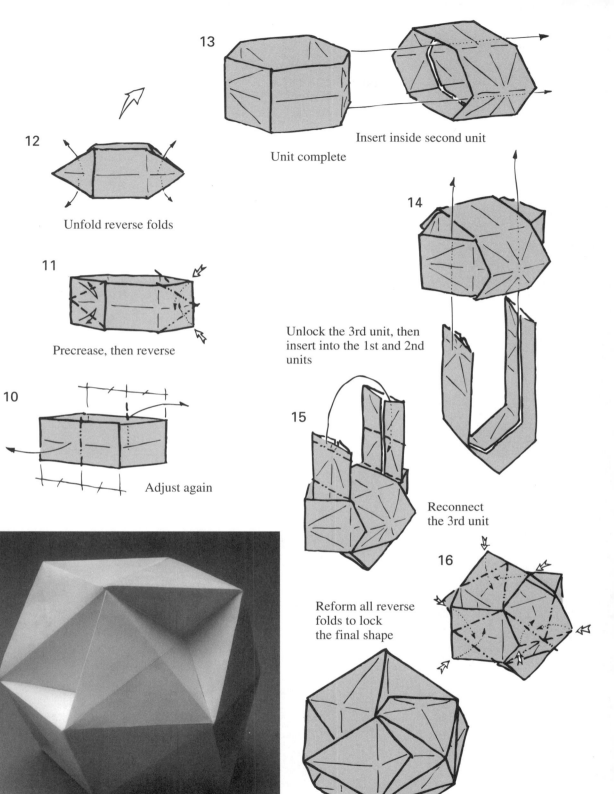

13

Insert inside second unit

Unit complete

12

Unfold reverse folds

11

Precrease, then reverse

10

Adjust again

14

Unlock the 3rd unit, then insert into the 1st and 2nd units

15

Reconnect the 3rd unit

16

Reform all reverse folds to lock the final shape

Double Star Flexicube

I had been introduced to this puzzle-like toy by Paul Jackson.
It later appeared commercially in plastic. I felt it impossible
to reproduce in origami terms until I saw a six-piece star puzzle
by David Mitchell. His design, reproducing in paper a wood-block
puzzle gave me a clue to folding this result. It needs a little care
in handling and flexing.

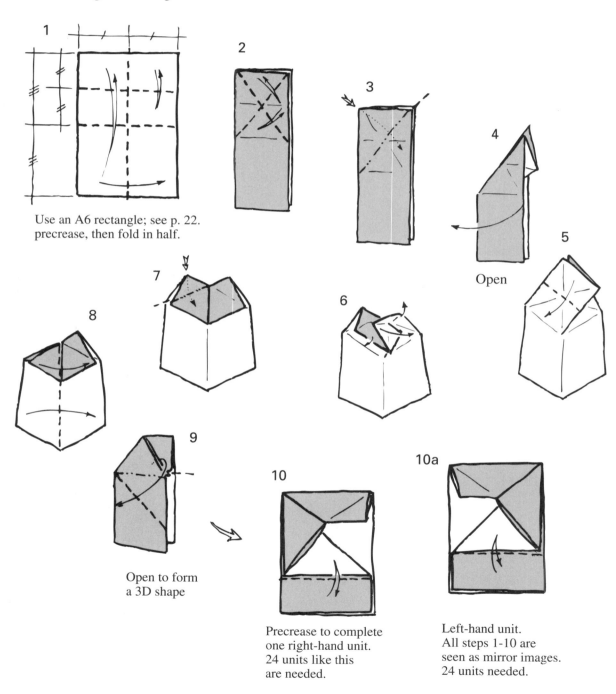

1

Use an A6 rectangle; see p. 22.
precrease, then fold in half.

2

3

4

Open

5

6

7

8

9

Open to form
a 3D shape

10

Precrease to complete
one right-hand unit.
24 units like this
are needed.

10a

Left-hand unit.
All steps 1-10 are
seen as mirror images.
24 units needed.

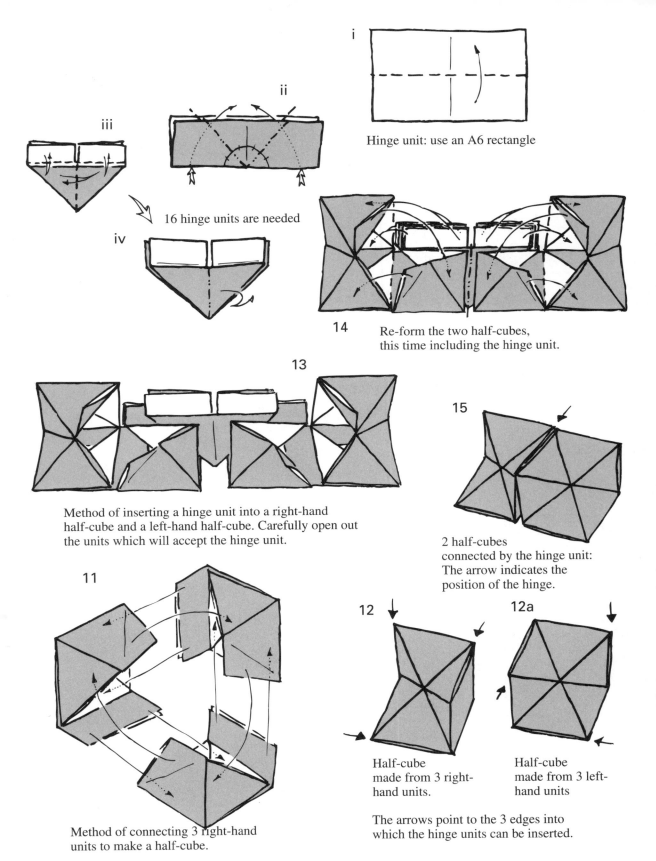

i

Hinge unit: use an A6 rectangle

ii

iii

16 hinge units are needed

iv

14   Re-form the two half-cubes,
this time including the hinge unit.

13

Method of inserting a hinge unit into a right-hand
half-cube and a left-hand half-cube. Carefully open out
the units which will accept the hinge unit.

15

2 half-cubes
connected by the hinge unit:
The arrow indicates the
position of the hinge.

11

Method of connecting 3 right-hand
units to make a half-cube.

12

Half-cube
made from 3 right-
hand units.

12a

Half-cube
made from 3 left-
hand units

The arrows point to the 3 edges into
which the hinge units can be inserted.

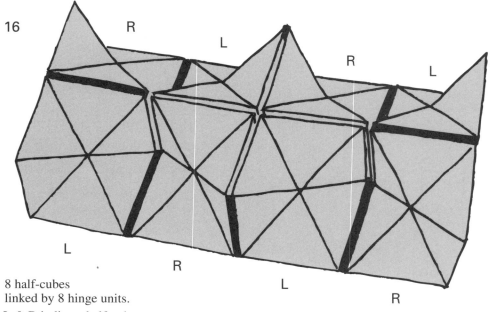

16

R

L

R

L

L

R

L

R

8 half-cubes
linked by 8 hinge units.

L & R indicate half-cubes
made from left and right handed units respectively.

The heavy black lines indicate the position of the hinge units   2 of these constructions are needed

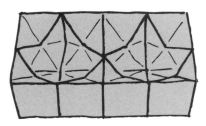

This shape
can contain the
shape shown
on the right

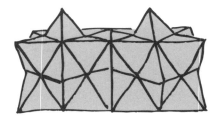

These structures can be formed
by flexing the construction shown in 16

This cube will contain this
three-dimensional star.

100

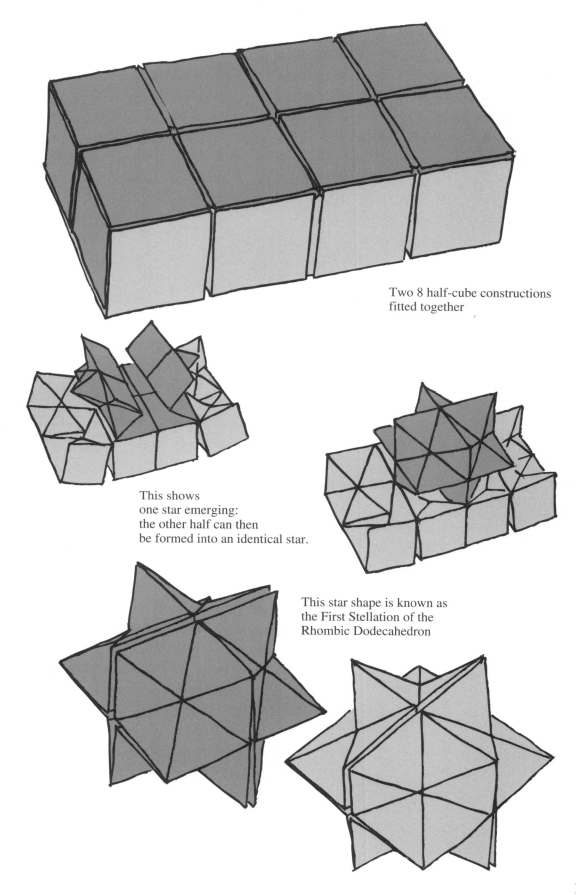

Two 8 half-cube constructions
fitted together

This shows
one star emerging:
the other half can then
be formed into an identical star.

This star shape is known as
the First Stellation of the
Rhombic Dodecahedron

Double Star Flexicube

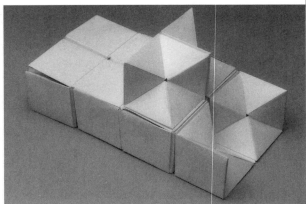

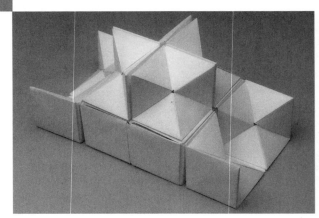

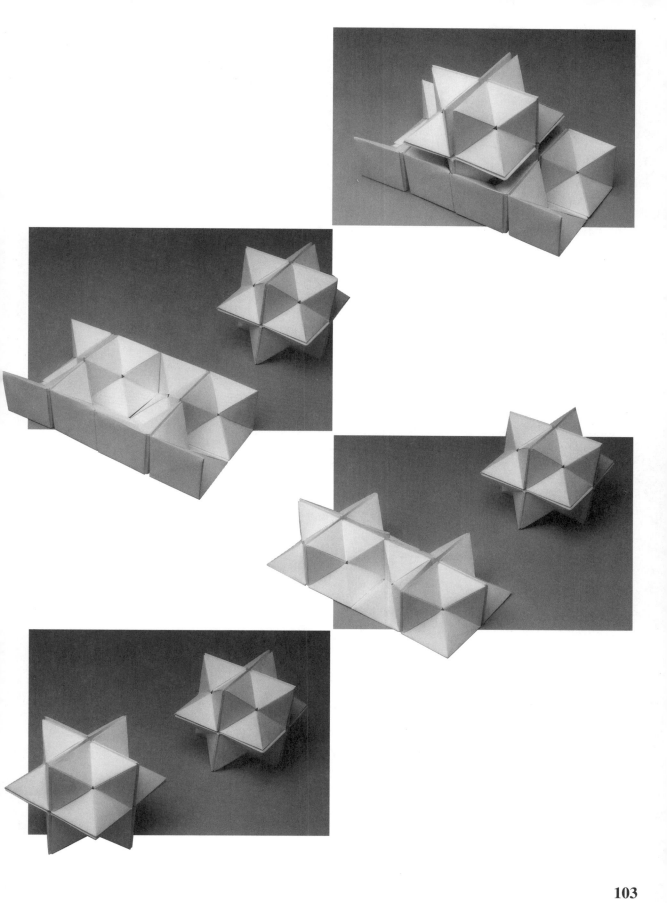

Wet Folding Techniques

To the purist who prefers not to introduce any outside tools to influence the direct dialogue between paper and folder, the technique known as 'Wet Folding" may not be immediately attractive. However it is an interesting and useful skill which isn't difficult to acquire. Indeed a lot of mystery has been attached to the process, which is in fact quite a straightforward one

Particularly suited to animals and living forms, wet folding has been pioneered by the Japanese master, Akira Yoshizawa. Its advantages include the ability to give both sharp creases and soft curves. The finished form will be much more solid than its dry paper counterpart, and large models can be folded from thickish sheets. These will support their weight and are less likely to collapse than the same subject folded conventionally.

Essentially the technique involves lightly wetting the paper before folding, folding swiftly and smoothly, and then allowing the result to dry. You should pay attention to the shape and three dimensionality of the model at all times.Yoshizawa has also used and described a development called "urauchi", where two layers of paper of different thicknesses are sealed together with thick flour paste. The layered sheet is then carefully stuck to a board by its edges with thin line of the same paste, and then left to dry. The sheet is then carefully removed from the board, now quite taught and wrinkle-free. It can then be dampened again by using a spray or a wet towel, prior to folding.

I suggest the following tips may help those new to the idea of wet folding techniques.

-Choose a thickish paper. I have used the heavier grades of Fabriano or Canson paper to good effect, and have found that even common brown wrapping paper works too.

-Don't over wet the paper: it should be floppy, though not dripping with moisture.

-Useful tools are a spray bottle which gives an even, drip-free mist, a towel, lightly moistened, paperclips or clothes pegs to hold layers together while drying, and possibly also a hair-dryer to speed drying of the finished model.

-It may be necessary to re-wet the paper during the folding process, but I prefer to avoid this as it's difficult to ensure that all layers within are evenly penetrated by the water.

-Make sure that you are completely familiar with the folding sequence of your chosen design: If folding from a book or diagrams, learn the method by heart before you begin.

-Fold swiftly and accurately, in the air if possible, as soon as the design has reached a manageable size.

I believe it's well worthwhile trying this process which will expand your knowledge of the behavior of paper while being folded. The results will be permanent and often well-suited formal exhibitions or displays.

Animals

This must be the most popular subject in origami: it is certainly one of the most challenging too. In the following pages I have tried to show a range of animals which I worked long and hard over in the 1970s and 1980s: I have tried to make them all three dimensional and with an element of life. Unfortunately it is not always easy to show the finer points of folding in the accepted diagramming style which I have used, but I hope that the photographs of the finished subjects will fill in any gaps in the information.

My only message is to persevere if your first folding attempt is unsuccessful. A second go will almost always give a better result. Please try your own variations too: this may open the door to your own creative origami career.

Lamb and Corgi (p. 106)

Lamb and Corgi

These are relatively simple animals, both in folding method and finished form. The reverse fold in step 12 needs careful positioning. I tried some variations with longer rectangles with the hope of making longer legged animals, but the results were not a success. The head and ears section has been used to form the base for the human figure; see p. 197.

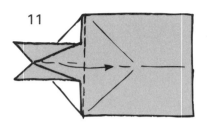

11

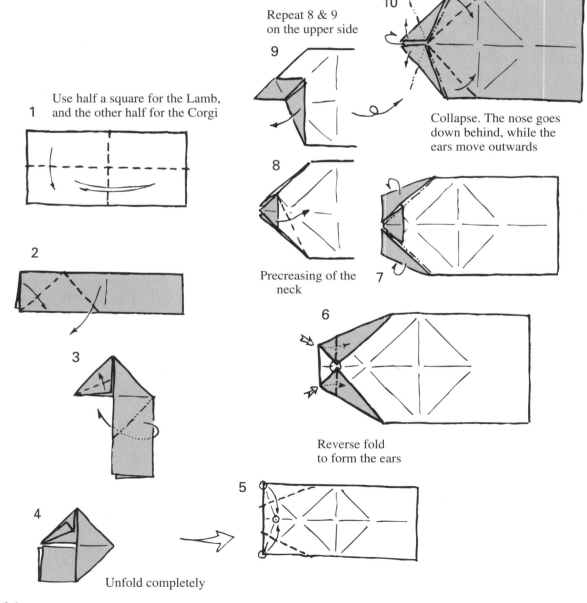

Repeat 8 & 9
on the upper side

9

10

Collapse. The nose goes
down behind, while the
ears move outwards

Use half a square for the Lamb,
1   and the other half for the Corgi

8

Precreasing of the
neck

7

2

6

Reverse fold
to form the ears

3

5

4

Unfold completely

106

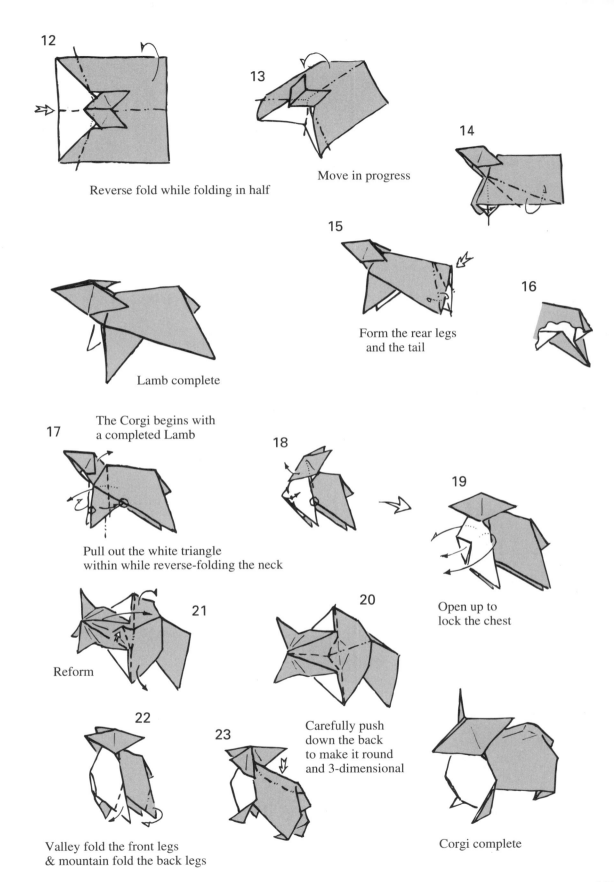

12
Reverse fold while folding in half

13
Move in progress

14

15
Form the rear legs
and the tail

16

Lamb complete

The Corgi begins with
a completed Lamb

17
Pull out the white triangle
within while reverse-folding the neck

18

19
Open up to
lock the chest

21
Reform

20

22
Valley fold the front legs
& mountain fold the back legs

23
Carefully push
down the back
to make it round
and 3-dimensional

Corgi complete

Another simply formed animal which uses
a variation of the fish base. The technique
forming ears was borrowed from Robert
Neale's Harlequin mask. The guinea pig
was made to order (and actually came
before the mouse) for some friends who
discovered they had a common interest
in these animals which they kept as pets.

Mouse

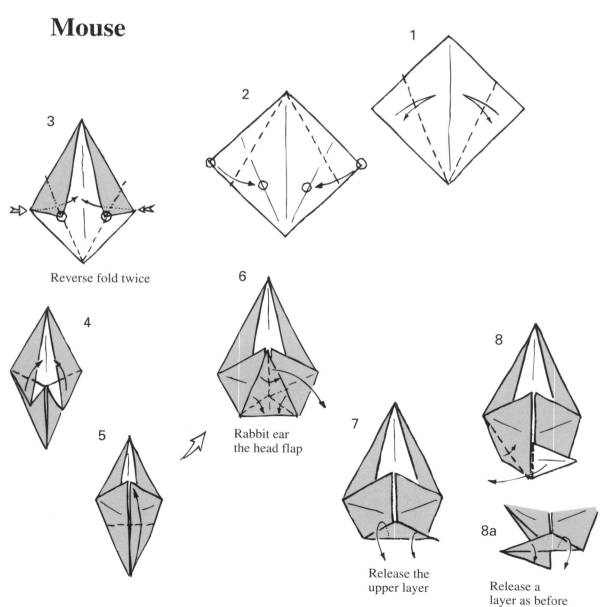

3

Reverse fold twice

2

1

4

5

6

Rabbit ear
the head flap

7

Release the
upper layer

8

8a

Release a
layer as before

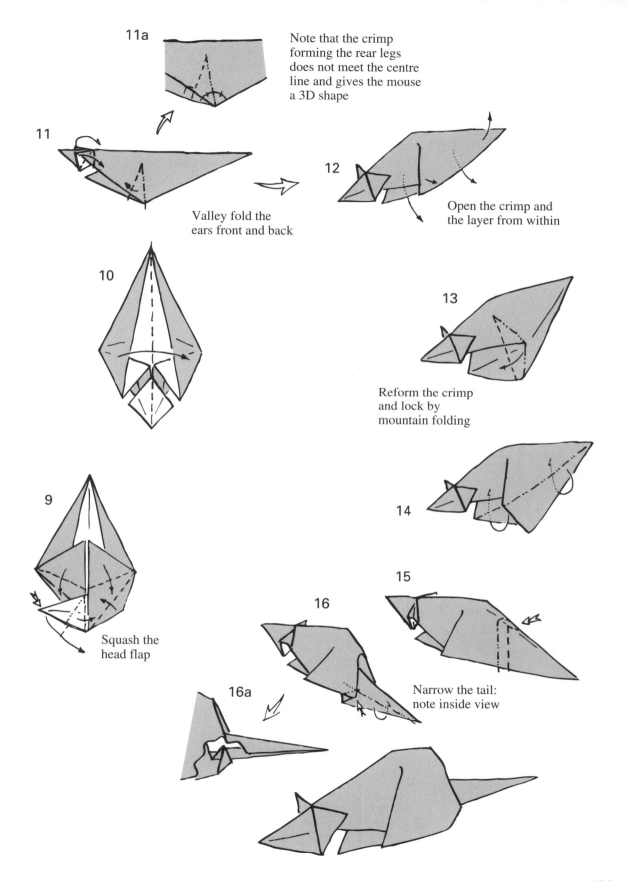

11a

Note that the crimp forming the rear legs does not meet the centre line and gives the mouse a 3D shape

11

Valley fold the ears front and back

12

Open the crimp and the layer from within

10

13

Reform the crimp and lock by mountain folding

9

Squash the head flap

14

15

16

Narrow the tail: note inside view

16a

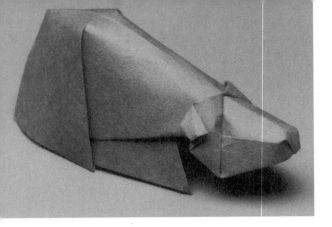

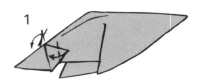

1

Start from step 14 of the Mouse

2

Squash the ears

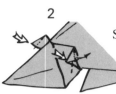

3

4

Form the eyes by
pushing in on the
folded edge

Lock the nose
by folding the
point underneath

5

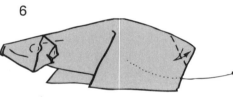

6

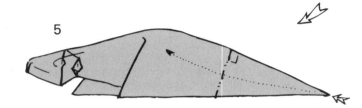

Guinea Pig

7

Pleat the pointed
flap to the left

8

then valley fold
inside the body
trapping a small
triangle within.

9

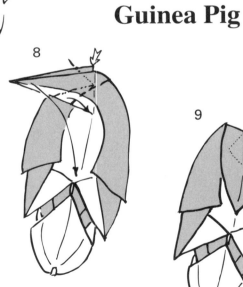

I was anxious to avoid all logical reference points when creating this animal, although I confess I have tidied up the method in these diagrams. The twisted head was a compromise to release the ears from below the head, but the positioning gives the rabbit a lively feel.

1

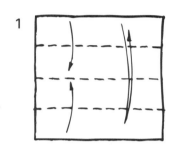

2

Reverse fold

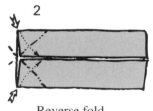

3

Form the rear legs
by a sort of petal-fold

Rabbit

Shorten the rear legs

4

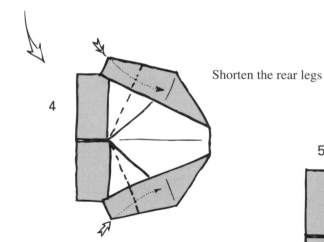

5

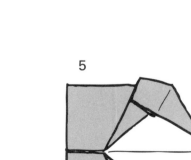

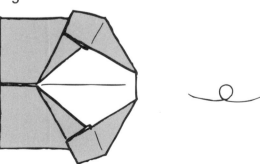

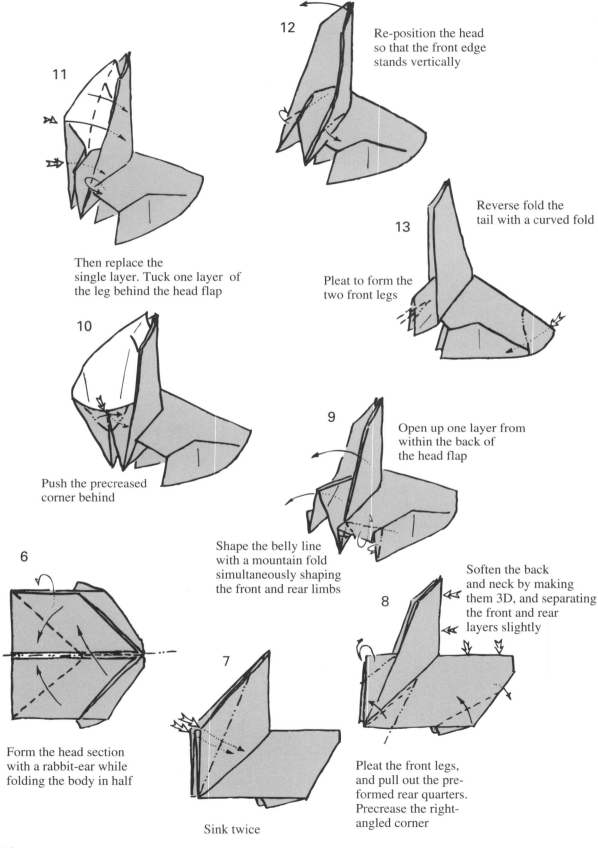

12

Re-position the head
so that the front edge
stands vertically

11

Then replace the
single layer. Tuck one layer of
the leg behind the head flap

13

Reverse fold the
tail with a curved fold

Pleat to form the
two front legs

10

Push the precreased
corner behind

9

Open up one layer from
within the back of
the head flap

Shape the belly line
with a mountain fold
simultaneously shaping
the front and rear limbs

Soften the back
and neck by making
them 3D, and separating
the front and rear
layers slightly

6

Form the head section
with a rabbit-ear while
folding the body in half

8

7

Pleat the front legs,
and pull out the pre-
formed rear quarters.
Precrease the right-
angled corner

Sink twice

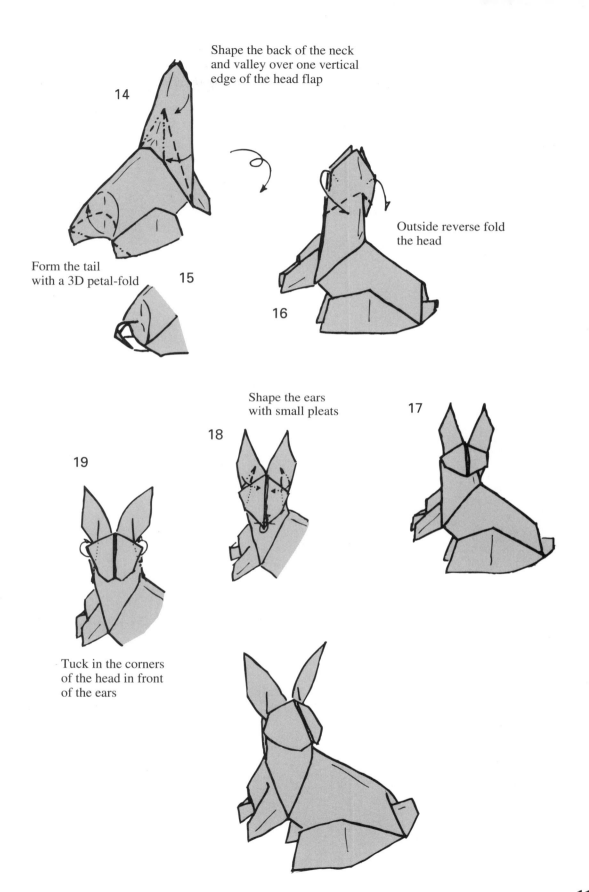

Shape the back of the neck
and valley over one vertical
edge of the head flap

14

Form the tail
with a 3D petal-fold

15

Outside reverse fold
the head

16

Shape the ears
with small pleats

18

17

19

Tuck in the corners
of the head in front
of the ears

Goose

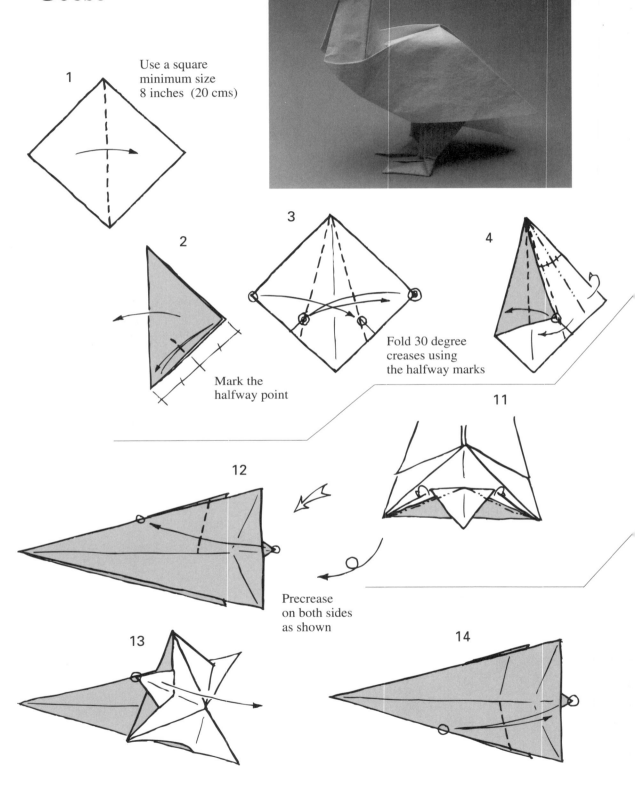

1 Use a square minimum size 8 inches (20 cms)

2 Mark the halfway point

3 Fold 30 degree creases using the halfway marks

4

11

12 Precrease on both sides as shown

13

14

114

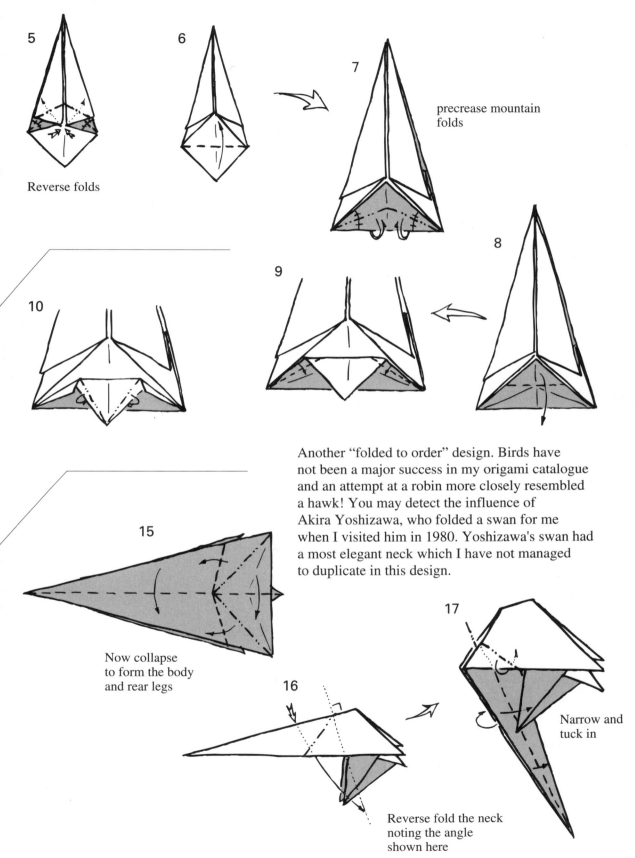

5

Reverse folds

6

7

precrease mountain folds

8

9

10

Another "folded to order" design. Birds have not been a major success in my origami catalogue and an attempt at a robin more closely resembled a hawk! You may detect the influence of Akira Yoshizawa, who folded a swan for me when I visited him in 1980. Yoshizawa's swan had a most elegant neck which I have not managed to duplicate in this design.

15

Now collapse to form the body and rear legs

16

Reverse fold the neck noting the angle shown here

17

Narrow and tuck in

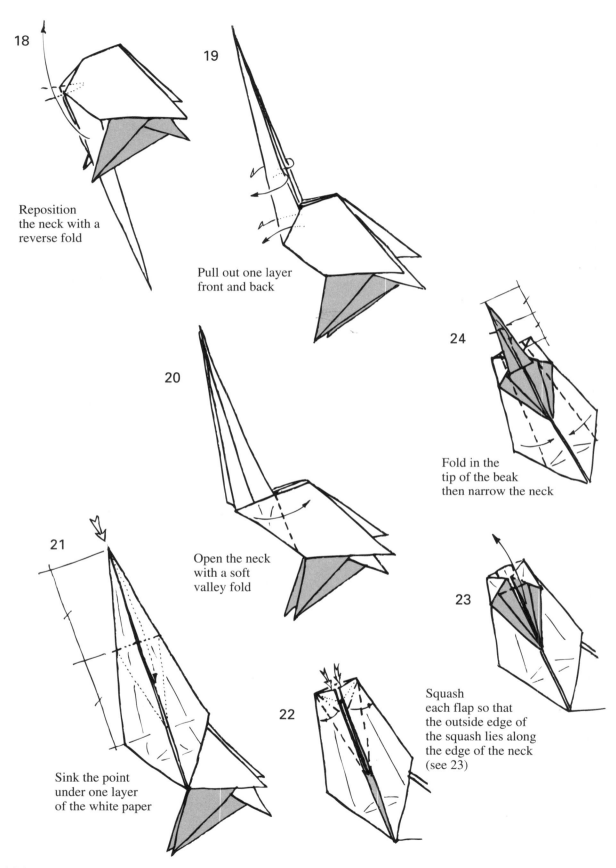

18

Reposition
the neck with a
reverse fold

19

Pull out one layer
front and back

20

Open the neck
with a soft
valley fold

24

Fold in the
tip of the beak
then narrow the neck

23

Squash
each flap so that
the outside edge of
the squash lies along
the edge of the neck
(see 23)

21

Sink the point
under one layer
of the white paper

22

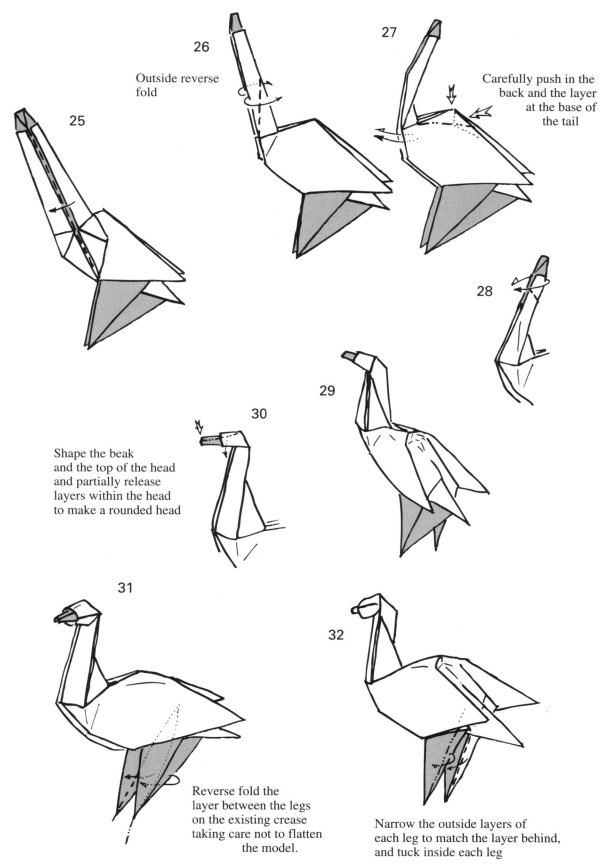

26

Outside reverse
fold

25

27

Carefully push in the
back and the layer
at the base of
the tail

28

29

30

Shape the beak
and the top of the head
and partially release
layers within the head
to make a rounded head

31

Reverse fold the
layer between the legs
on the existing crease
taking care not to flatten
the model.

32

Narrow the outside layers of
each leg to match the layer behind,
and tuck inside each leg

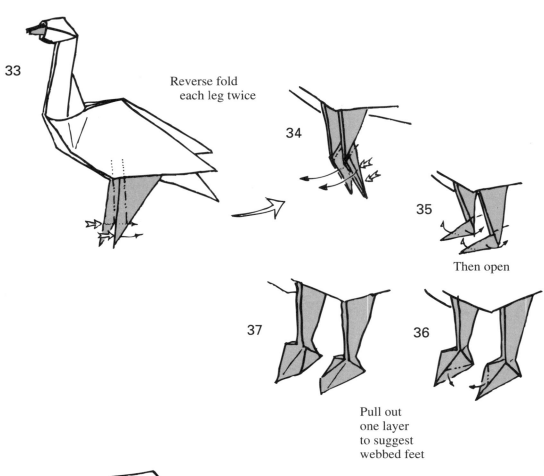

33

Reverse fold
each leg twice

34

35

Then open

37

36

Pull out
one layer
to suggest
webbed feet

Squirrel

A development of the mouse/guinea pig:
the formation of the head and ears needs
care, but if done successfully gives a dramatic
move in 26. Further difficulties may emerge in
the shaping of the back of the head but a second
or third attempt should allow you to obtain a good
result.

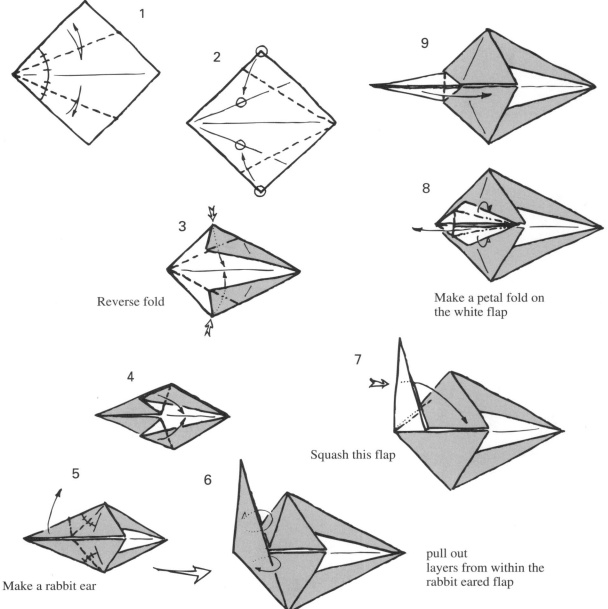

1

2

3

Reverse fold

4

5

Make a rabbit ear

6

7

Squash this flap

pull out
layers from within the
rabbit eared flap

8

Make a petal fold on
the white flap

9

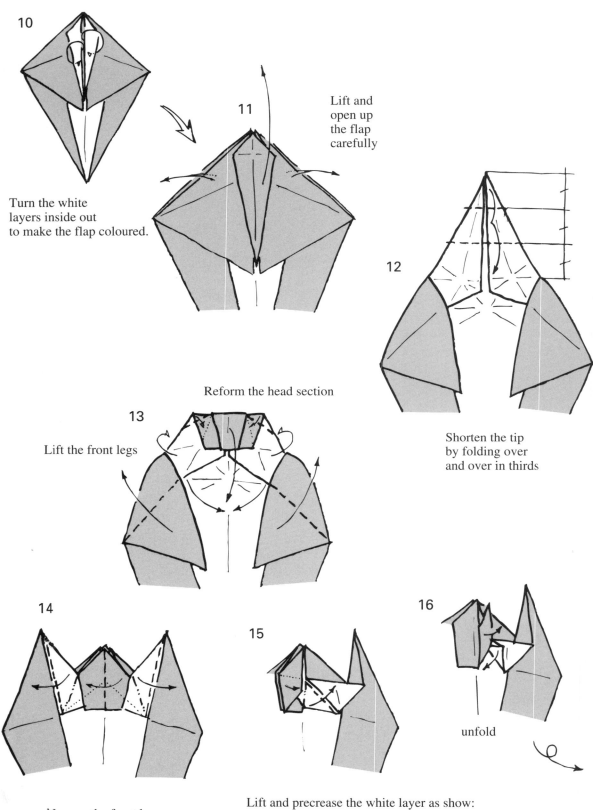

10

Turn the white
layers inside out
to make the flap coloured.

11

Lift and
open up
the flap
carefully

12

Shorten the tip
by folding over
and over in thirds

Reform the head section

13

Lift the front legs

14

Narrow the front legs
and fold the lead in
half to the left.

15

16

unfold

Lift and precrease the white layer as show:
this causes the head to open slightly and the
triangular area lying inside the head to stand
vertically.

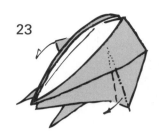

23

pleat the rear legs again

22

Push over the diamond shape
and collapse the tail

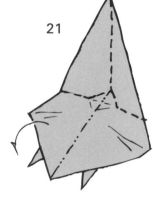

21

Reform the back
and tail using
new creases around
the precreased diamond
shape at the base of the tail

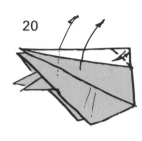

20

Precrease the
small corner
and then open up

19

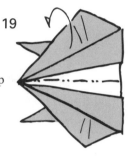

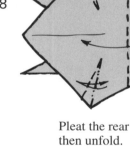

18

Pleat the rear legs forward
then unfold.

Fold the tip of the tail
to the head.

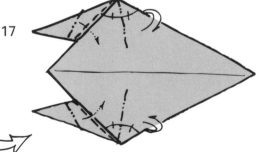

17

Pleat the front legs into
the layers between the body.

Precrease the rear leg section
noting that the crease does not
extend to the centre line

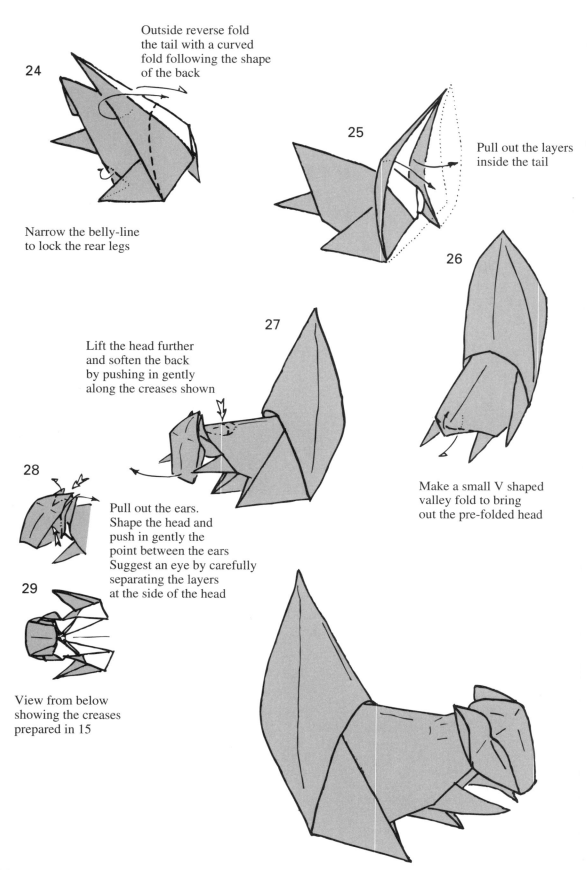

24

Outside reverse fold
the tail with a curved
fold following the shape
of the back

Narrow the belly-line
to lock the rear legs

25

Pull out the layers
inside the tail

26

Make a small V shaped
valley fold to bring
out the pre-folded head

27

Lift the head further
and soften the back
by pushing in gently
along the creases shown

28

Pull out the ears.
Shape the head and
push in gently the
point between the ears
Suggest an eye by carefully
separating the layers
at the side of the head

29

View from below
showing the creases
prepared in 15

In my early creative experiences, the *blintz bird
base seemed to be a saviour for all subjects. I had
been deeply impressed by George Rhoad's Elephant
in *The Best of Origami* by Sam Randlett, and had
enjoyed reading a treatise on blintzes by Gershon Legman
printed by Dokuohtei Nakano in his publication,
The Origami Companion, in the 1970s. I later found the
blintz to be more a hindrance than a help, producing
models which are thick and uneconomical. This dog
is however a successful treatment of half of a blintz bird
base and was designed to complete the Fox Hunt scene with
the two models on the following pages.
※ see 8, p. 125.

Foxhound

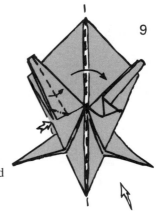

9

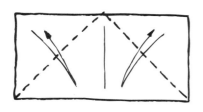

1

Start with a 2x1 rectangle
minimum size 8x4 inches (20x10 cm)

Narrow and
squash the
front legs

8

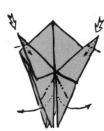
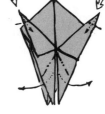

Reverse fold
the back legs

2

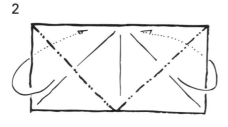

7

Valley fold the
front legs to lie
along the outside edges

3

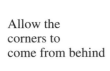

Allow the
corners to
come from behind

6

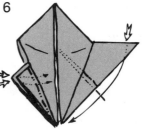

Sink the 2 corners
on the left, &
repeat 5 & 6
on the right

4

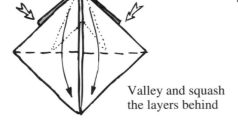

5

Half of a
Blintz Bird Base

Valley and squash
the layers behind

Reverse fold

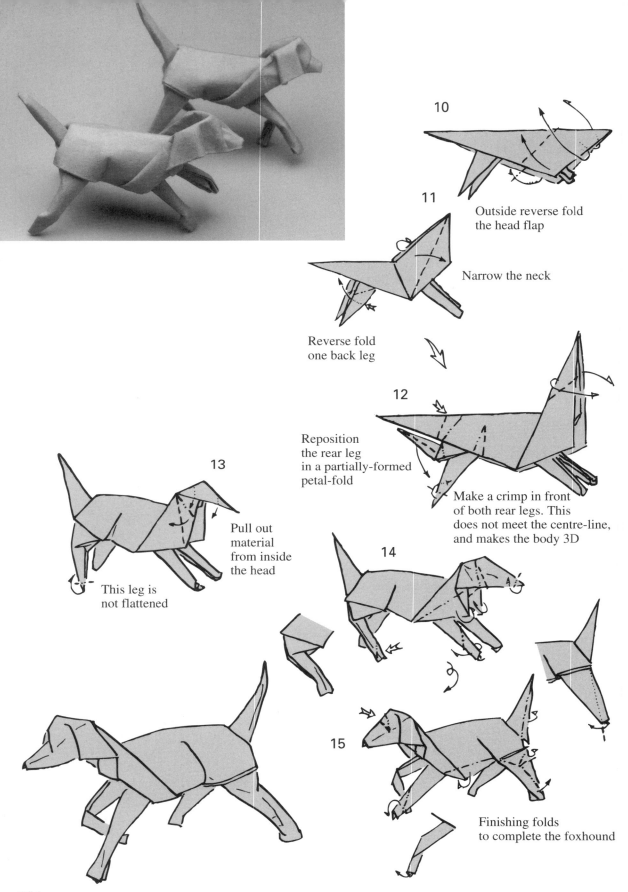

10

Outside reverse fold
the head flap

Narrow the neck

11

Reverse fold
one back leg

12

Reposition
the rear leg
in a partially-formed
petal-fold

Make a crimp in front
of both rear legs. This
does not meet the centre-line,
and makes the body 3D

13

Pull out
material
from inside
the head

This leg is
not flattened

14

15

Finishing folds
to complete the foxhound

1

Make a waterbomb base

Fox

2

Pre-crease each corner
to the central point

3

Rotate

4

5

Open out completely
to the coloured side

6

Re-form following
these crease lines,
at the same time
lifting each corner

7

Bring the points
together below

8

Lift the rear corner

Reverse fold
two edges

9

This shape is known as the
Blintz Bird Base

One of the first animals I made with the blintz bird base is this Fox. I was forced into using the twisted head as the ear flaps emerged under the head. This idea was later more successfully developed into forward facing creatures in the Elephant and Rhino, but the Dragon and Rabbit use similar techniques and look sideways or backwards. In the context of the Foxhunt scene, the head posture of the fox fits well.

125

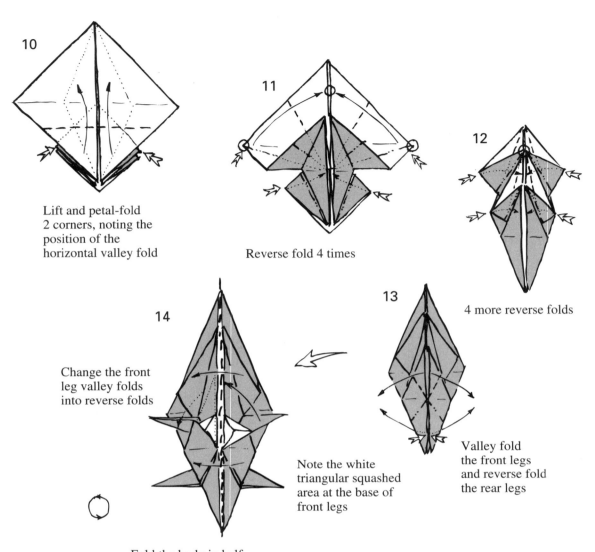

10

Lift and petal-fold
2 corners, noting the
position of the
horizontal valley fold

11

Reverse fold 4 times

12

4 more reverse folds

13

Valley fold
the front legs
and reverse fold
the rear legs

14

Change the front
leg valley folds
into reverse folds

Note the white
triangular squashed
area at the base of
front legs

Fold the body in half

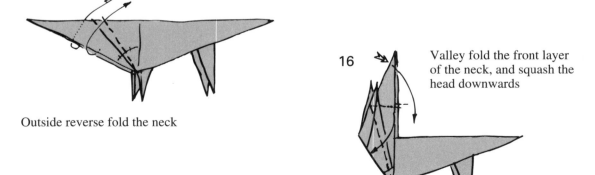

15

Outside reverse fold the neck

16

Valley fold the front layer
of the neck, and squash the
head downwards

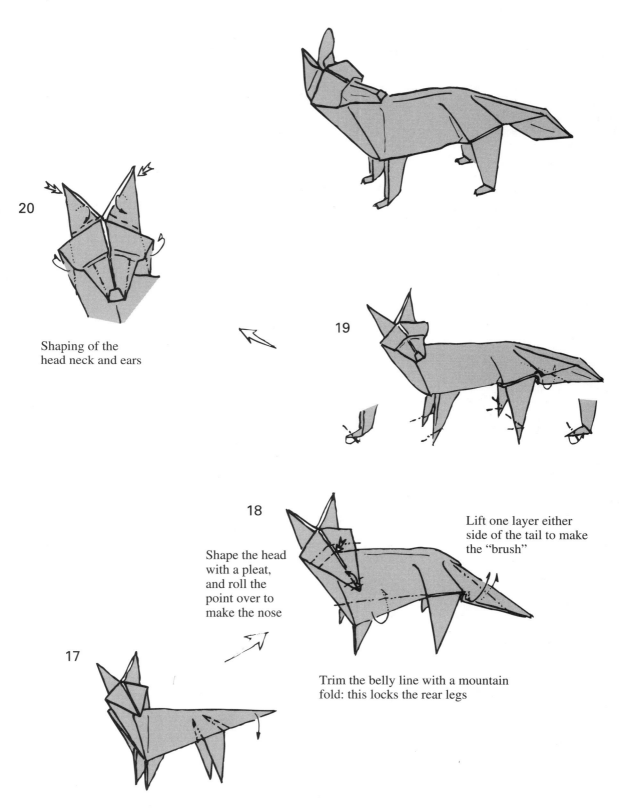

20

Shaping of the
head neck and ears

19

18

Shape the head
with a pleat,
and roll the
point over to
make the nose

Lift one layer either
side of the tail to make
the "brush"

Trim the belly line with a mountain
fold: this locks the rear legs

17

Make small pleats (not extending to the centre line)
either side of the rear legs. The tail will move down

Horseman

In the 60s and 70s it was fashionable to make dual subject models such as this. The style was pioneered by US folders Neal Elias and Fred Rohm. Although this horse and rider is presentable, it has many unsatisfactory aspects such as the white rear legs and tail if the design is made from coloured/white paper. It is also excessively bulky and has a very longwinded folding sequence. Following other dabblings with the multi subject style, I decided that the compromises to the individual parts were too great. I now prefer to make each subject from a separate sheet. To paraphrase Akira Yoshizawa, the man and the horse exist separately in nature, so why should we seek to join them?

Start with a large 2x1 rectangle coloured both sides: brown wrapping paper works well.
Minimum size 12x24 inches (30x60 cms)

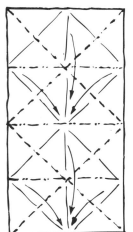

1

Precrease diagonals verticals and horizontals as shown, then form into a double waterbomb base

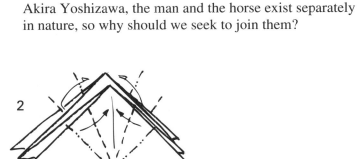

2

Pleat to the centre line front and back

3

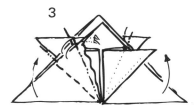

Crimp the centre points between the layers

4

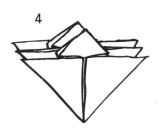

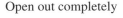

Open out completely

5

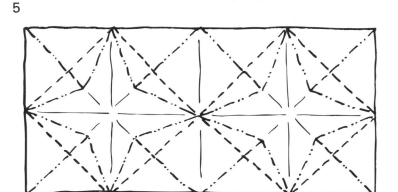

Reform the existing creases like this, then collapse by lifting each corner and the centres of the 2 long sides. (similar to Fox, step 7)

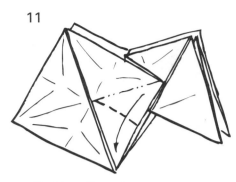

11

Start to collapse by
forming these creases

10

Pleat front and back

9

Open up front and back

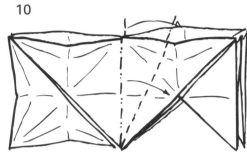

8

Reverse fold
8 right-angled
corners

Lift the
hidden
corner

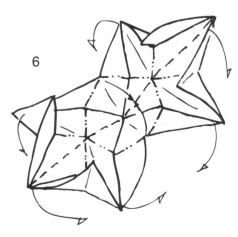

6

Bring six corners together

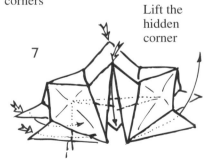

7

Reverse fold 4 times
This is a double
Blintz Bird Base.

12

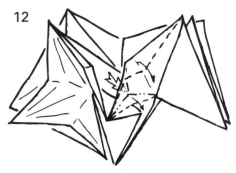

Push in gently
reforming the creases as shown, and continue collapsing
the left and right sides
of the construction

13

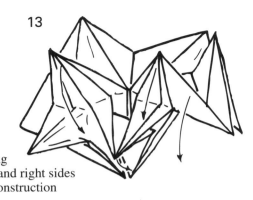

14

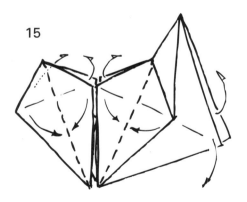

Almost complete
Repeat 11,12 & 13
on the back

15

Open and rotate both sides

16

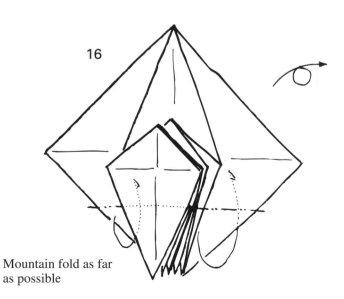

Mountain fold as far
as possible

130

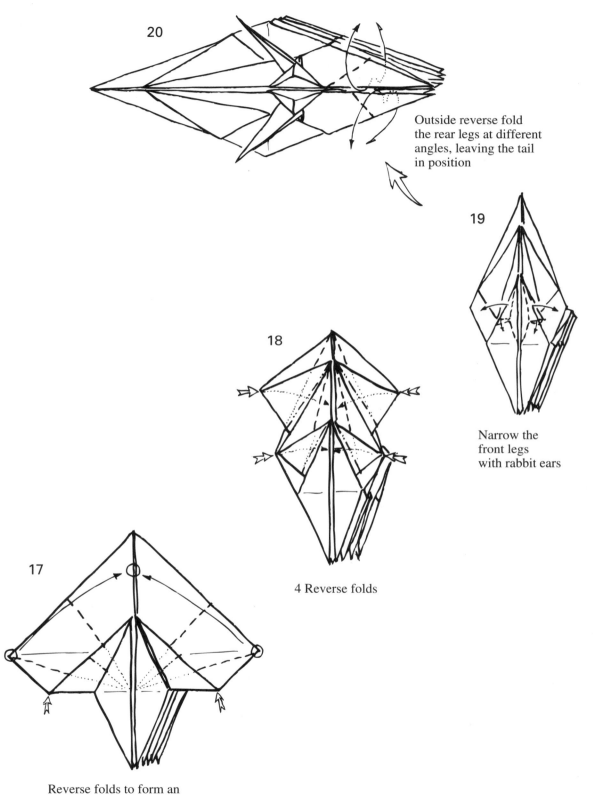

20

Outside reverse fold
the rear legs at different
angles, leaving the tail
in position

19

Narrow the
front legs
with rabbit ears

18

4 Reverse folds

17

Reverse folds to form an
asymmetric preliminary base

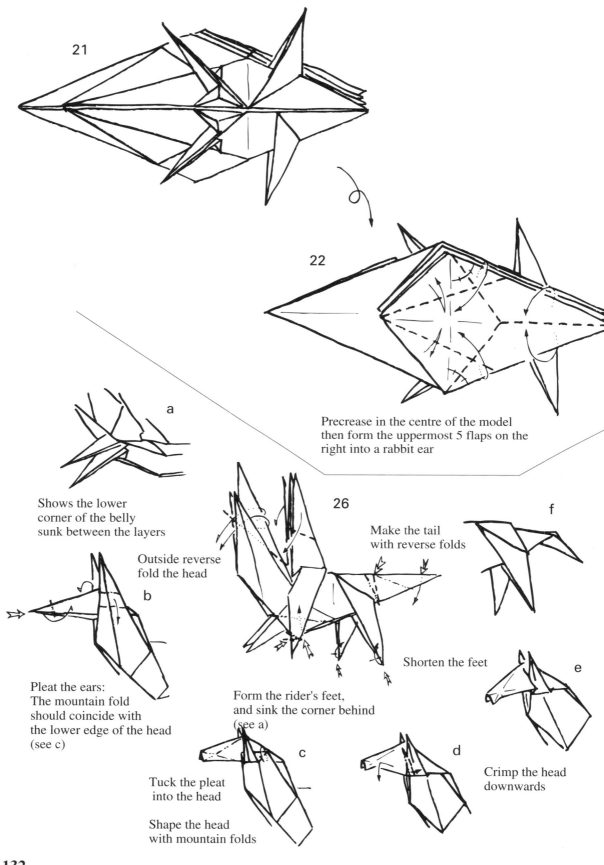

21

22

Precrease in the centre of the model
then form the uppermost 5 flaps on the
right into a rabbit ear

a

Shows the lower
corner of the belly
sunk between the layers

Outside reverse
fold the head

b

Pleat the ears:
The mountain fold
should coincide with
the lower edge of the head
(see c)

26

Make the tail
with reverse folds

f

Shorten the feet

e

Form the rider's feet,
and sink the corner behind
(see a)

c

d

Crimp the head
downwards

Tuck the pleat
into the head

Shape the head
with mountain folds

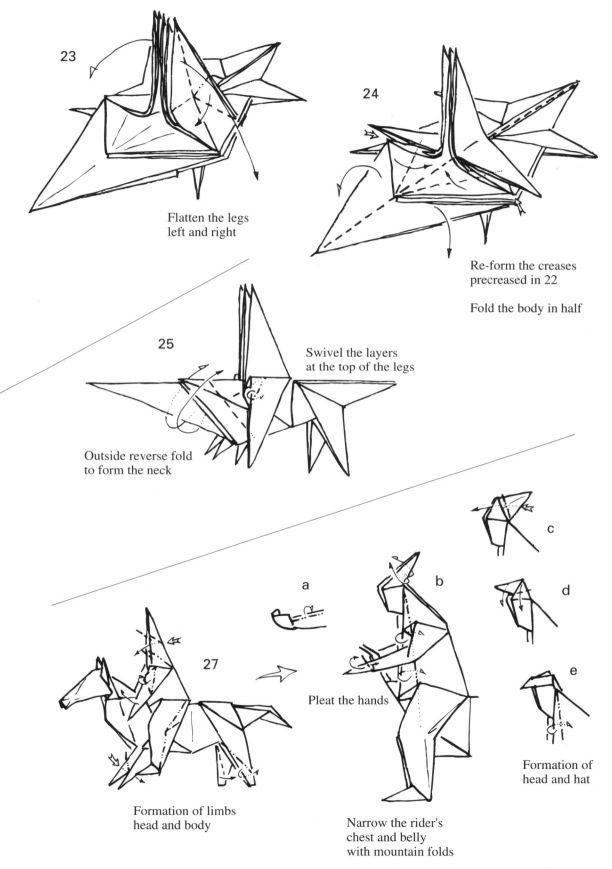

23

Flatten the legs
left and right

24

Re-form the creases
precreased in 22

Fold the body in half

25

Swivel the layers
at the top of the legs

Outside reverse fold
to form the neck

c

a

b

d

e

27

Pleat the hands

Formation of
head and hat

Formation of limbs
head and body

Narrow the rider's
chest and belly
with mountain folds

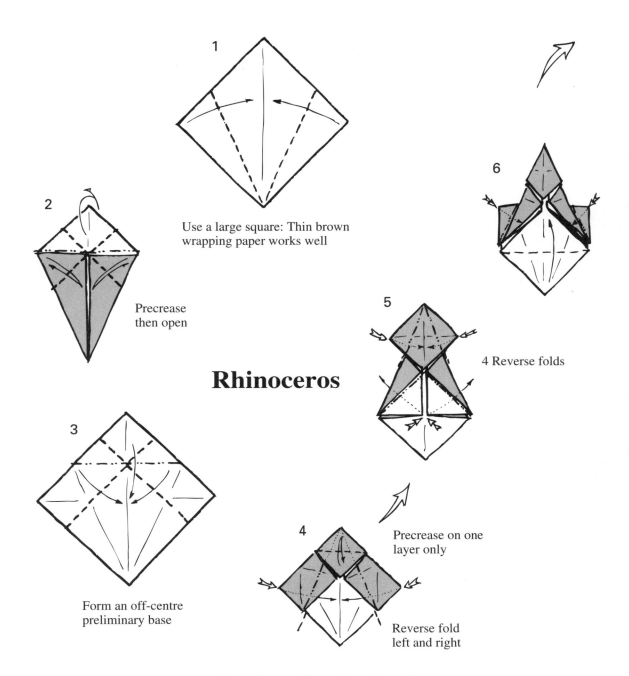

1

Use a large square: Thin brown
wrapping paper works well

2

Precrease
then open

Rhinoceros

3

Form an off-centre
preliminary base

4

Reverse fold
left and right

5

4 Reverse folds

6

Precrease on one
layer only

Some years ago I visited Chester Zoo, where I recall being very
impressed with the Rhino, who stood motionless in his enclosure.
I made sketches of the animal which later gave me information
for this design. Technically the base used has been stimulating for me.
The head has to revolve through 180 degrees to release the head and
horns. This time, however, unlike the fox, rabbit and dragon, the
animal looks forward, although this has been achieved at the
expense of quite a lot of bulkiness at the nape of the neck. The stresses
in the paper here can be used to pose the head slightly to one side,
as if the Rhino is considering whether to charge at the spectator!

135

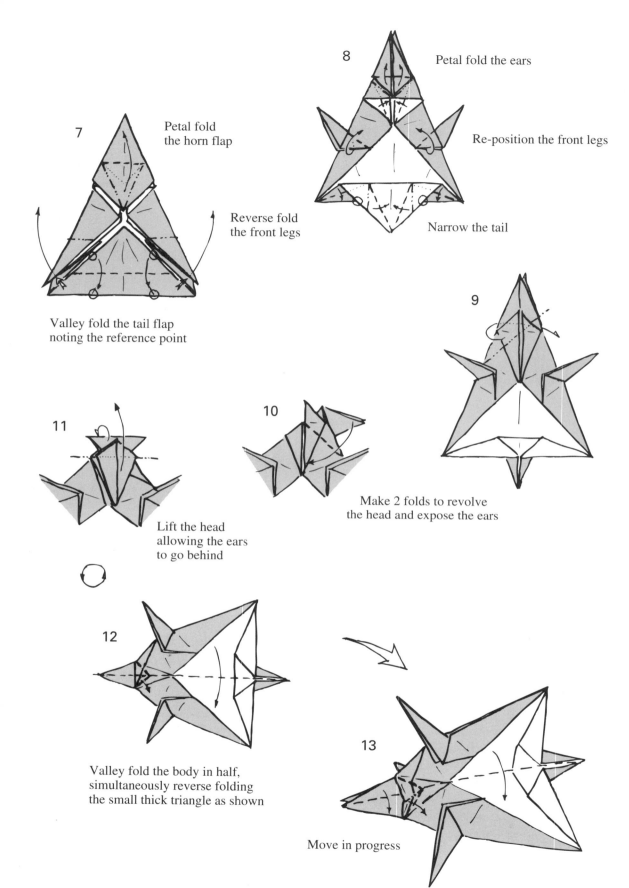

7

Petal fold
the horn flap

Reverse fold
the front legs

Valley fold the tail flap
noting the reference point

8

Petal fold the ears

Re-position the front legs

Narrow the tail

9

11

Lift the head
allowing the ears
to go behind

10

Make 2 folds to revolve
the head and expose the ears

12

Valley fold the body in half,
simultaneously reverse folding
the small thick triangle as shown

13

Move in progress

These drawings show the formation of the front and back legs

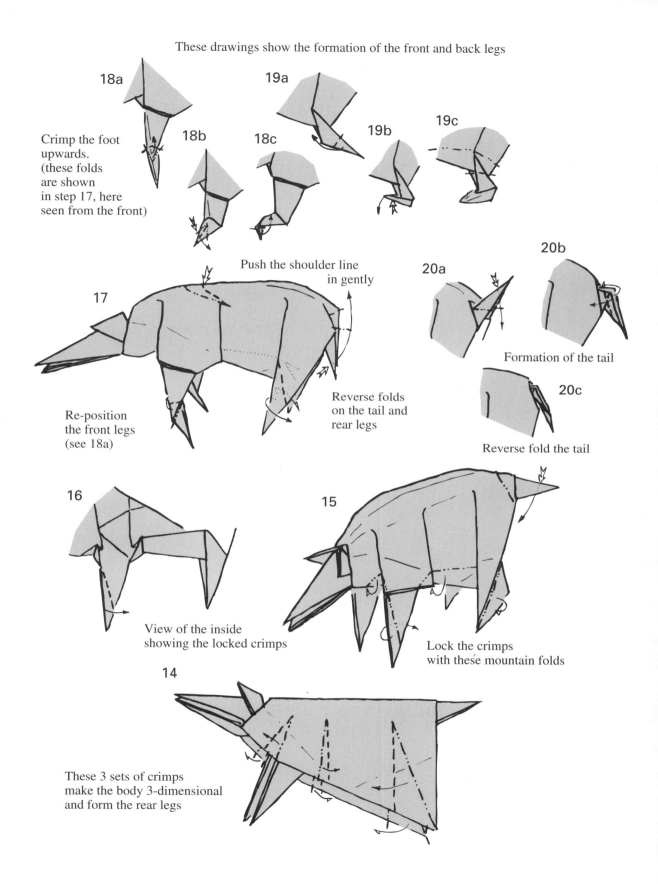

18a

Crimp the foot
upwards.
(these folds
are shown
in step 17, here
seen from the front)

18b

18c

19a

19b

19c

20a

20b

Formation of the tail

20c

Reverse fold the tail

17

Push the shoulder line
in gently

Re-position
the front legs
(see 18a)

Reverse folds
on the tail and
rear legs

16

View of the inside
showing the locked crimps

15

Lock the crimps
with these mountain folds

14

These 3 sets of crimps
make the body 3-dimensional
and form the rear legs

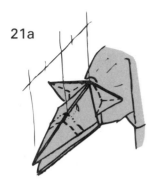

21a

Pleat the smaller horn

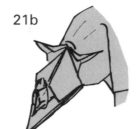

21b

Raise the smaller
horn with a rabbit ear

Pull out layers from within
the smaller horn

21c

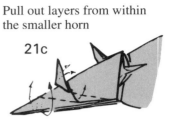

Valley fold the corner
to make the eye

Outside reverse fold
the larger horn

21d

Open the ears, shape the
head and eyes, and crimp
the larger horn slightly

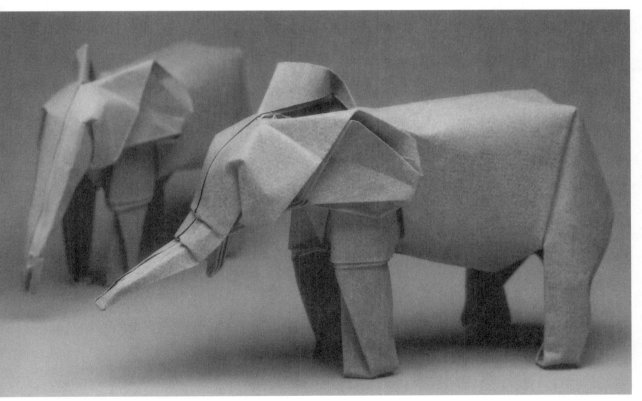

Elephant

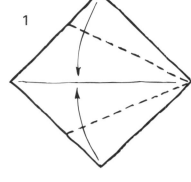

1

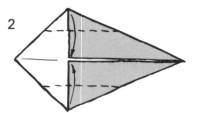

2

Use a large square of thickish paper
Minimum square size 12 inches (30 cm)

3

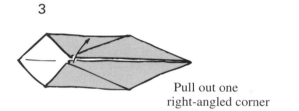

Pull out one
right-angled corner

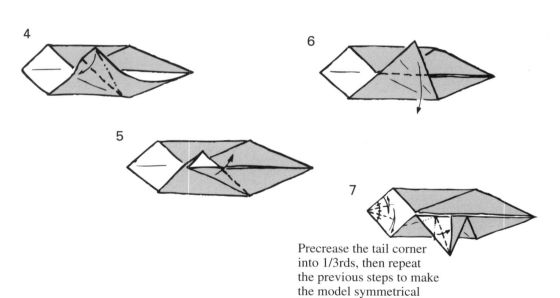

4

6

5

7

Precrease the tail corner
into 1/3rds, then repeat
the previous steps to make
the model symmetrical

I spent a lot of time developing this animal which I wanted to
have a fully three-dimensional construction, having a cylindrical body
with a closed stomach, as far as possible. The head and ears revolve
as before, and the animal looks forward. In folding this, you will need
to experiment, adjusting the illustrated folds during the formation of the
body to get the best result. Try again if your first attempt fails to satisfy.

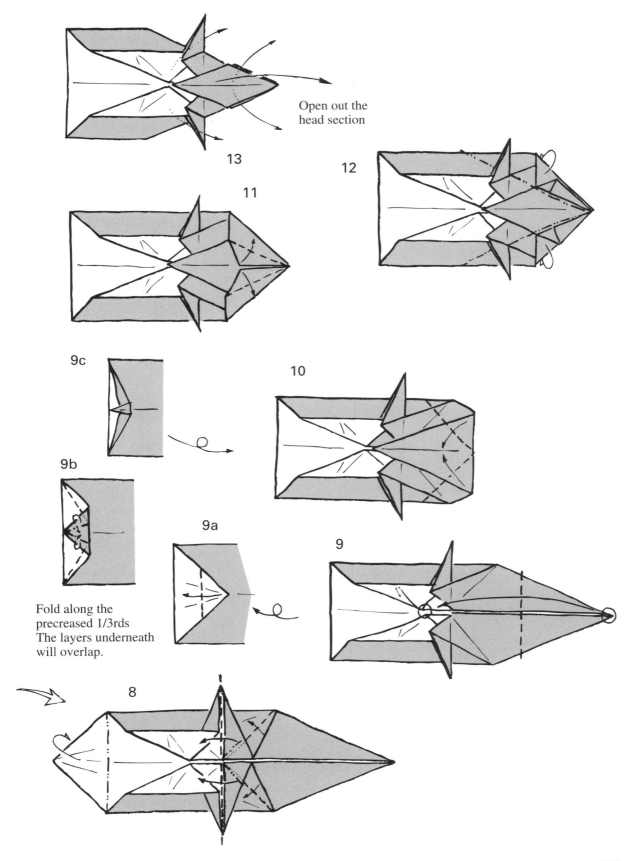

Open out the
head section

13

12

11

9c

10

9b

9a

9

Fold along the
precreased 1/3rds
The layers underneath
will overlap.

8

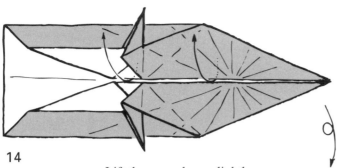

14

Lift the upper layer slightly

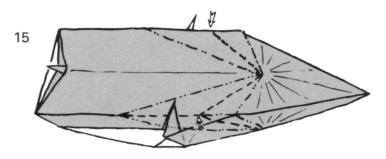

15

Sink along the precreased lines

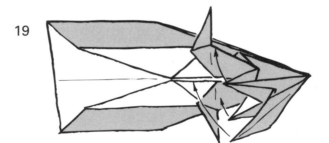

19

Collapsing almost complete

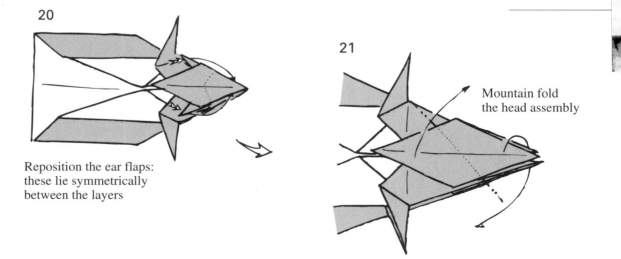

20

Reposition the ear flaps:
these lie symmetrically
between the layers

21

Mountain fold
the head assembly

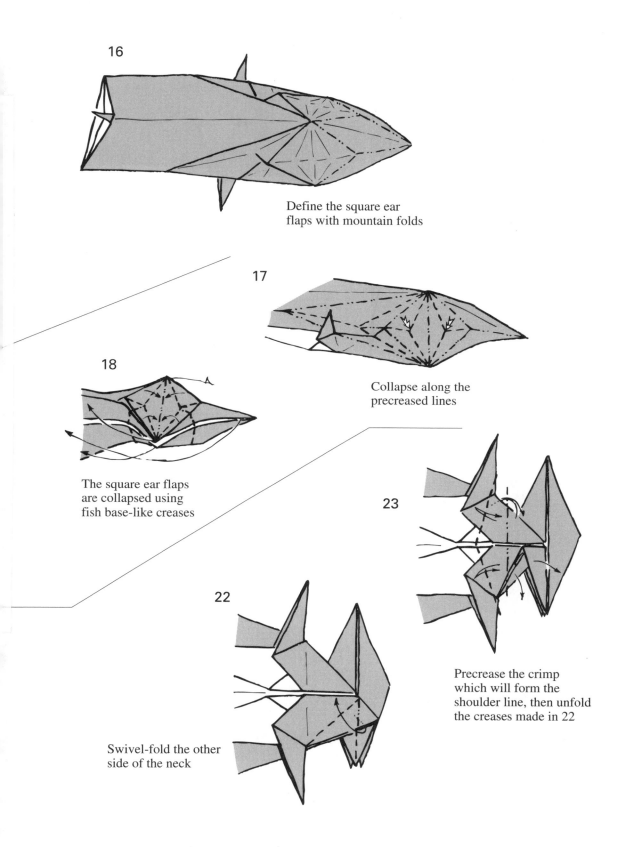

16

Define the square ear
flaps with mountain folds

17

Collapse along the
precreased lines

18

The square ear flaps
are collapsed using
fish base-like creases

23

Precrease the crimp
which will form the
shoulder line, then unfold
the creases made in 22

22

Swivel-fold the other
side of the neck

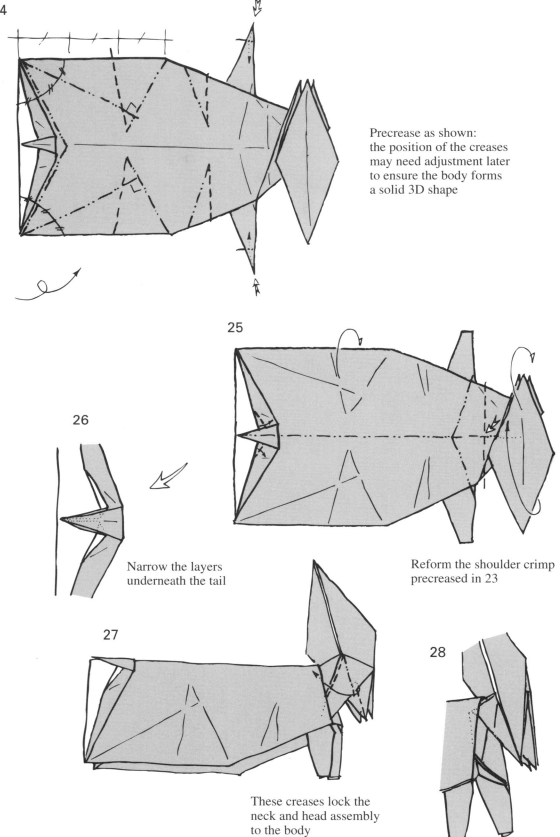

24

Precrease as shown:
the position of the creases
may need adjustment later
to ensure the body forms
a solid 3D shape

25

26

Narrow the layers
underneath the tail

Reform the shoulder crimp
precreased in 23

27

These creases lock the
neck and head assembly
to the body

28

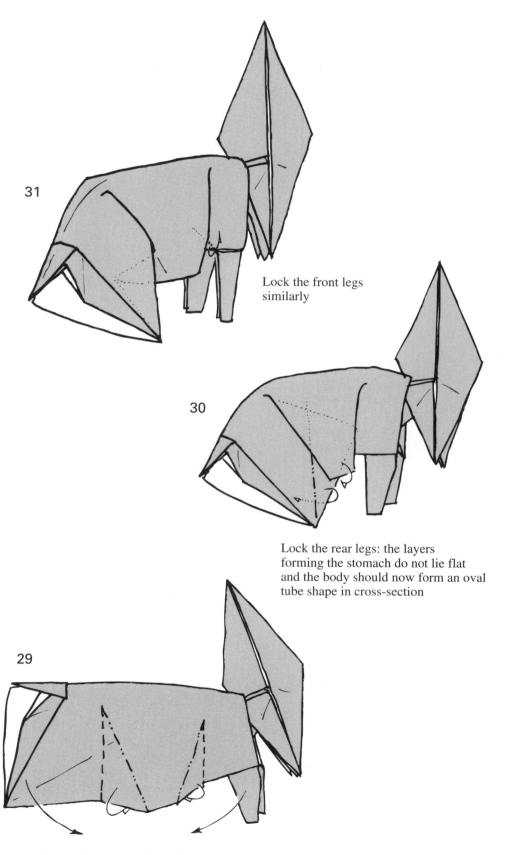

31

Lock the front legs
similarly

30

Lock the rear legs: the layers
forming the stomach do not lie flat
and the body should now form an oval
tube shape in cross-section

29

Start to form the body and leg crimps

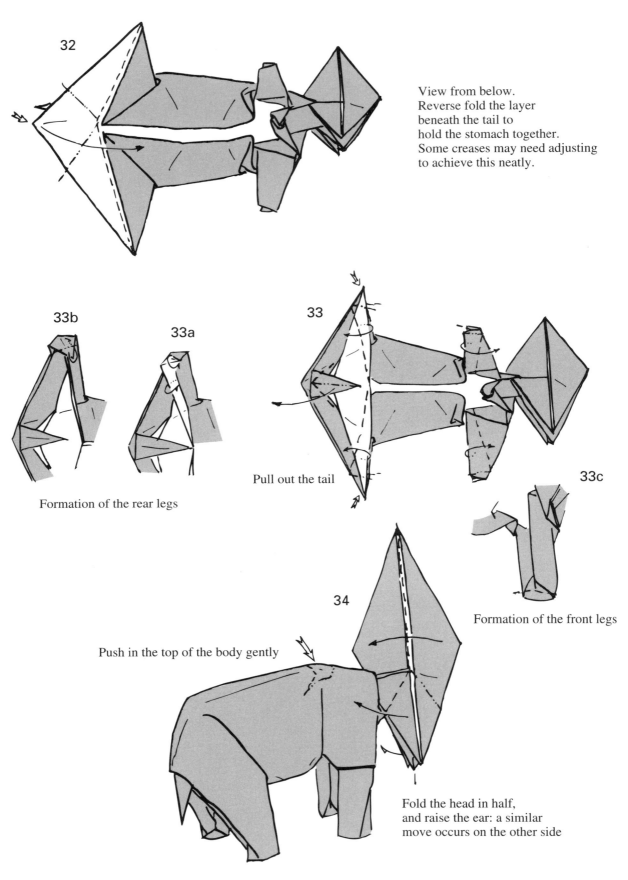

32

View from below.
Reverse fold the layer
beneath the tail to
hold the stomach together.
Some creases may need adjusting
to achieve this neatly.

33b

33a

Formation of the rear legs

33

Pull out the tail

33c

Formation of the front legs

34

Push in the top of the body gently

Fold the head in half,
and raise the ear: a similar
move occurs on the other side

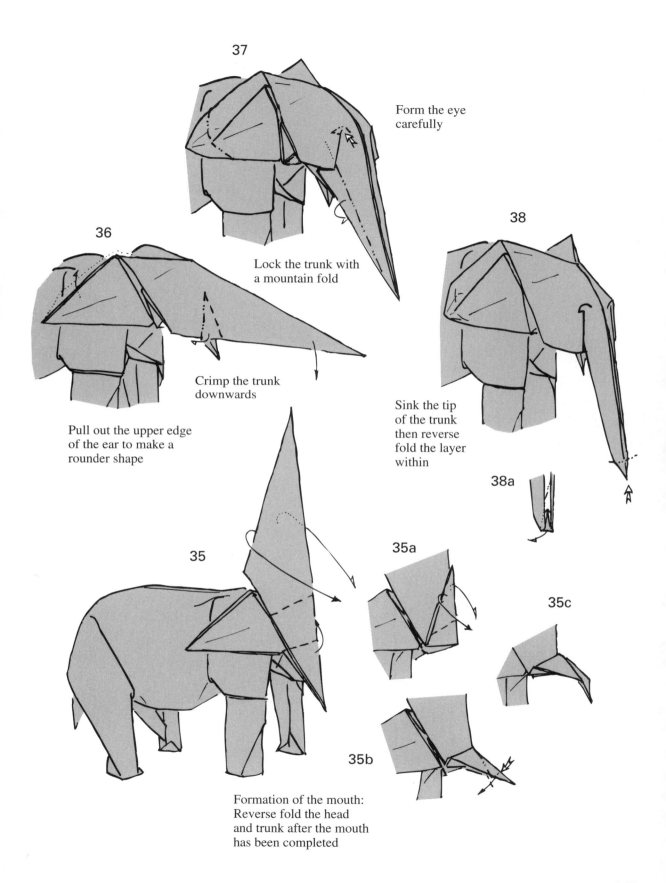

37

Form the eye
carefully

Lock the trunk with
a mountain fold

38

36

Crimp the trunk
downwards

Pull out the upper edge
of the ear to make a
rounder shape

Sink the tip
of the trunk
then reverse
fold the layer
within

38a

35

35a

35c

35b

Formation of the mouth:
Reverse fold the head
and trunk after the mouth
has been completed

Square Versus Equilateral Triangle

As I have mentioned, I was preoccupied with the use of the blintz bird base when I first began folding animals. Successful examples of animals folded from this starting point included in this book are the fox and the reindeer. But I soon exhausted my ideas, finding the many disadvantages of this approach. Apart from a growing reluctance to use the over-familiar shapes provided by the base, I found that I was limited by its bulkiness, and the short limbs which my animals seemed to have.

Attempting some experiments with tri-section of the standard bird base geometry, I found that I could economize by changing the shape of the starting sheet to an equilateral triangle. This opened many new doors for me, and I found that the new shapes provided by the natural folds in the paper were much more attractive, and furthermore, I obtained animals with much slenderer limbs.

Three of the most successful animals I folded follow: I'm pleased to include here a poem inspired by the Horse. (p. 168) .

Dave Brill's Horse

But this is just a horse,
This thing of paper plain
For these folds form
The sinews of a stallion,
A wild free living beast.
Thus can life shine through
The constraints of our art.

John Smith

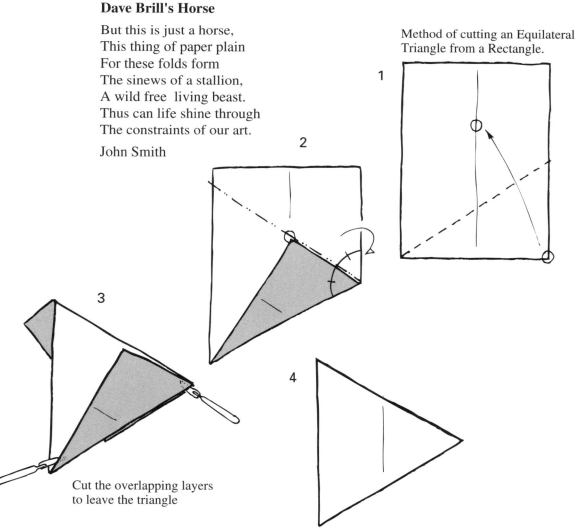

Method of cutting an Equilateral Triangle from a Rectangle.

Cut the overlapping layers to leave the triangle

149

Lioness

1

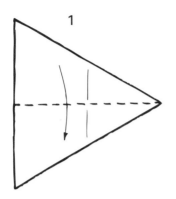

Start with a large
equilateral triangle
cut from an A2 sheet
of thickish paper

2

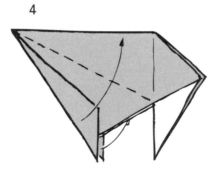

3

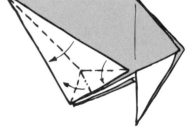

Form rabbit ear folds
on the layers at
the front and back

4

5

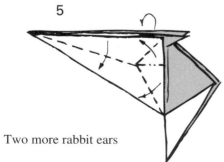

Two more rabbit ears

6

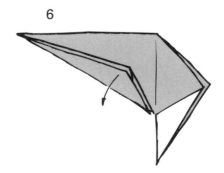

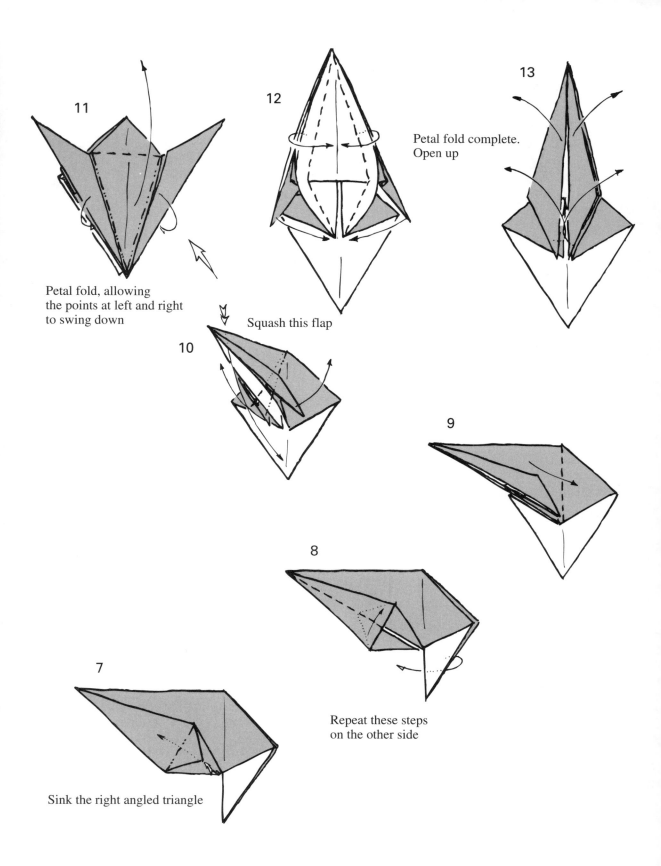

11

Petal fold, allowing
the points at left and right
to swing down

12

Petal fold complete.
Open up

13

Squash this flap

10

9

8

Repeat these steps
on the other side

7

Sink the right angled triangle

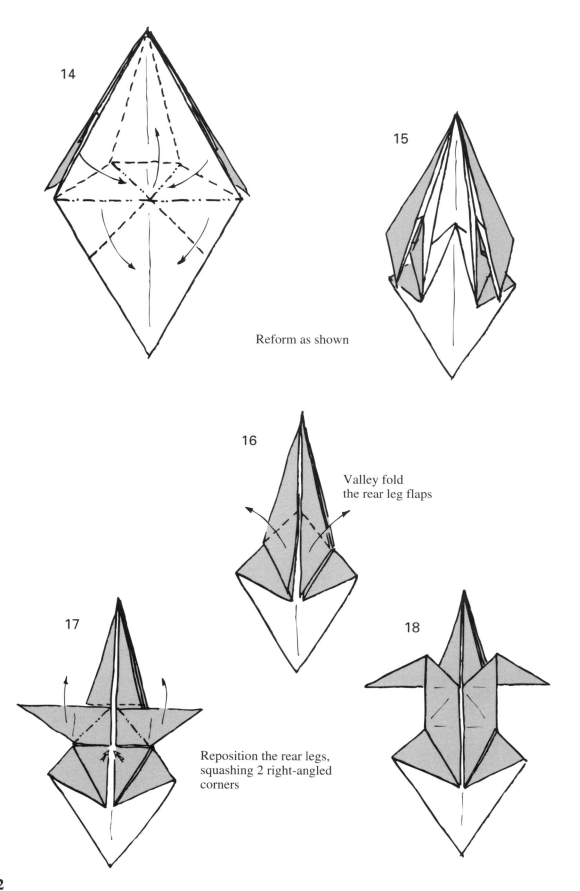

14

15

Reform as shown

16

Valley fold
the rear leg flaps

17

Reposition the rear legs,
squashing 2 right-angled
corners

18

21

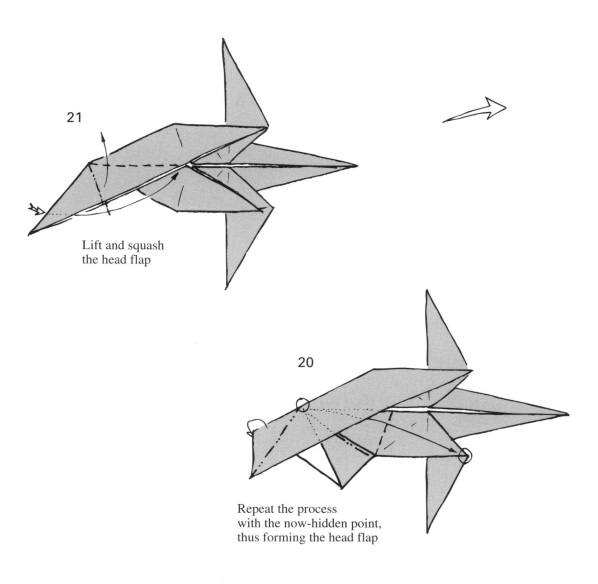

Lift and squash
the head flap

20

Repeat the process
with the now-hidden point,
thus forming the head flap

19

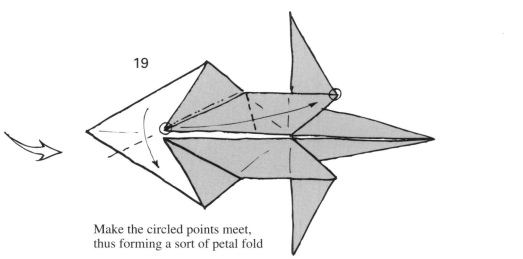

Make the circled points meet,
thus forming a sort of petal fold

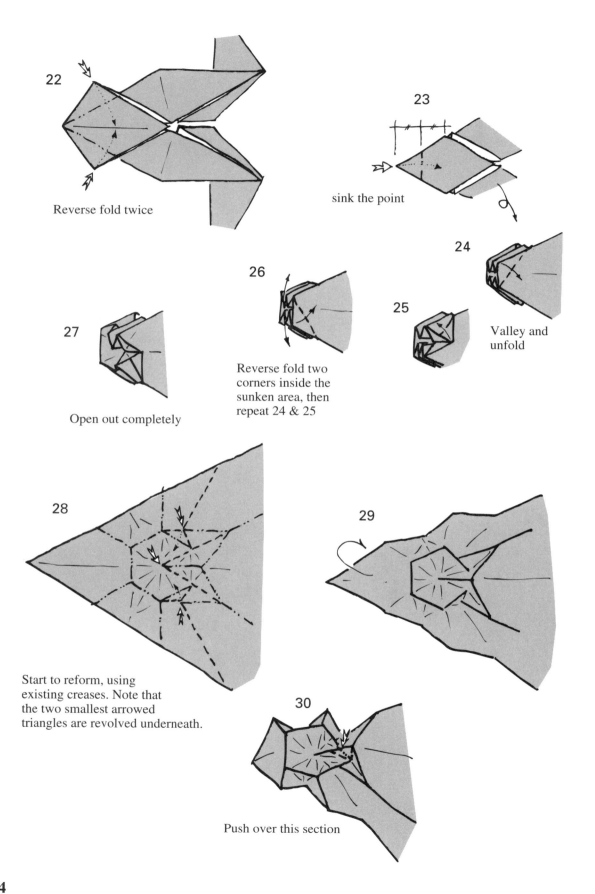

22
Reverse fold twice

23
sink the point

24
Valley and unfold

25

26
Reverse fold two corners inside the sunken area, then repeat 24 & 25

27
Open out completely

28
Start to reform, using existing creases. Note that the two smallest arrowed triangles are revolved underneath.

29

30
Push over this section

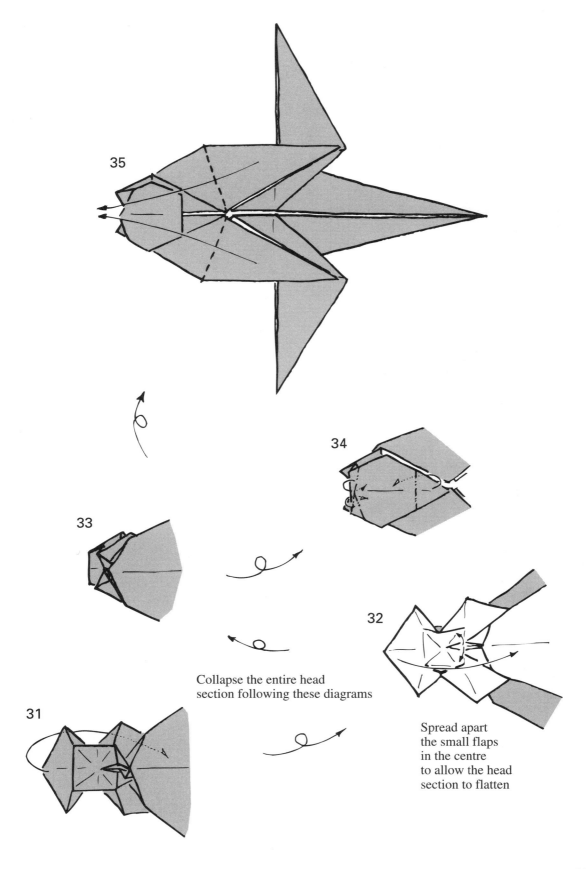

35

34

33

Collapse the entire head
section following these diagrams

32

Spread apart
the small flaps
in the centre
to allow the head
section to flatten

31

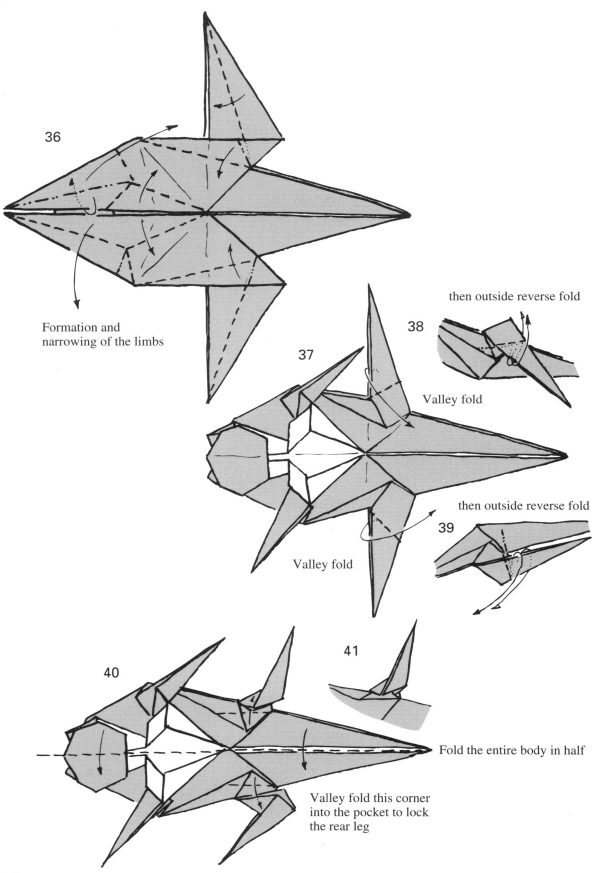

36

Formation and narrowing of the limbs

37

Valley fold

38

then outside reverse fold

Valley fold

39

then outside reverse fold

40

41

Fold the entire body in half

Valley fold this corner into the pocket to lock the rear leg

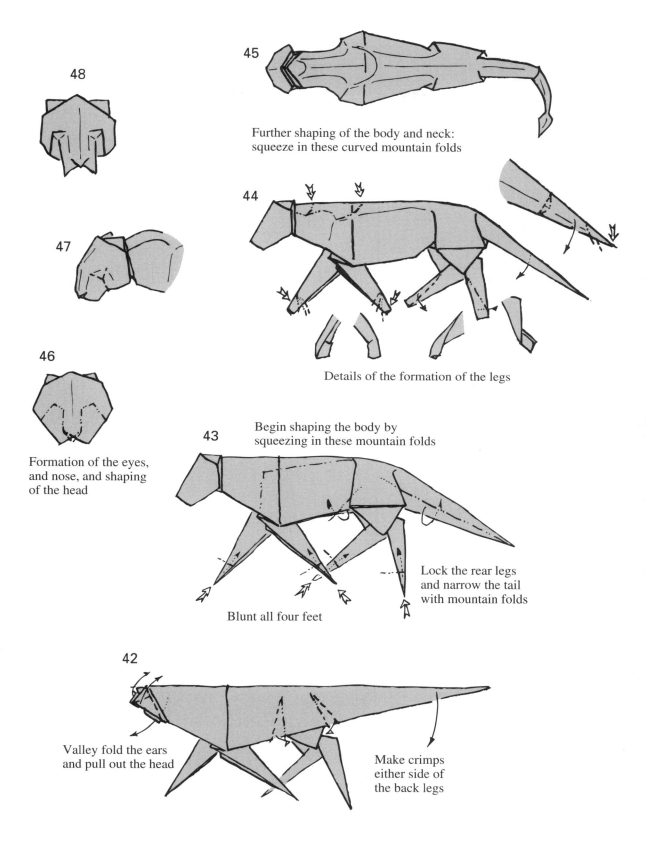

48

45

Further shaping of the body and neck:
squeeze in these curved mountain folds

47

44

Details of the formation of the legs

46

Formation of the eyes,
and nose, and shaping
of the head

43

Begin shaping the body by
squeezing in these mountain folds

Lock the rear legs
and narrow the tail
with mountain folds

Blunt all four feet

42

Valley fold the ears
and pull out the head

Make crimps
either side of
the back legs

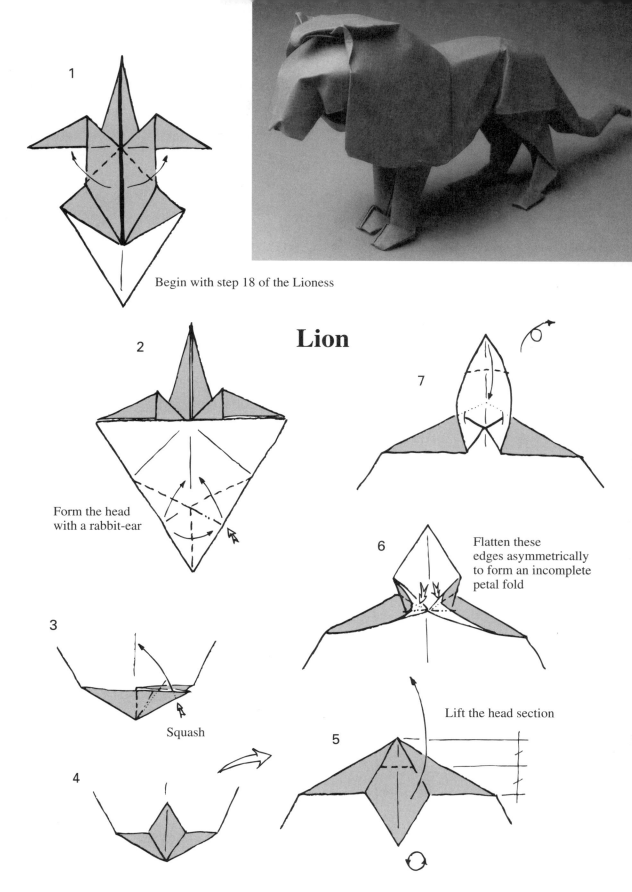

1

Begin with step 18 of the Lioness

Lion

2

Form the head
with a rabbit-ear

7

6

Flatten these
edges asymmetrically
to form an incomplete
petal fold

3

Squash

Lift the head section

4

5

159

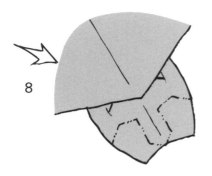

8

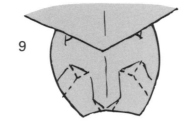

9

Formation of the features
- a similar process to the lioness

10

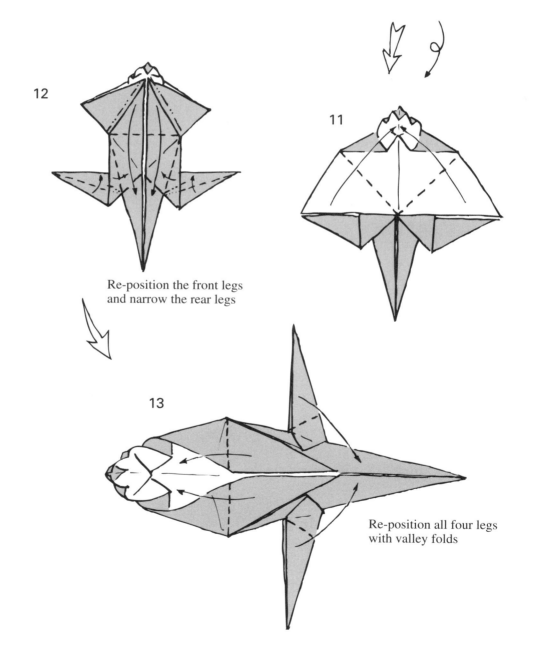

12

Re-position the front legs
and narrow the rear legs

11

13

Re-position all four legs
with valley folds

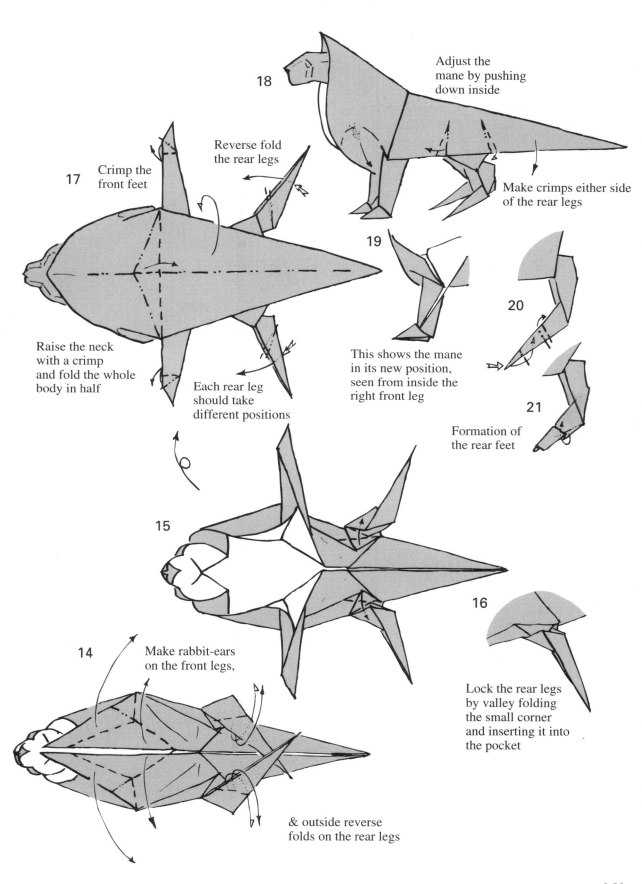

18

Adjust the
mane by pushing
down inside

Reverse fold
the rear legs

17   Crimp the
front feet

Make crimps either side
of the rear legs

Raise the neck
with a crimp
and fold the whole
body in half

Each rear leg
should take
different positions

19

This shows the mane
in its new position,
seen from inside the
right front leg

20

21

Formation of
the rear feet

15

16

14   Make rabbit-ears
on the front legs,

Lock the rear legs
by valley folding
the small corner
and inserting it into
the pocket

& outside reverse
folds on the rear legs

161

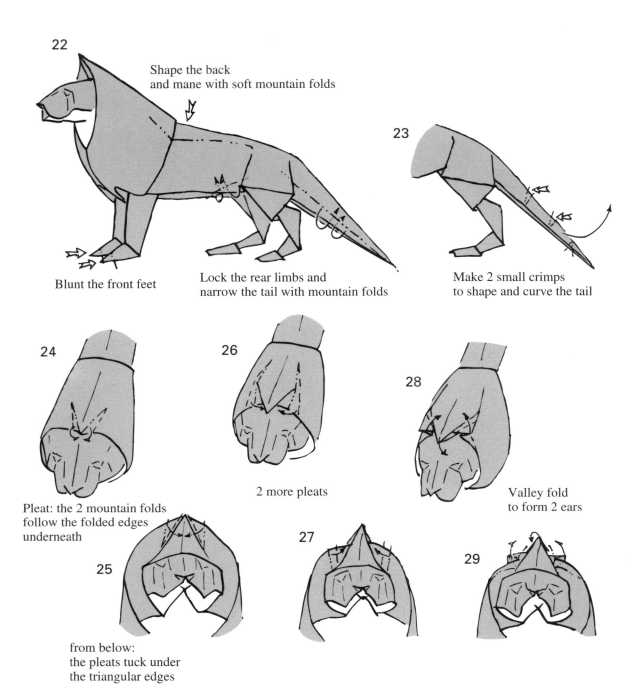

22

Shape the back
and mane with soft mountain folds

23

Blunt the front feet

Lock the rear limbs and
narrow the tail with mountain folds

Make 2 small crimps
to shape and curve the tail

24

26

28

Pleat: the 2 mountain folds
follow the folded edges
underneath

2 more pleats

Valley fold
to form 2 ears

25

27

29

from below:
the pleats tuck under
the triangular edges

Lion Cub

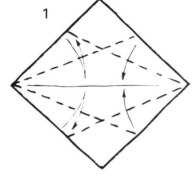
1

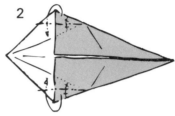
2

4

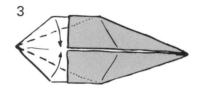
3

Valley fold within the layers

5

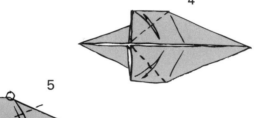

6

Open up the upper half
of the square

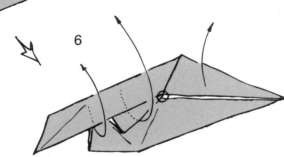

Having made what I considered to be quite
satisfactory adult lions, it followed that I should
complete the family with a cub. My first attempts
were made from the right-angled triangle formed
by cutting a square along the diagonal, but the version
shown here emerged some years later. This has a better
folding sequence and a new method for obtaining
depth to the body. (steps 26, 27 and 28).

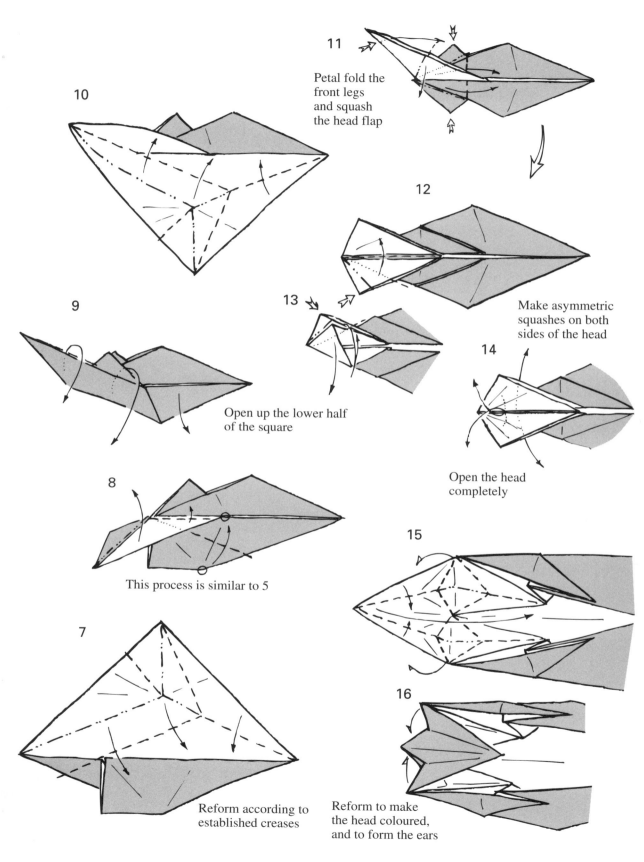

11

Petal fold the
front legs
and squash
the head flap

10

12

Make asymmetric
squashes on both
sides of the head

9

13

Open up the lower half
of the square

14

Open the head
completely

8

This process is similar to 5

15

7

Reform according to
established creases

16

Reform to make
the head coloured,
and to form the ears

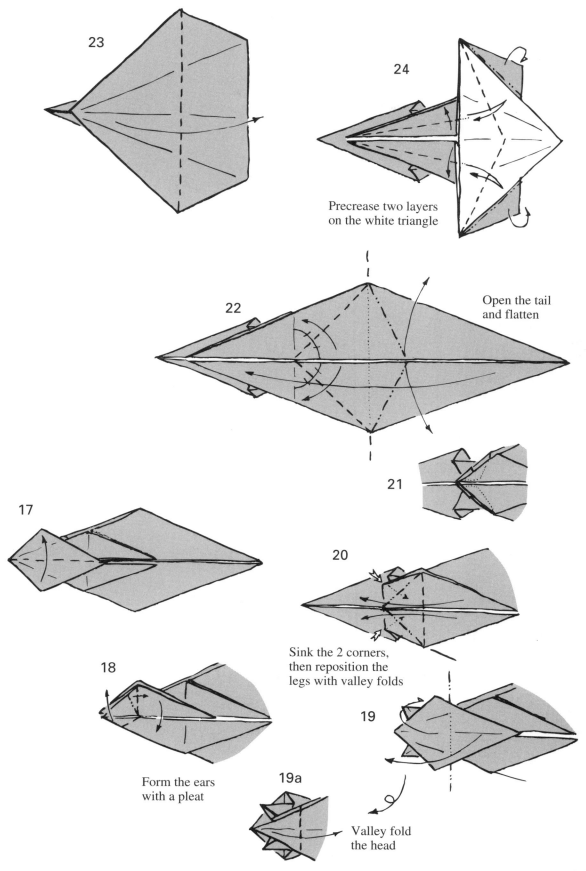

23

24

Precrease two layers
on the white triangle

22

Open the tail
and flatten

21

17

20

Sink the 2 corners,
then reposition the
legs with valley folds

18

19

Form the ears
with a pleat

19a

Valley fold
the head

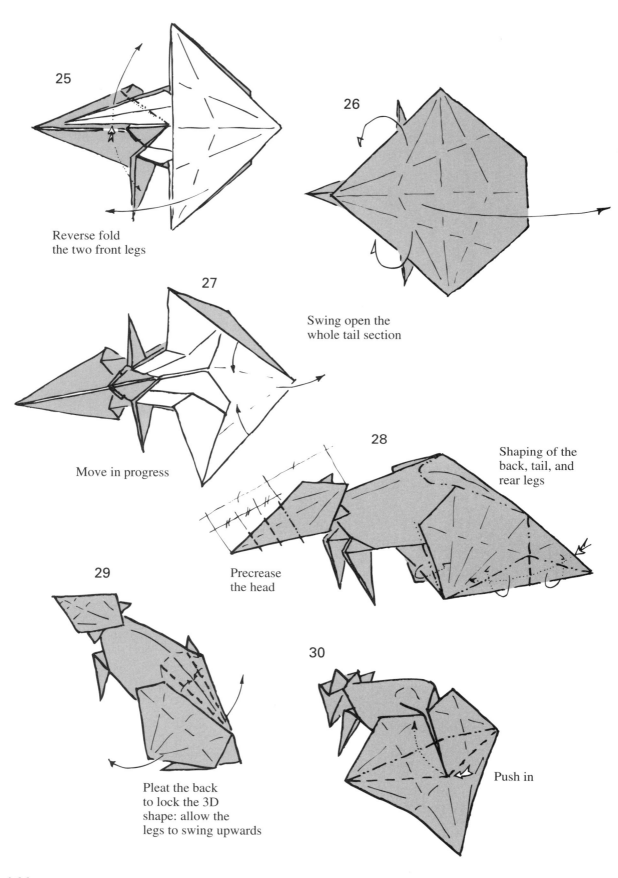

25

Reverse fold
the two front legs

26

Swing open the
whole tail section

27

Move in progress

28

Precrease
the head

Shaping of the
back, tail, and
rear legs

29

Pleat the back
to lock the 3D
shape: allow the
legs to swing upwards

30

Push in

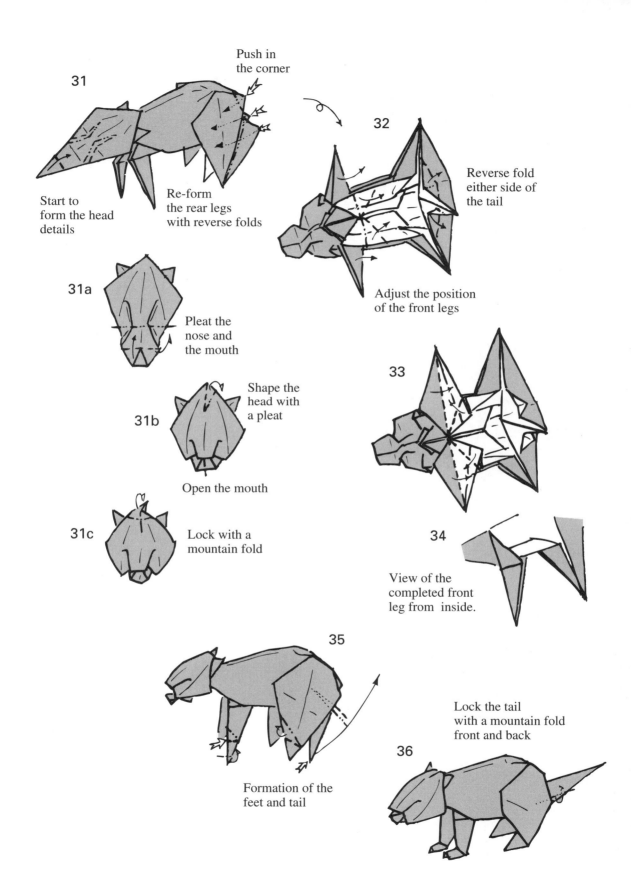

31 Start to form the head details

Push in the corner

Re-form the rear legs with reverse folds

32 Reverse fold either side of the tail

Adjust the position of the front legs

31a Pleat the nose and the mouth

31b Shape the head with a pleat

Open the mouth

33

31c Lock with a mountain fold

34 View of the completed front leg from inside.

35 Formation of the feet and tail

Lock the tail with a mountain fold front and back

36

I had made an earlier version of a horse with a bowed head but was prompted to revise it when I saw a photograph of a galloping horse: I was keen that the new version should have the flowing grace of the horse in the photo. This horse is used in two groups of folds shown later in this book: the Showjumper scene, and St George and the Dragon. some adjustment of the limbs may be necessary to achieve the required effect in each case.

4

Reverse fold

Valley fold

Start from step 18
of the lioness

Petal fold the front legs
and adjust the rear leg positions

Horse

1

Make a rabbit-ear
on the head flap

3

Mountain fold
this leg

2

Valley fold
the head flap

Swivel the
left-hand leg
and sink the
right-hand leg

168

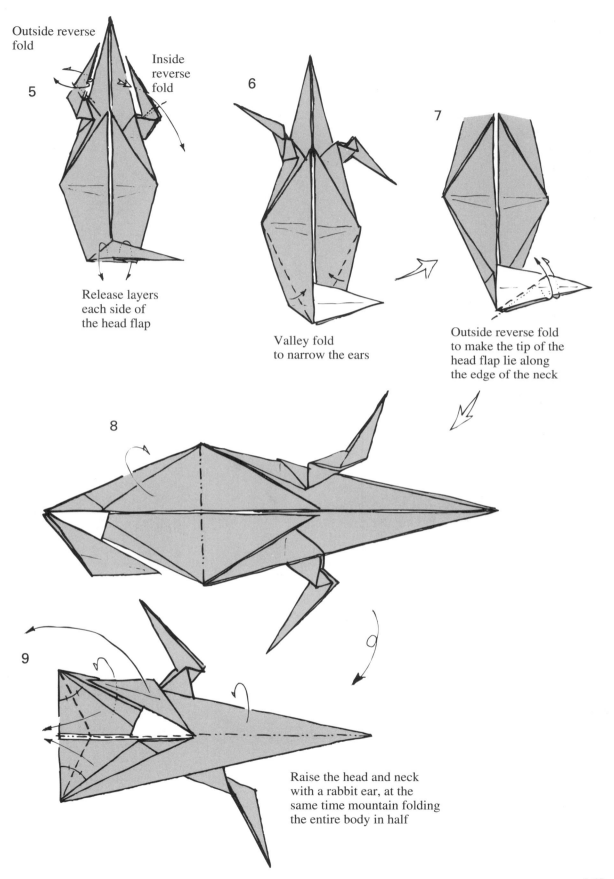

Outside reverse fold

Inside reverse fold

5

Release layers each side of the head flap

6

Valley fold to narrow the ears

7

Outside reverse fold to make the tip of the head flap lie along the edge of the neck

8

9

Raise the head and neck with a rabbit ear, at the same time mountain folding the entire body in half

169

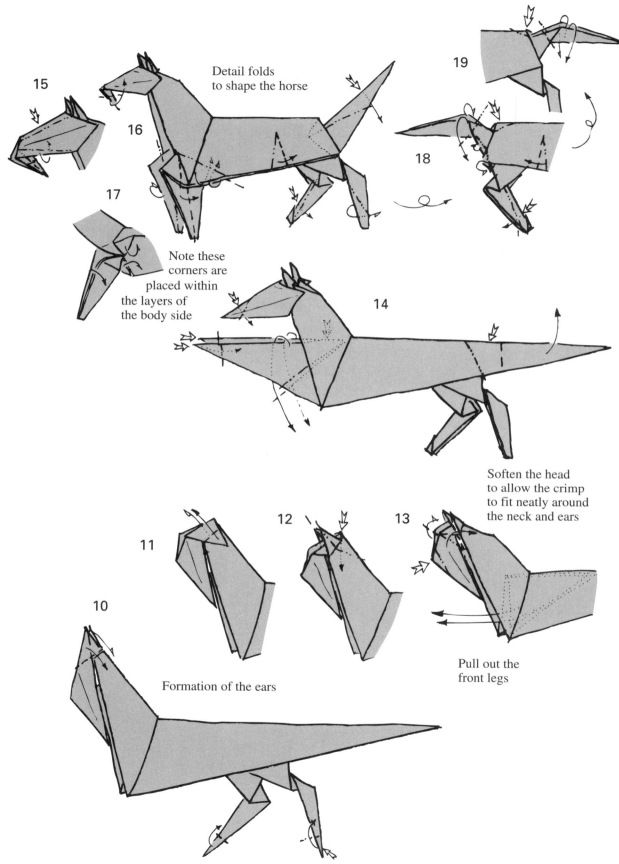

15

16

Detail folds
to shape the horse

19

18

17

Note these
corners are
placed within
the layers of
the body side

14

Soften the head
to allow the crimp
to fit neatly around
the neck and ears

11

12

13

10

Formation of the ears

Pull out the
front legs

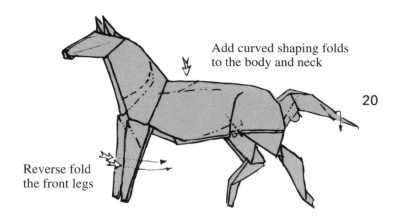

Add curved shaping folds
to the body and neck

20

Reverse fold
the front legs

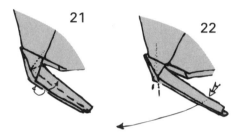

21

22

Narrow the front legs
then reverse fold
the left hand leg.
The right hand leg can
remain pointing backwards

Open the tips of the feet
to suggest hooves. (see final diagram)

The basis for this design was originally an unsuccessful
experiment for a cat! I visited veteran origami researcher
Gershon Legman at his home in Valbonne, in the south of
France in August 1982: he suggested that I try a dragon
with a three-pronged tail. This is a subsequent development
with a single point at the tail. I found that the Dragon's wings
flapped by accident. The twisted head is used to good effect
in the St George and Dragon scene.

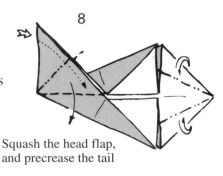

8

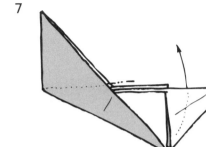

Squash the head flap,
and precrease the tail

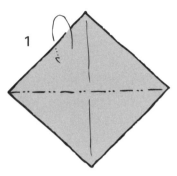

1

Dragon

7

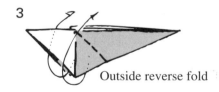

Start with a large square
at least 12 inches (30 cm) each side

2

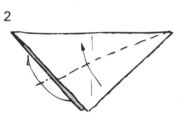

6

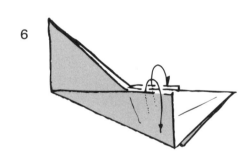

Re-position the layers
from inside

3

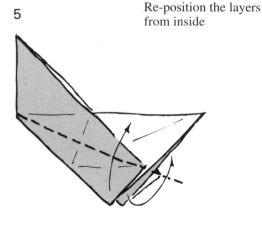

Outside reverse fold

5

4

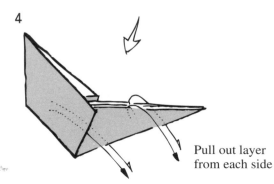

Pull out layer
from each side

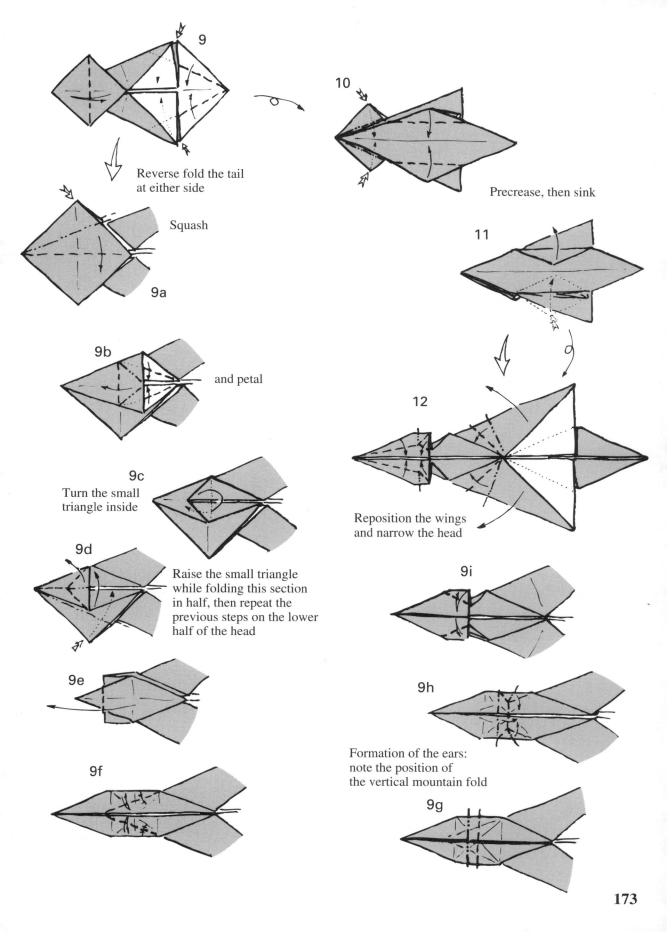

9

Reverse fold the tail
at either side

10

Precrease, then sink

Squash

9a

11

9b

and petal

12

9c

Turn the small
triangle inside

Reposition the wings
and narrow the head

9d

Raise the small triangle
while folding this section
in half, then repeat the
previous steps on the lower
half of the head

9i

9e

9h

9f

Formation of the ears:
note the position of
the vertical mountain fold

9g

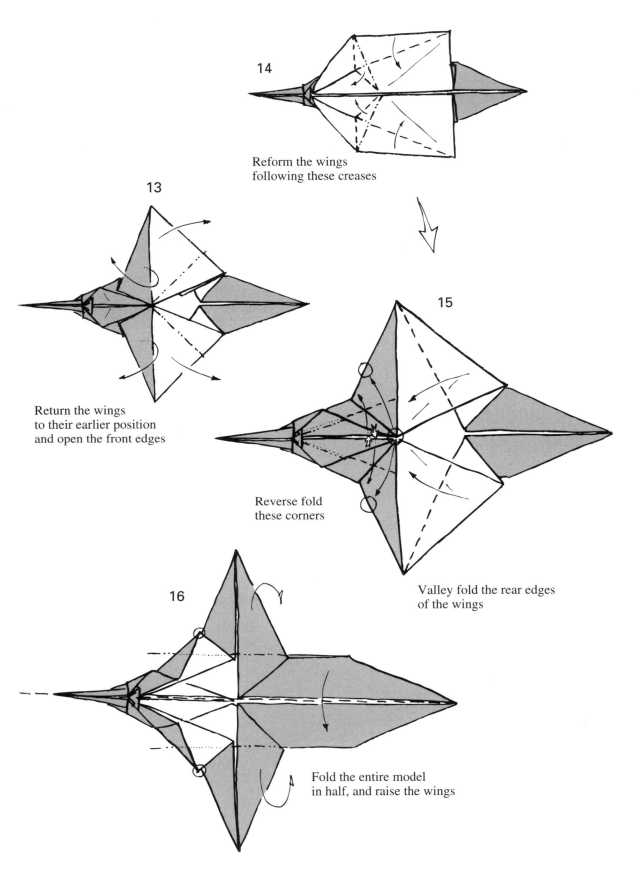

14

Reform the wings
following these creases

13

Return the wings
to their earlier position
and open the front edges

15

Reverse fold
these corners

Valley fold the rear edges
of the wings

16

Fold the entire model
in half, and raise the wings

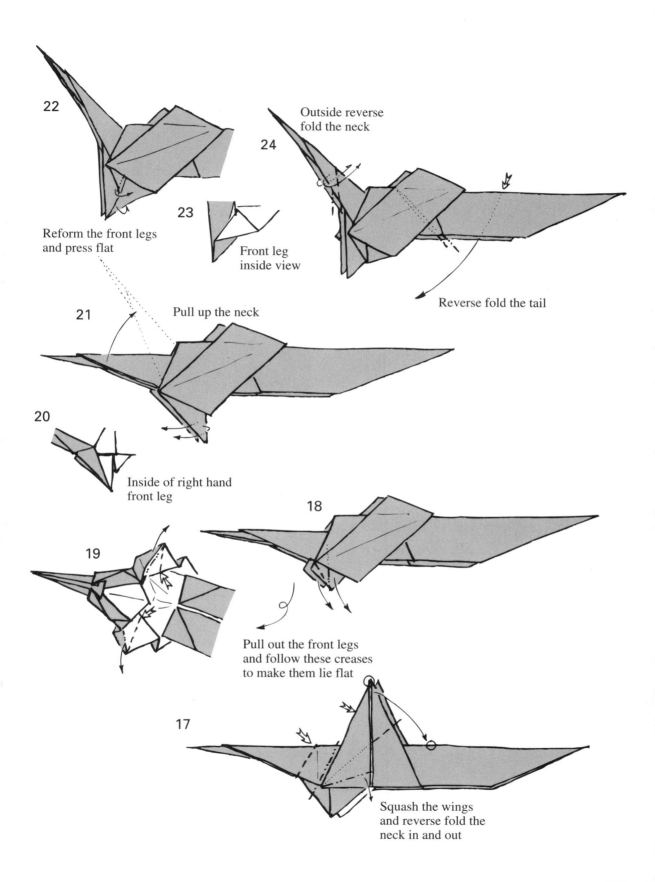

22

24

Outside reverse
fold the neck

23

Reform the front legs
and press flat

Front leg
inside view

Reverse fold the tail

21

Pull up the neck

20

Inside of right hand
front leg

18

19

Pull out the front legs
and follow these creases
to make them lie flat

17

Squash the wings
and reverse fold the
neck in and out

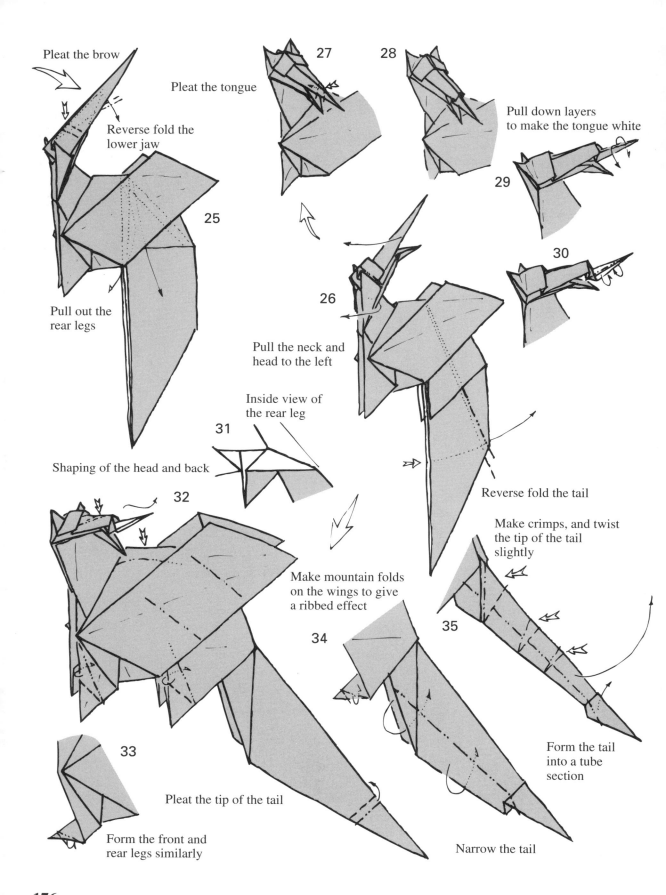

Pleat the brow

Pleat the tongue

27

28

Reverse fold the
lower jaw

Pull down layers
to make the tongue white

29

25

26

30

Pull out the
rear legs

Pull the neck and
head to the left

Inside view of
the rear leg

31

Shaping of the head and back

32

Reverse fold the tail

Make crimps, and twist
the tip of the tail
slightly

35

Make mountain folds
on the wings to give
a ribbed effect

34

Form the tail
into a tube
section

33

Pleat the tip of the tail

Form the front and
rear legs similarly

Narrow the tail

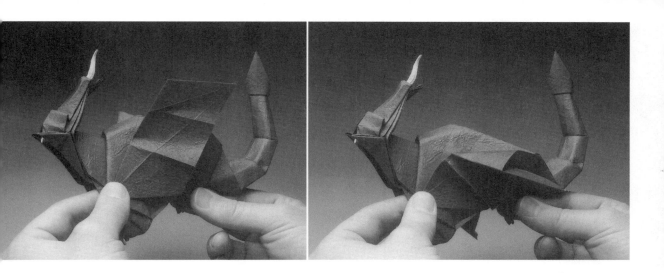

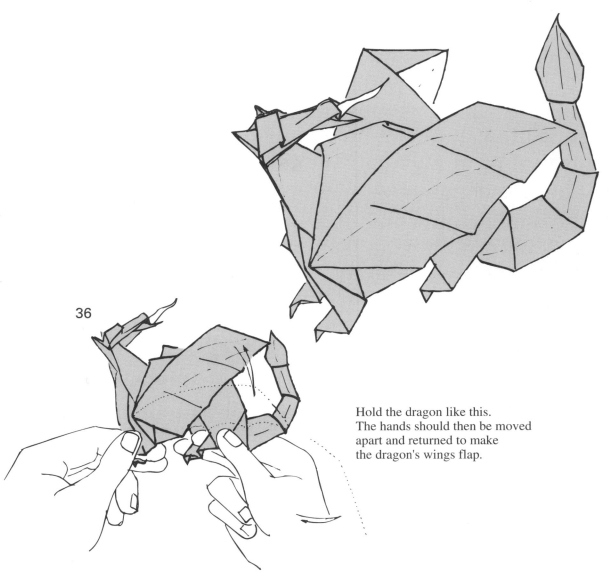

36

Hold the dragon like this.
The hands should then be moved
apart and returned to make
the dragon's wings flap.

Rules Traditional and Personal

One of the main attractions of origami is the limitations which are understood by the Japanese word: "ORIGAMI = to fold paper. "The logical assumptions which follow form the basis of the traditional rules:

No Cutting, No Gluing,No Decoration.
The restrictions particularly appeal to me: this purest form of origami means that no complicated tools or raw materials are required, neither need there be lengthy preparation time. It is a dialogue, a method of communication between you and the simplest raw material, the square of paper. From time to time, even the strictest origami purist will give a little leeway and allow himself a small cut or maybe a drawn decoration: indeed it's perhaps a healthy state of affairs for rules to be bent from time to time. In this way, further lessons can often be learnt which will enrich future attempts. But in every case, the end result must be strong enough to allow any taking of liberties. Maybe the most common transgression is the cut: my opinion is that is this almost the worst: apart from the commonly-cited criticism that cutting destroys the purity of the square, my objection to it is a practical one. If a cut is made in error, the work has to be discarded and begun again. If an error is made with a fold, then it is quite possible to unfold the error and remake it correctly.

An individual will inevitably add his own rules to the accepted traditional ones. He will have his own standards and will not wish to cheat himself and compromise. It is the creator's own responsibility to elevate state of the art and move its limits further and further away, and the restrictions which are imposed by himself will enrich his creative efforts. These rules are personal and it could be suggested that is inappropriate to criticize or suggest that he changes them.

My self-imposed rules include:
Economy: It may be difficult to understand this from a book containing a more advanced level of work. But my principle is to make the maximum use of the paper. I dislike unused paper or hidden layers: for example corners "blintzed" or taken to the center of the square in the early stages of the process and not subsequently released and used. Similarly the technique of tidying up a square corner to make a curved shape I find distasteful. The shape of the paper is often better left as it is.

Avoid Classic Geometry and Bases: The classic fish-, bird-, and frog-bases which seem to be such a useful starting point in creative work carry their own problems. Models made from them usually are recogniseably from these traditional forms: all rely on the division of the right-angle into equal halves or quarters giving 45 degree or 22.5 degree angles which in themselves produce common shapes: too familiar for my liking. I have preferred the exploration of 60 or 30 degree angles, equilateral triangles, and pentagonal geometries, and finding out how they can relate to the square. This exploration leads to much more unfamiliar shapes, more interesting to my eye at least.

Volume or three-dimensionality: Many origami animals seem to have been run over by a steam roller and I have frequently asked the question "why bother going to the trouble of making four legs, two ears and a pair of horns, when one lies exactly over the other?" It has seemed to me that if a flat animal is made, silhouette style, half that number of details would have been enough. Pressured by my critics and contemporaries in the British Origami Society, I have accepted the principle of the *closed back* when folding animals: this allows a degree of moulding and promotes the folding of animals with a three dimensional structure.

In other non-living subjects, I still feel that a three-dimensional approach is necessary. Philip Shen has said that he dislikes the volume of any origami subject to be achieved by many thicknesses, and a structural and economical style is evident in his own geometric work. I admire Shen's origami and agree with this comment, particularly because of my own preferences for the paper being used in the most effective way.

Let the Paper Speak: I now subscribe to the belief that the folds in any good design are hidden in the paper, with natural reference points or geometries. Creatively I attempt to allow the next creases to form themselves almost as if without my influence. I feel the paper should never be forced to do what it doesn't want to do. The best models have a naturalness or an inevitability which gives them their strength of design.

The rules which the creator will establish for himself will inevitably shift and change; if he uses his eyes, removing blinkers to see the world around him rather than concentrating on existing origami styles, his original creative style will develop naturally and effectively.

Human Figures

For some reason, unlike animals, human figures in origami are less common subjects, and frequently the results are less satisfactory. Is this because we are too familiar with the human form, and less able to accept any liberties which are taken with proportion and detail? Why is there not a really satisfactory figure in origami?

There are certainly many practical difficulties in folding the figure: I have found that arms are frequently too short, and the neck is an awkward aspect to deal with. Kunihiko Kasahara tells me that he considers that a folder would become truly great in his eyes if that folder could achieve a satisfactory female nude...

My interest in the human figure in origami stems back to the influence of Eric Kenneway, who was able somehow to draw with the paper: it's true that his figures were all flat, but they had a style that was truly unique. Much of Kenneway's unpublished work is extremely difficult to reproduce, employing much free-folding, and lack of logical reference points.

I feel that this area represents a true challenge to those seeking to push origami to new boundaries, and I hope that you may be stimulated to carry on the research by my attempts in this chapter.

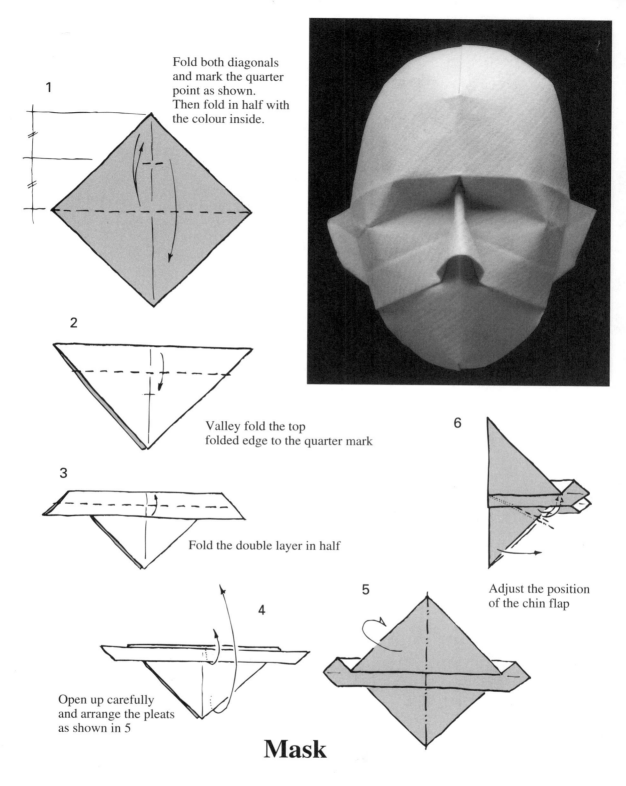

1

Fold both diagonals and mark the quarter point as shown. Then fold in half with the colour inside.

2

Valley fold the top folded edge to the quarter mark

3

Fold the double layer in half

4

Open up carefully and arrange the pleats as shown in 5

5

6

Adjust the position of the chin flap

Mask

I was impressed by Yoshihide Momotani's masks: full of character.
This is my own attempt making use of similar cross-pleat ideas.
Quite a number of expression changes are possible: try using thick paper and handling the material quite clumsily to experiment.

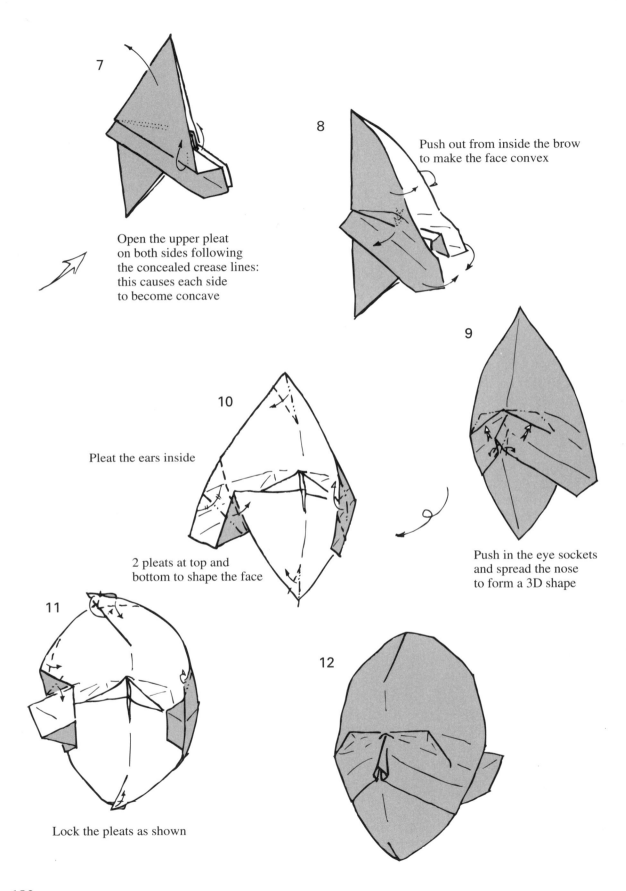

7

Open the upper pleat
on both sides following
the concealed crease lines:
this causes each side
to become concave

8

Push out from inside the brow
to make the face convex

9

Push in the eye sockets
and spread the nose
to form a 3D shape

10

Pleat the ears inside

2 pleats at top and
bottom to shape the face

11

Lock the pleats as shown

12

Christmas Tree Fairy

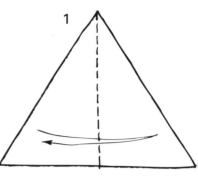

1

Use an equilateral
triangle, side length 20 inches (48 cm).
Textured gold foil works well.

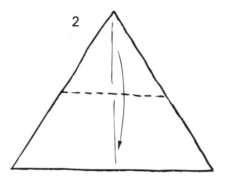

2

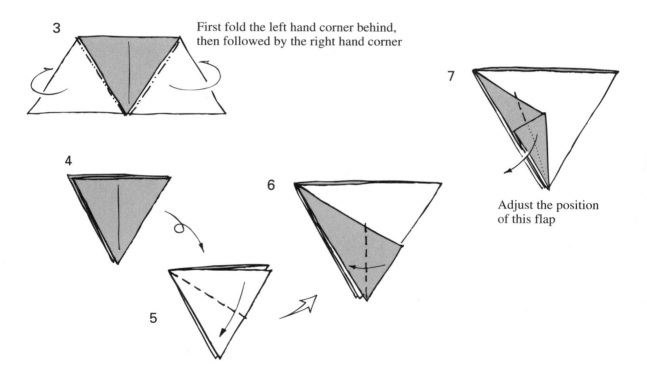

3

First fold the left hand corner behind,
then followed by the right hand corner

4

5

6

7

Adjust the position
of this flap

Having spent a lot of time making this decoration for the top
of a Christmas tree, I realised with horror that I had forgotten to give
the Fairy any wings! I did attempt to make the figure with the crown
and wand from a single sheet, but the results were ghastly. I prefer the
3 sheet ensemble which doesn't compromise the individual elements.

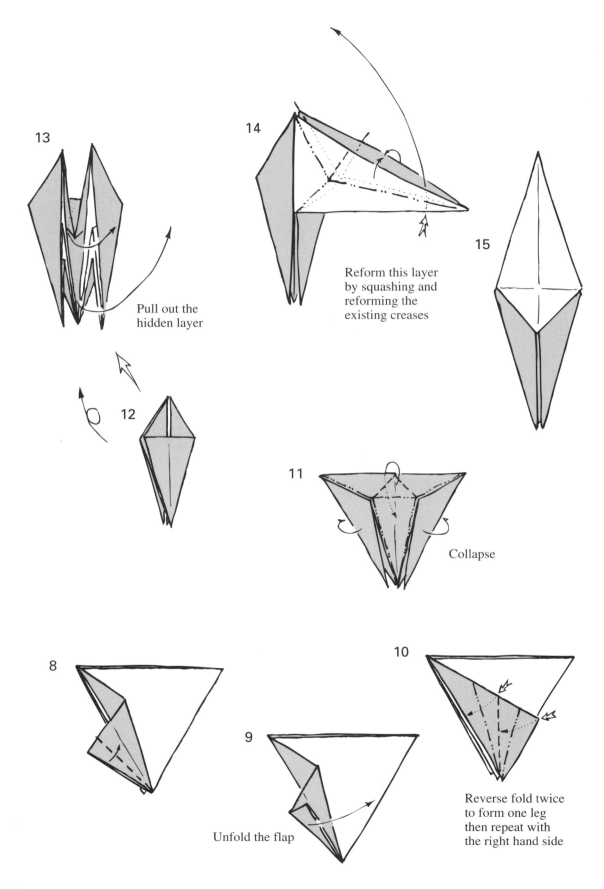

13

Pull out the
hidden layer

14

Reform this layer
by squashing and
reforming the
existing creases

15

12

11

Collapse

8

9

Unfold the flap

10

Reverse fold twice
to form one leg
then repeat with
the right hand side

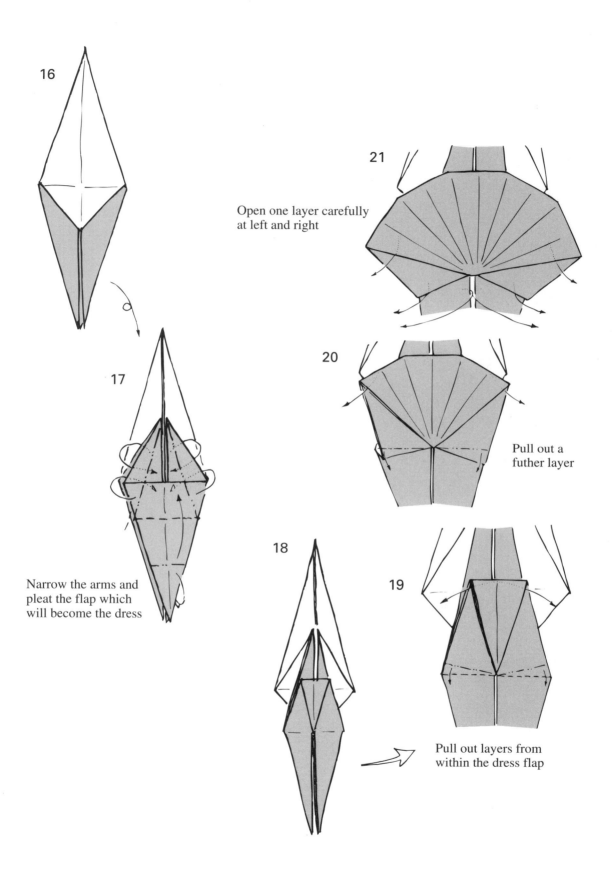

16

17

Narrow the arms and
pleat the flap which
will become the dress

18

19

Pull out layers from
within the dress flap

20

Pull out a
futher layer

21

Open one layer carefully
at left and right

185

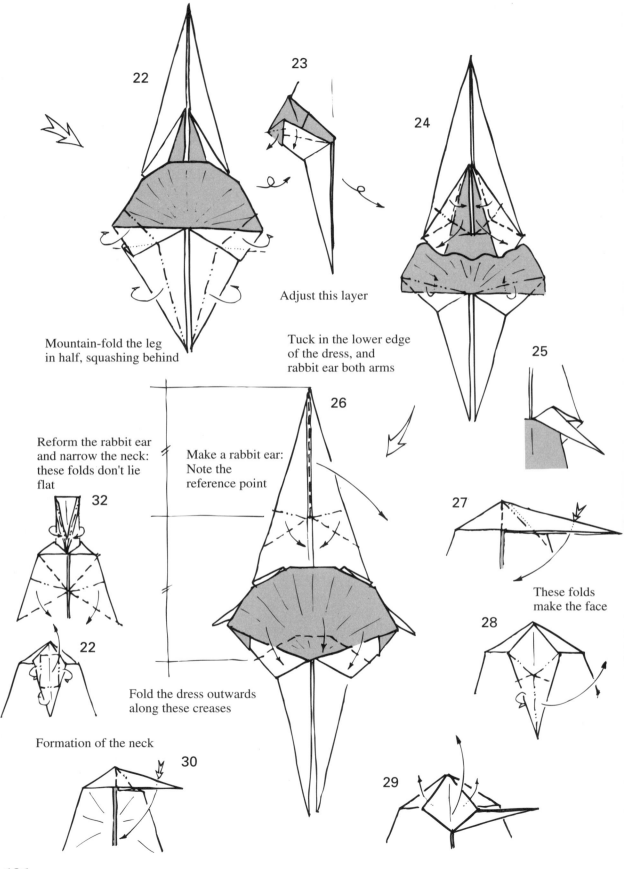

22

Mountain-fold the leg
in half, squashing behind

23

Adjust this layer

24

Tuck in the lower edge
of the dress, and
rabbit ear both arms

25

Reform the rabbit ear
and narrow the neck:
these folds don't lie
flat

32

26

Make a rabbit ear:
Note the
reference point

27

These folds
make the face

28

22

Fold the dress outwards
along these creases

Formation of the neck

29

30

186

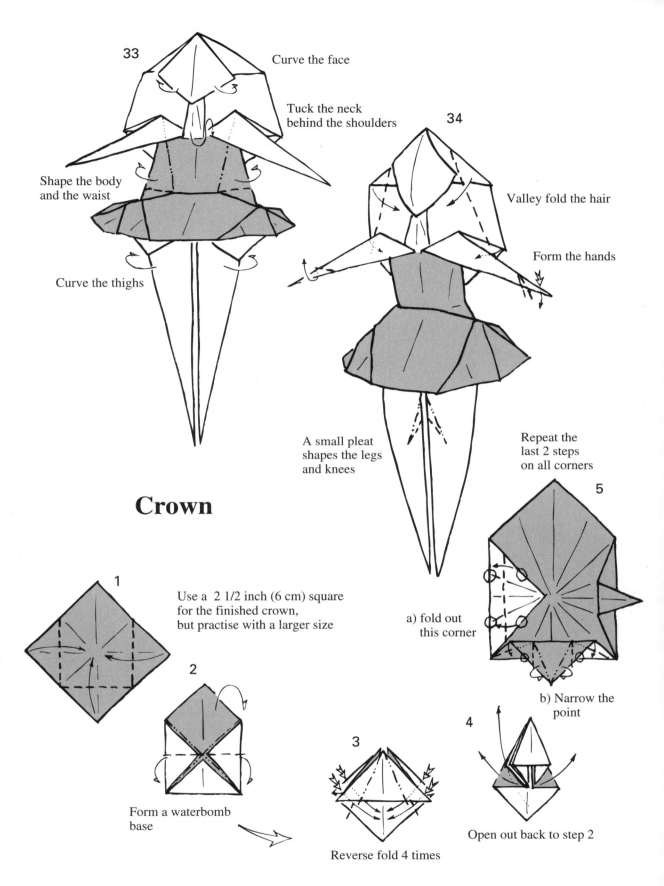

33

Curve the face

Tuck the neck
behind the shoulders

34

Valley fold the hair

Shape the body
and the waist

Form the hands

Curve the thighs

A small pleat
shapes the legs
and knees

Repeat the
last 2 steps
on all corners

Crown

5

Use a 2 1/2 inch (6 cm) square
for the finished crown,
but practise with a larger size

a) fold out
this corner

1

b) Narrow the
point

2

3

4

Form a waterbomb
base

Reverse fold 4 times

Open out back to step 2

1

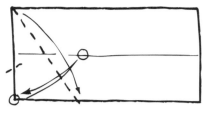

Precrease a 60 degree valley fold
then mark 1/3rd as shown

Use a 2x1 rectangle,
2 1/2x5 inches (6x12 cm)
for the finished model, but
practise with a larger size

Wand

2

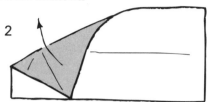

5

4

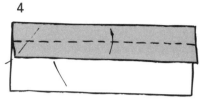

Divide into 1/3rds, then 1/6ths

3

Crown (continued)

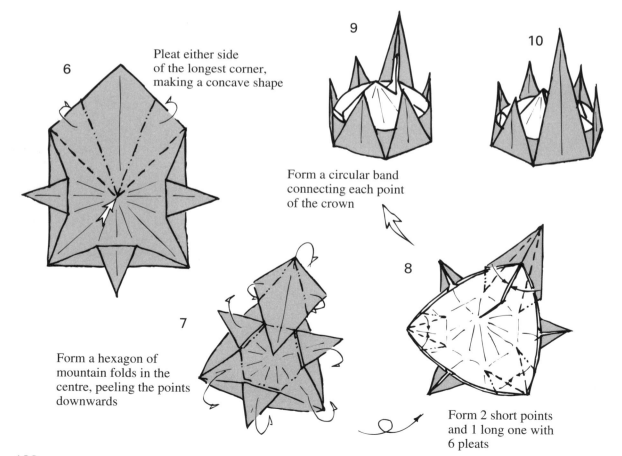

6

Pleat either side
of the longest corner,
making a concave shape

9

10

Form a circular band
connecting each point
of the crown

8

7

Form a hexagon of
mountain folds in the
centre, peeling the points
downwards

Form 2 short points
and 1 long one with
6 pleats

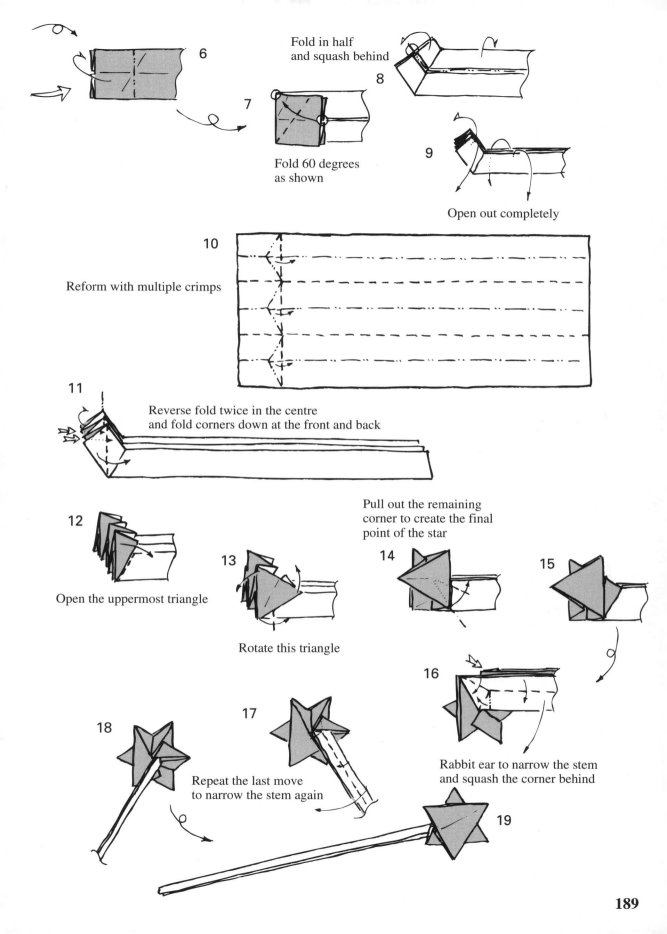

6

7

Fold in half
and squash behind

8

Fold 60 degrees
as shown

9

Open out completely

10

Reform with multiple crimps

11

Reverse fold twice in the centre
and fold corners down at the front and back

12

Open the uppermost triangle

13

Rotate this triangle

Pull out the remaining
corner to create the final
point of the star

14

15

16

Rabbit ear to narrow the stem
and squash the corner behind

17

Repeat the last move
to narrow the stem again

18

19

Glue the crown and wand in
position, and attatch the
figure to the tree behind the waist.

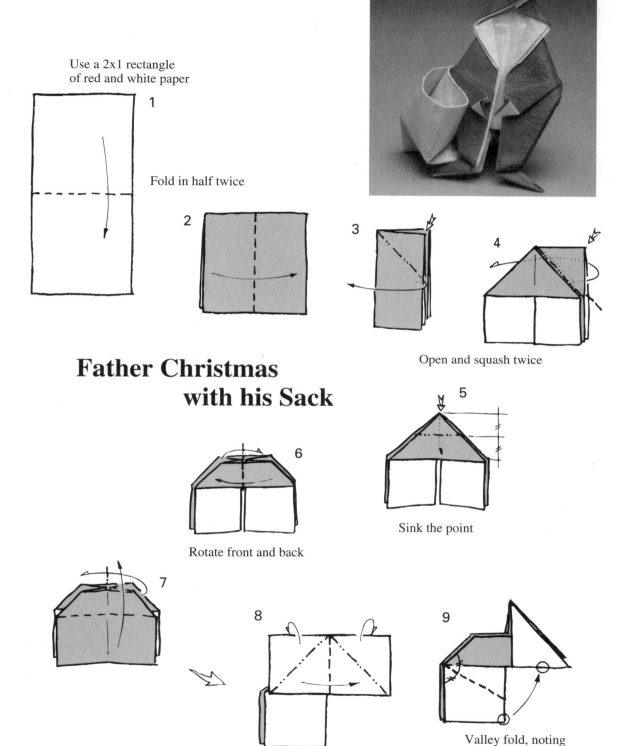

Use a 2x1 rectangle
of red and white paper

1

Fold in half twice

2

3

4

Open and squash twice

Father Christmas
with his Sack

5

Sink the point

6

Rotate front and back

7

8

9

Valley fold, noting
the location point

Another product of the British Origami Society "Whodunnit" column.
The idea was to provide an open sack for a present.

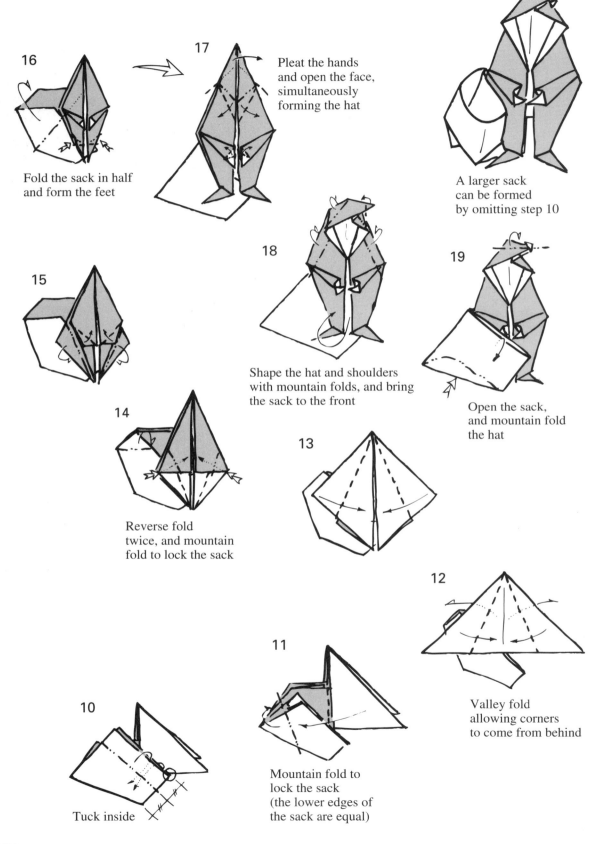

16

Fold the sack in half
and form the feet

17

Pleat the hands
and open the face,
simultaneously
forming the hat

A larger sack
can be formed
by omitting step 10

18

Shape the hat and shoulders
with mountain folds, and bring
the sack to the front

19

Open the sack,
and mountain fold
the hat

15

14

Reverse fold
twice, and mountain
fold to lock the sack

13

12

Valley fold
allowing corners
to come from behind

11

Mountain fold to
lock the sack
(the lower edges of
the sack are equal)

10

Tuck inside

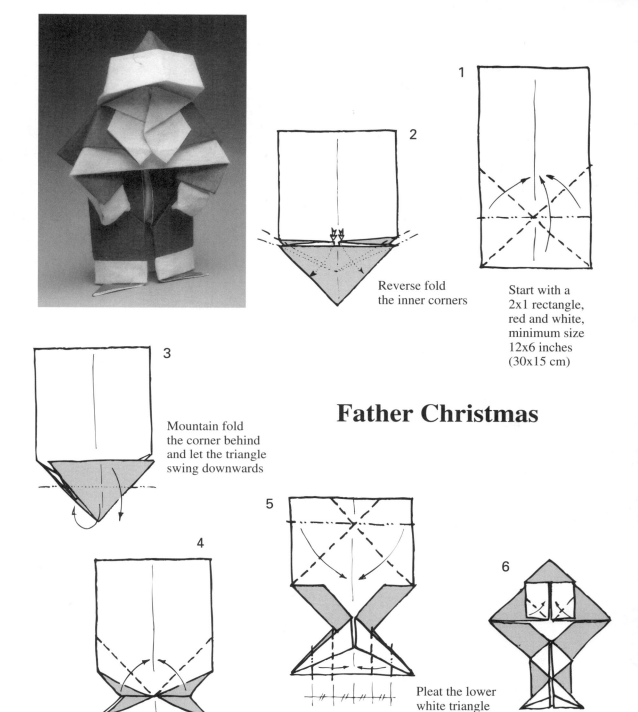

2 Reverse fold the inner corners

1 Start with a 2x1 rectangle, red and white, minimum size 12x6 inches (30x15 cm)

Father Christmas

3 Mountain fold the corner behind and let the triangle swing downwards

4

5 Pleat the lower white triangle

6

I made a Father Christmas figure for an early version of the sleigh, and reindeer group and intended to make drawings of this for this book. However I realised that the original figure was far too slim and I therefore had to redesign the figure before starting the drawings. The only common ground with original is the initial few steps and the head.

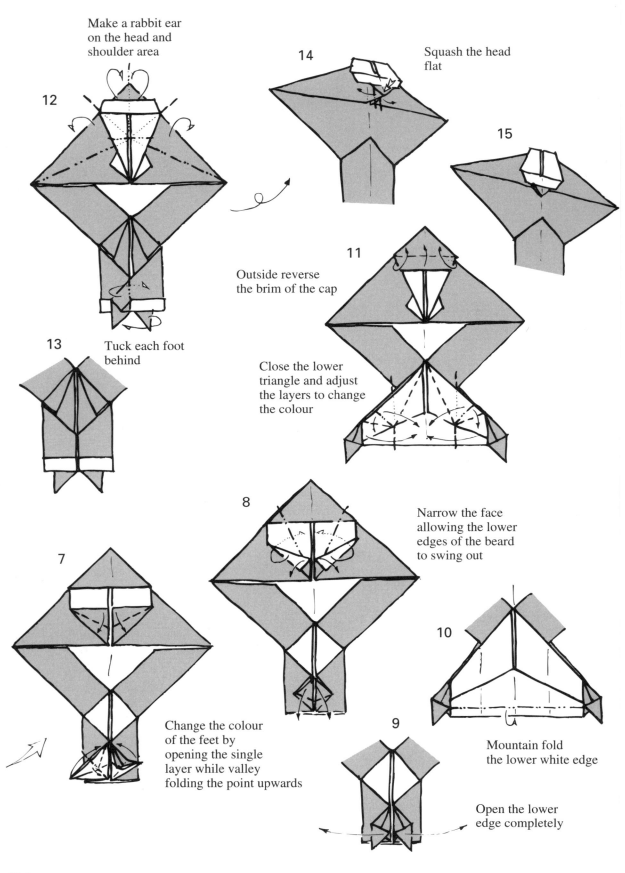

Make a rabbit ear
on the head and
shoulder area

12

14

Squash the head
flat

15

Outside reverse
the brim of the cap

11

Close the lower
triangle and adjust
the layers to change
the colour

13

Tuck each foot
behind

8

Narrow the face
allowing the lower
edges of the beard
to swing out

7

10

Change the colour
of the feet by
opening the single
layer while valley
folding the point
upwards

9

Mountain fold
the lower white edge

Open the lower
edge completely

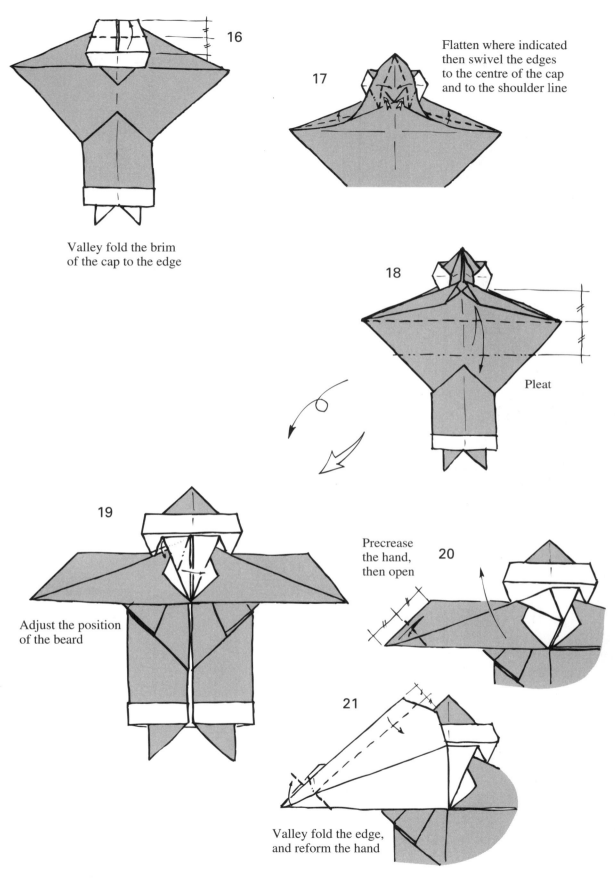

16

Valley fold the brim
of the cap to the edge

17

Flatten where indicated
then swivel the edges
to the centre of the cap
and to the shoulder line

18

Pleat

19

Adjust the position
of the beard

20

Precrease
the hand,
then open

21

Valley fold the edge,
and reform the hand

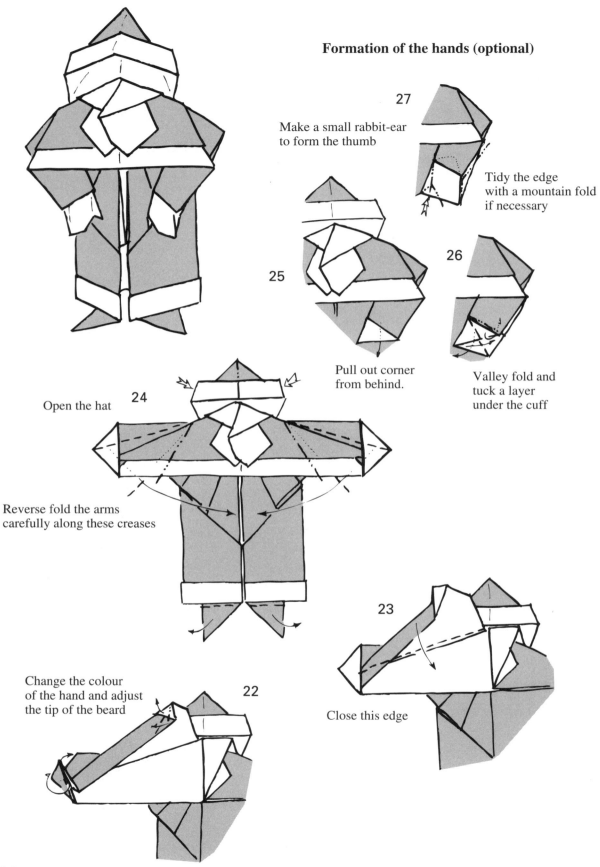

Formation of the hands (optional)

27

Make a small rabbit-ear
to form the thumb

Tidy the edge
with a mountain fold
if necessary

25

26

Pull out corner
from behind.

Valley fold and
tuck a layer
under the cuff

24

Open the hat

Reverse fold the arms
carefully along these creases

23

Close this edge

Change the colour
of the hand and adjust
the tip of the beard

22

Basic Form for Figures

1

Precrease mountain fold
diagonals from the white side
then fold in half

2

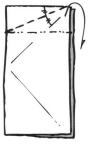

Pleat

3

Valley fold

5

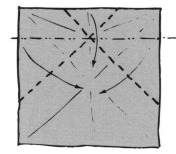

Reform according to these creases

4

Open out

6

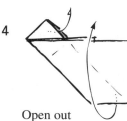

Adjust the position of the arms

7

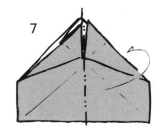

Mountain fold in half

8

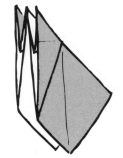

Although I have generally resisted the principle
of the base as a creative starting point, preferring to
design directly from the starting sheet, this figure
base has been useful. Many of the figures which
follow were designed for commissions to illustrate
the calendar for British paper manufacturer Bowater-
Scott in 1984 and 1985. The base uses the head and ears
from the corgi and lamb, but these flaps are used to make
limbs for the various figures.

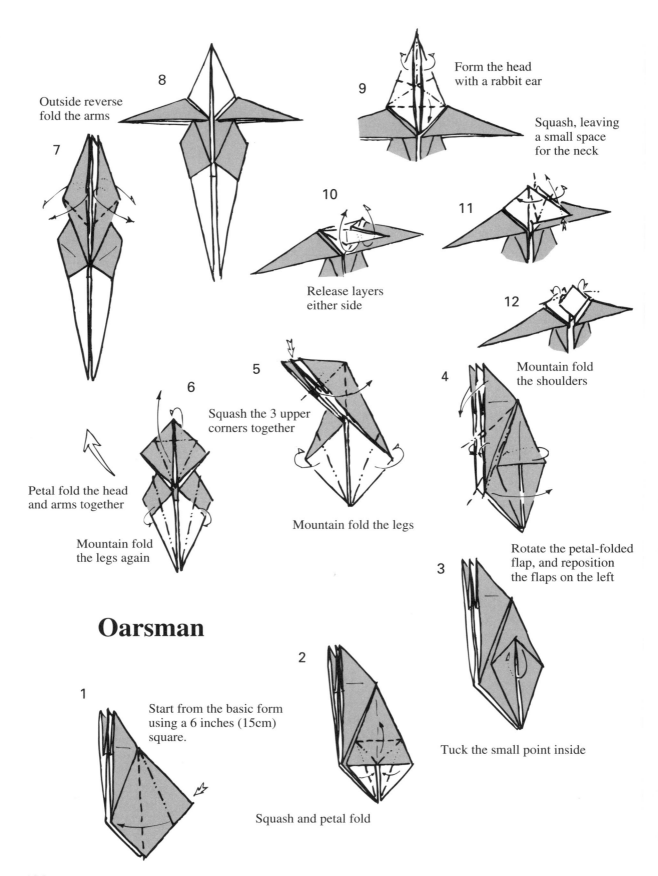

8

Outside reverse
fold the arms

7

9 Form the head
with a rabbit ear

Squash, leaving
a small space
for the neck

10

Release layers
either side

11

12

Mountain fold
the shoulders

6

5 Squash the 3 upper
corners together

4

Petal fold the head
and arms together

Mountain fold
the legs again

Mountain fold the legs

Rotate the petal-folded
flap, and reposition
the flaps on the left

3

Oarsman

2

1

Start from the basic form
using a 6 inches (15cm)
square.

Tuck the small point inside

Squash and petal fold

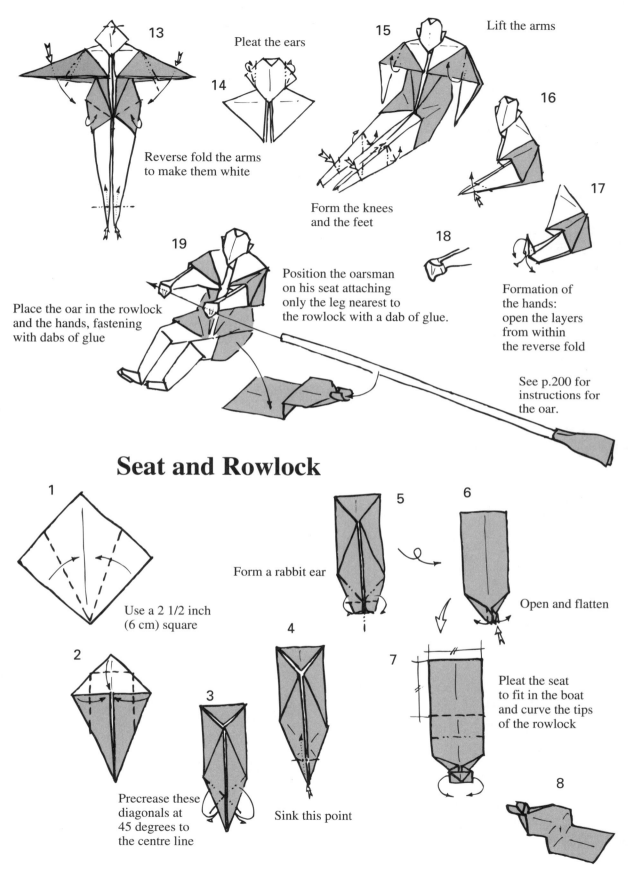

13

Reverse fold the arms
to make them white

14 Pleat the ears

15 Lift the arms

Form the knees
and the feet

16

17

18 Formation of
the hands:
open the layers
from within
the reverse fold

See p.200 for
instructions for
the oar.

19

Place the oar in the rowlock
and the hands, fastening
with dabs of glue

Position the oarsman
on his seat attaching
only the leg nearest to
the rowlock with a dab of glue.

Seat and Rowlock

1 Use a 2 1/2 inch
(6 cm) square

2

3 Precrease these
diagonals at
45 degrees to
the centre line

4 Sink this point

5 Form a rabbit ear

6 Open and flatten

7 Pleat the seat
to fit in the boat
and curve the tips
of the rowlock

8

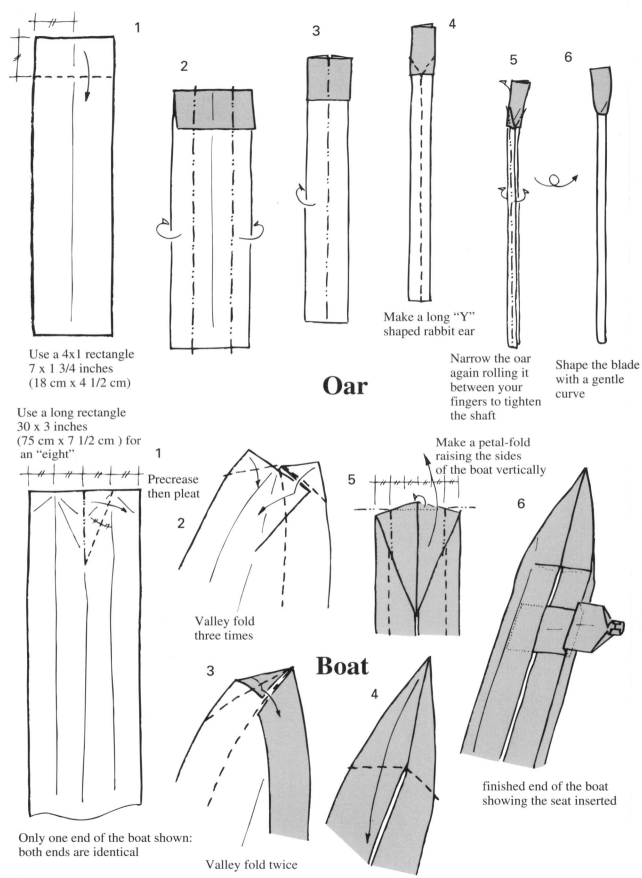

Oar

1

Use a 4x1 rectangle
7 x 1 3/4 inches
(18 cm x 4 1/2 cm)

2

3

4

Make a long "Y"
shaped rabbit ear

5

Narrow the oar
again rolling it
between your
fingers to tighten
the shaft

6

Shape the blade
with a gentle
curve

Boat

Use a long rectangle
30 x 3 inches
(75 cm x 7 1/2 cm) for
an "eight"

1

Precrease
then pleat

2

Valley fold
three times

3

Valley fold twice

4

5

Make a petal-fold
raising the sides
of the boat vertically

6

finished end of the boat
showing the seat inserted

Only one end of the boat shown:
both ends are identical

Cox

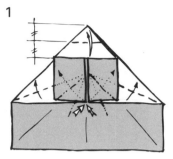

1

Start with step 6
of the figure basic form (p.197)

Reverse fold
left and right
and precrease
the top point

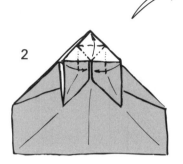

2

Make an incomplete
petal fold

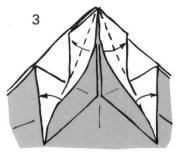

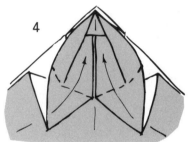

3

Fold the raw edges
to the outside edges

4

Reposition the arm flaps

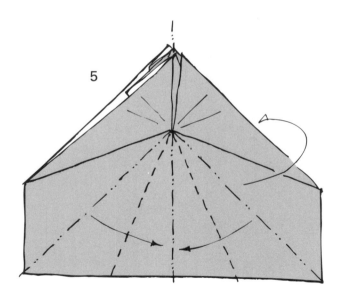

5

Fold in half, and pleat at the lower centre

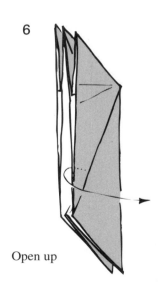

6

Open up

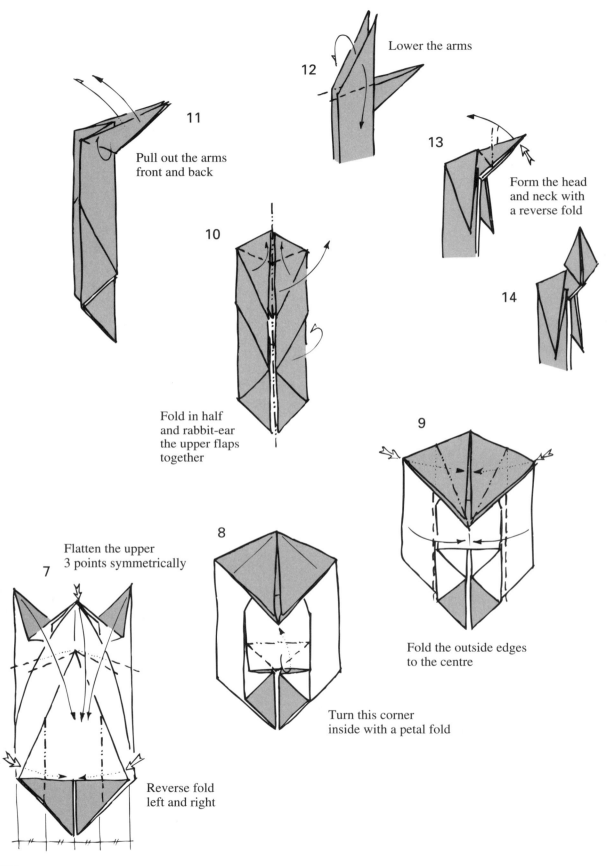

Lower the arms

12

11

Pull out the arms
front and back

13

Form the head
and neck with
a reverse fold

14

10

Fold in half
and rabbit-ear
the upper flaps
together

9

Flatten the upper
3 points symmetrically

7

8

Fold the outside edges
to the centre

Turn this corner
inside with a petal fold

Reverse fold
left and right

15 Open all layers
of the head and
valley fold down

Outside reverse fold
the legs upwards

Pull out the inner
layer of the leg
to make the outside
white, and repeat
behind

16 Lift and open
the upper part
of the head

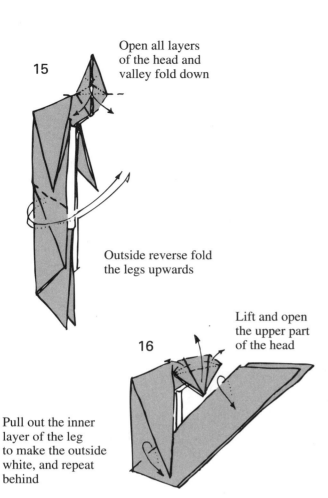

The Oxford and Cambridge Boat Race

This historic event takes place every spring
on the River Thames in London. The crews are
from the universities of Oxford and Cambridge,
and are identified by their colours of dark and
light blue respectively.
To make an origami version of the Boat Race,
(see pp.12 & 13) make two boats, with
eight oarsmen for each boat. The cox faces the
oarsmen whose oars are arranged alternately
left and right.

Formation of
the cap

18

19

17 Pleat the feet,
then fold
the legs down

Reverse fold
the hands

Shape the arms
with a soft
mountain fold

20 Adjust the position
of the body by pulling
it back slightly so that
the figure sits easily

Narrow the legs

Open the hands

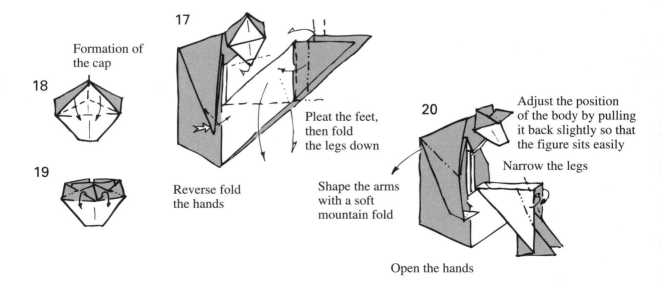

Three Wise Men

See p.15 for a photograph of the Wise Men scene
which is completed by the Square Silver Star (p.232)

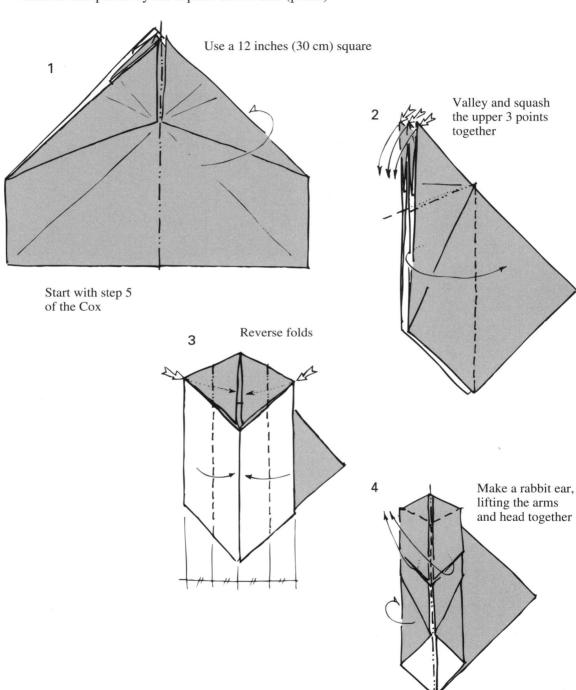

Use a 12 inches (30 cm) square

1

Start with step 5
of the Cox

2 Valley and squash
the upper 3 points
together

3 Reverse folds

4 Make a rabbit ear,
lifting the arms
and head together

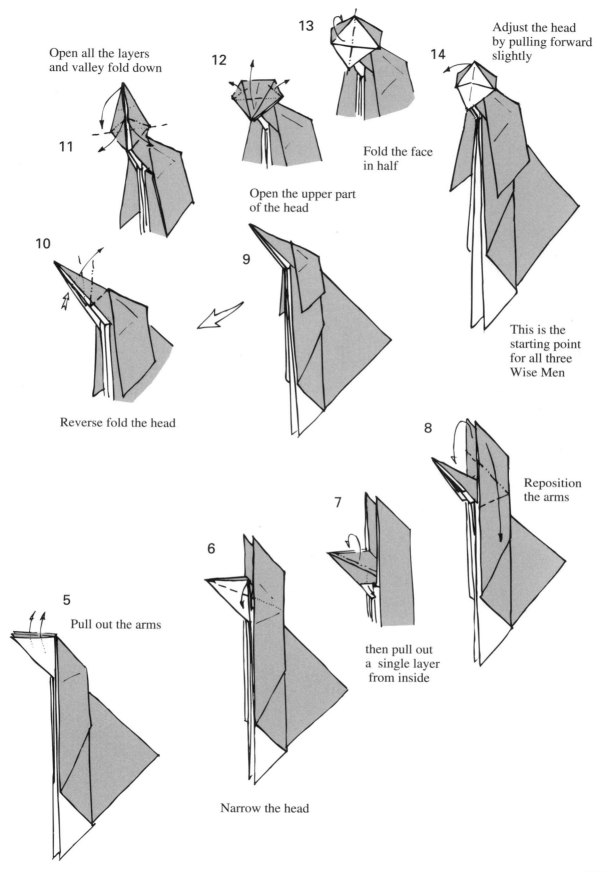

Open all the layers
and valley fold down

11

13

12

14

Adjust the head
by pulling forward
slightly

Fold the face
in half

Open the upper part
of the head

10

9

This is the
starting point
for all three
Wise Men

Reverse fold the head

8

Reposition
the arms

7

6

5

Pull out the arms

then pull out
a single layer
from inside

Narrow the head

205

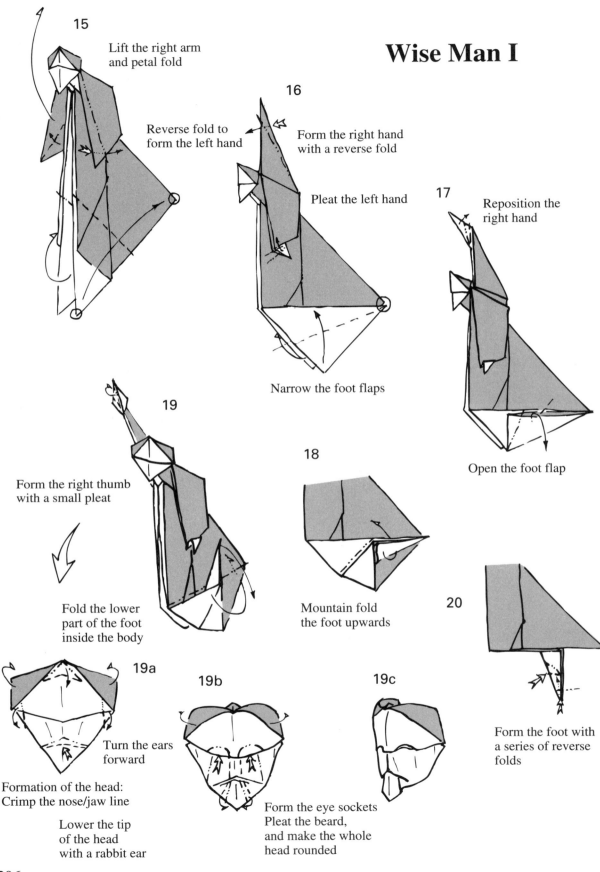

15

Lift the right arm
and petal fold

Wise Man I

16

Reverse fold to
form the left hand

Form the right hand
with a reverse fold

Pleat the left hand

17

Reposition the
right hand

Narrow the foot flaps

Open the foot flap

19

Form the right thumb
with a small pleat

Fold the lower
part of the foot
inside the body

18

Mountain fold
the foot upwards

20

19a

Turn the ears
forward

Formation of the head:
Crimp the nose/jaw line

Lower the tip
of the head
with a rabbit ear

19b

19c

Form the foot with
a series of reverse
folds

Form the eye sockets
Pleat the beard,
and make the whole
head rounded

Wise Man II

2

Pleat the hand

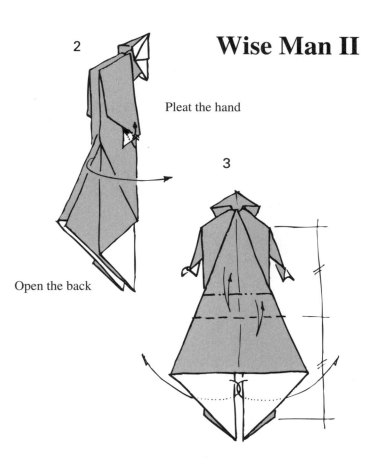

1

Reverse fold
the back

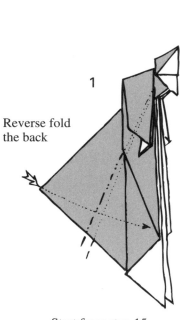

Open the back

Start from step 15
of the 1st Wise Man

3

Precrease the waist-
line folds then open
from the front

21

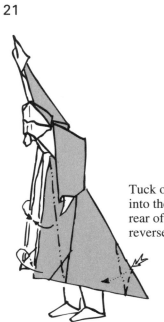

Tuck one side of the cloak
into the other: Form the
rear of the cloak with 2
reverse folds

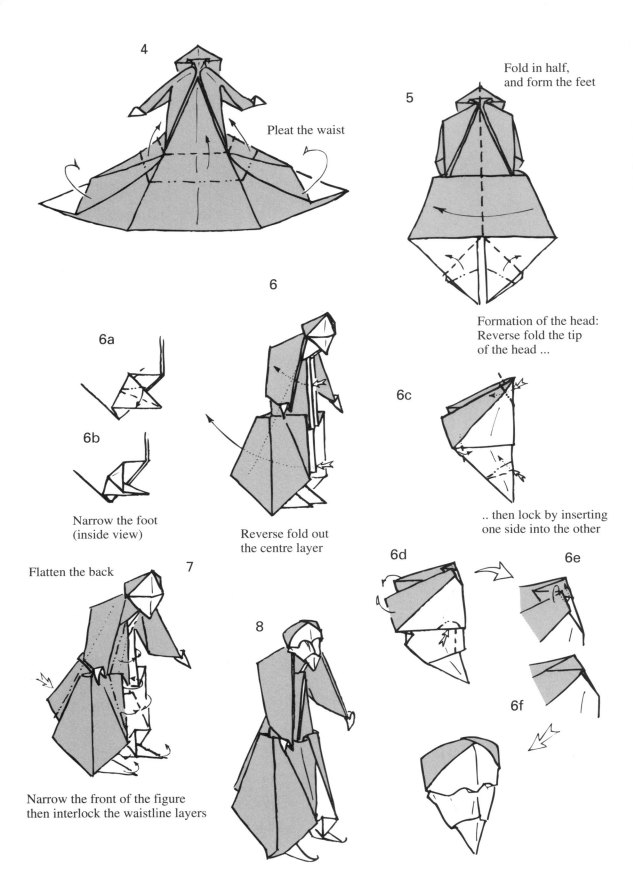

4

Pleat the waist

5

Fold in half,
and form the feet

6

6a

6b

Narrow the foot
(inside view)

Reverse fold out
the centre layer

Formation of the head:
Reverse fold the tip
of the head ...

6c

.. then lock by inserting
one side into the other

6d

6e

6f

Flatten the back

7

8

Narrow the front of the figure
then interlock the waistline layers

Wise Man III

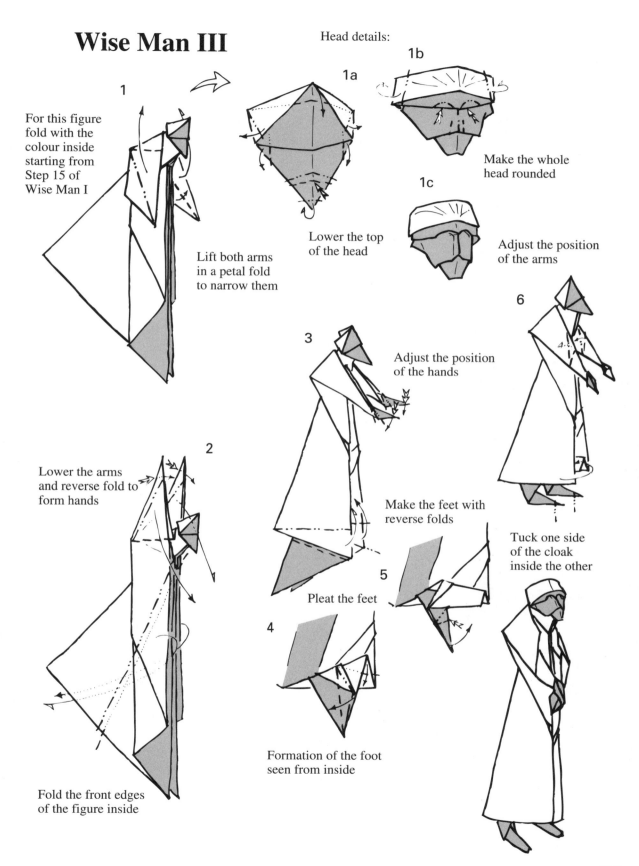

Head details:

1

For this figure fold with the colour inside starting from Step 15 of Wise Man I

1a

Lift both arms in a petal fold to narrow them

Lower the top of the head

1b

Make the whole head rounded

1c

Adjust the position of the arms

6

3

Adjust the position of the hands

2

Lower the arms and reverse fold to form hands

Make the feet with reverse folds

Tuck one side of the cloak inside the other

5

Pleat the feet

4

Formation of the foot seen from inside

Fold the front edges of the figure inside

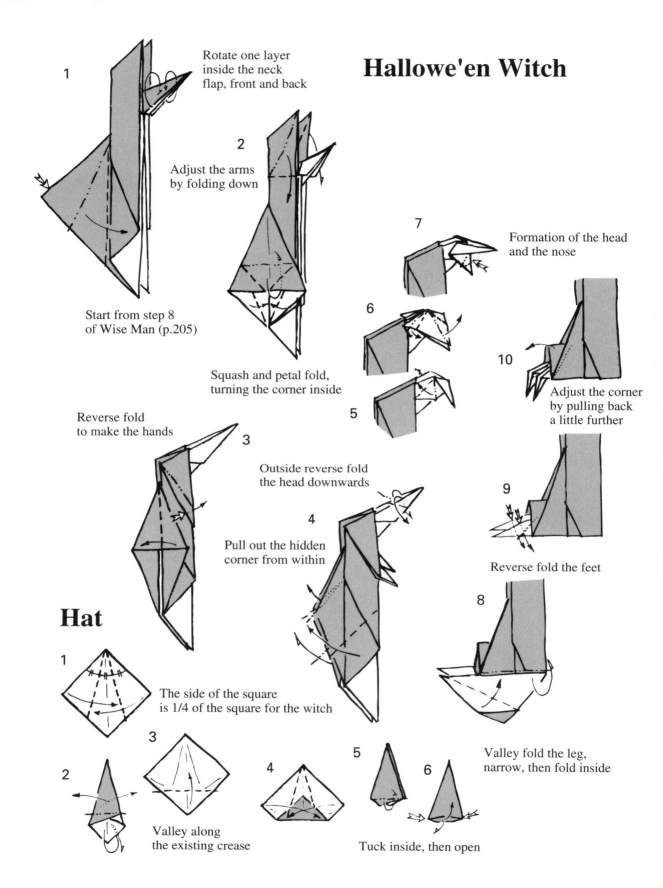

1 Rotate one layer inside the neck flap, front and back

Hallowe'en Witch

2 Adjust the arms by folding down

Start from step 8 of Wise Man (p.205)

Squash and petal fold, turning the corner inside

Reverse fold to make the hands

3

Outside reverse fold the head downwards

4 Pull out the hidden corner from within

7 Formation of the head and the nose

6

5

10 Adjust the corner by pulling back a little further

9 Reverse fold the feet

8

Hat

1 The side of the square is 1/4 of the square for the witch

2

3 Valley along the existing crease

4

5

6 Tuck inside, then open

Valley fold the leg, narrow, then fold inside

210

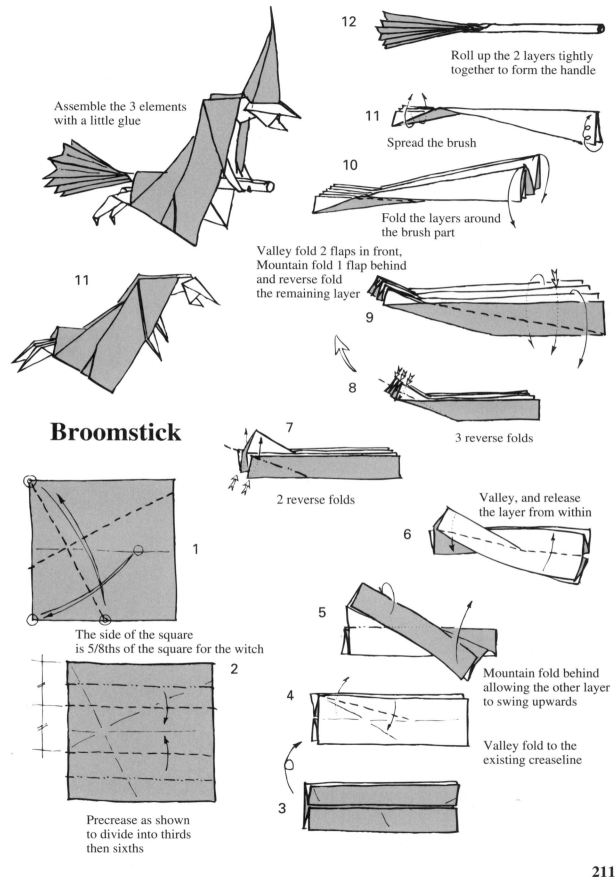

12

Roll up the 2 layers tightly together to form the handle

11

Spread the brush

10

Fold the layers around the brush part

Valley fold 2 flaps in front, Mountain fold 1 flap behind and reverse fold the remaining layer

9

Assemble the 3 elements with a little glue

11

8

7

3 reverse folds

2 reverse folds

Valley, and release the layer from within

6

Broomstick

5

1

The side of the square is 5/8ths of the square for the witch

Mountain fold behind allowing the other layer to swing upwards

Valley fold to the existing creaseline

2

4

3

Precrease as shown to divide into thirds then sixths

Showjumper

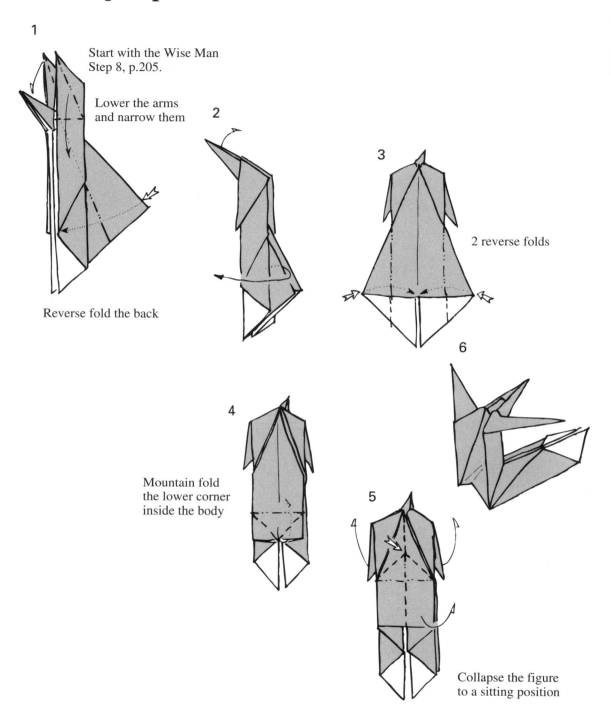

1

Start with the Wise Man
Step 8, p.205.

Lower the arms
and narrow them

Reverse fold the back

2

3

2 reverse folds

4

Mountain fold
the lower corner
inside the body

5

6

Collapse the figure
to a sitting position

To complete the Show jumper scene, make a Horse (p.168), and add
a small fence: I used a variation of Fujimoto's cube to make
the upright gate posts, adding strips to form the bars of the gate.

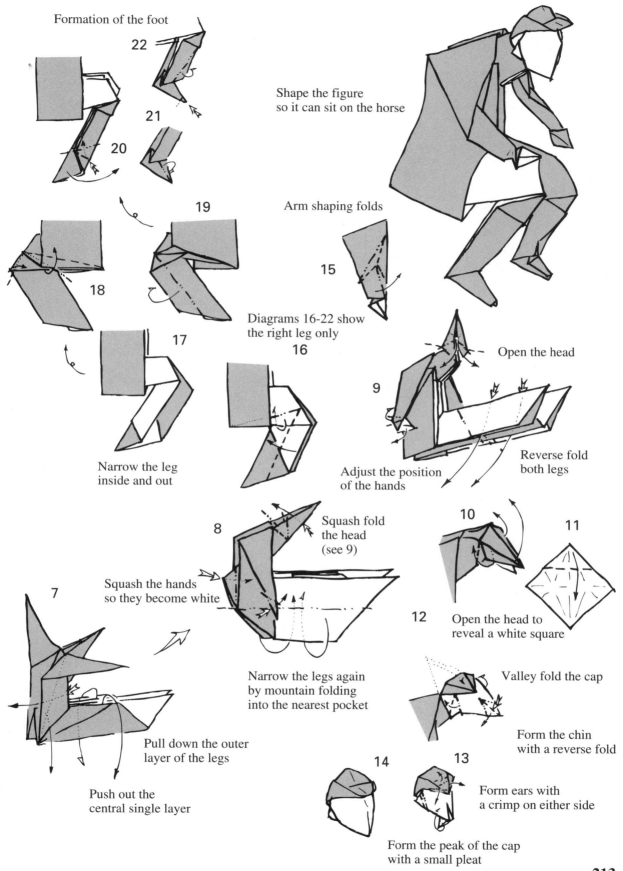

Formation of the foot

22

21

20

Shape the figure
so it can sit on the horse

19

Arm shaping folds

18

15

17

Diagrams 16-22 show
the right leg only

16

Narrow the leg
inside and out

9

Open the head

Reverse fold
both legs

Adjust the position
of the hands

8

Squash fold
the head
(see 9)

Squash the hands
so they become white

10

11

12

Open the head to
reveal a white square

7

Narrow the legs again
by mountain folding
into the nearest pocket

Valley fold the cap

Form the chin
with a reverse fold

Pull down the outer
layer of the legs

14

13

Form ears with
a crimp on either side

Push out the
central single layer

Form the peak of the cap
with a small pleat

St. George

Like the showjumper, St. George needs to be mounted on a Horse (p.168). The St. George and Dragon scene on the cover of this book is completed by a Dragon (p.172)

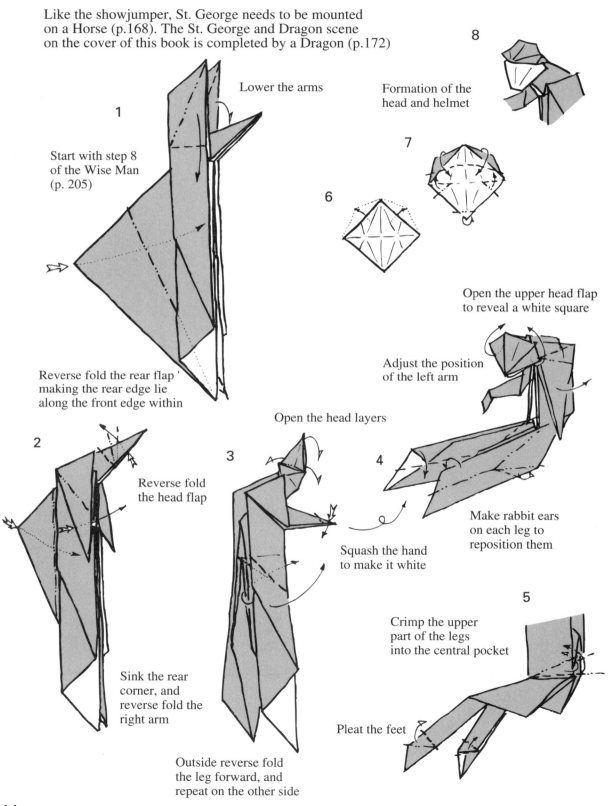

1

Start with step 8 of the Wise Man (p. 205)

Lower the arms

Reverse fold the rear flap making the rear edge lie along the front edge within

2

Reverse fold the head flap

Sink the rear corner, and reverse fold the right arm

3

Open the head layers

Squash the hand to make it white

Outside reverse fold the leg forward, and repeat on the other side

4

Open the upper head flap to reveal a white square

Adjust the position of the left arm

Make rabbit ears on each leg to reposition them

5

Crimp the upper part of the legs into the central pocket

Pleat the feet

6

7

8

Formation of the head and helmet

214

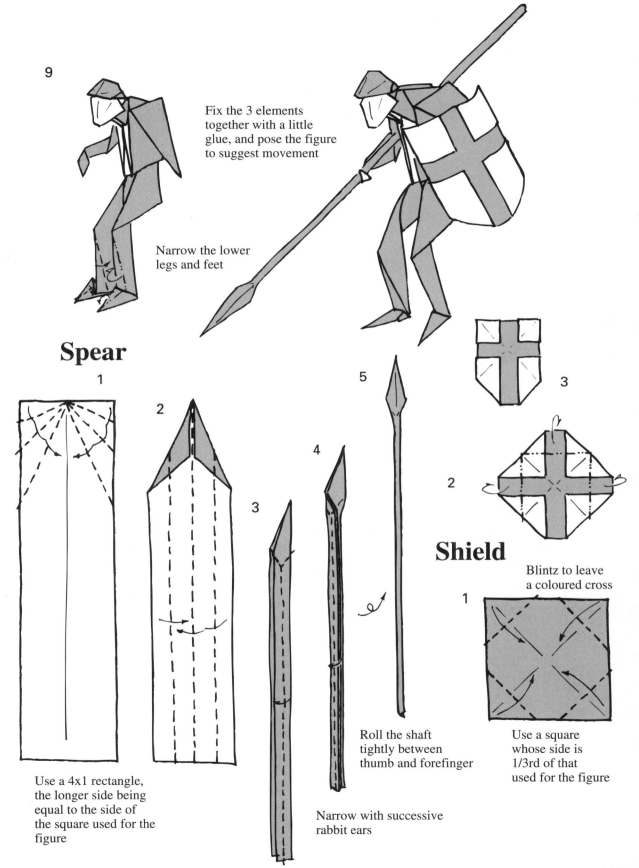

9

Fix the 3 elements together with a little glue, and pose the figure to suggest movement

Narrow the lower legs and feet

Spear

1

2

3

4

5

Use a 4x1 rectangle, the longer side being equal to the side of the square used for the figure

Narrow with successive rabbit ears

Roll the shaft tightly between thumb and forefinger

Shield

3

2

1

Blintz to leave a coloured cross

Use a square whose side is 1/3rd of that used for the figure

Geppetto

Start with a 2 x 1 rectangle: suggested size 16 x 8 inches (40 x 20 cm)

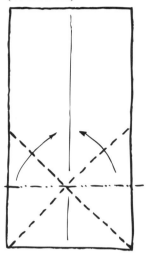

1

Fold a waterbomb base at one end of the rectangle

2

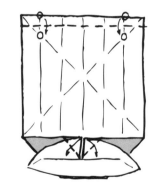

Sink the point

Precrease the other end of the rectangle into 1/6ths

3 Precrease 2 diagonals

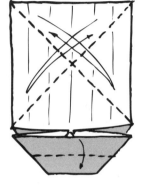

Fold down the raw edge

4

Valley fold the top edge and the 2 central corners

Mountain fold the 2 edges behind at each side

5

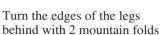

Turn the edges of the legs behind with 2 mountain folds

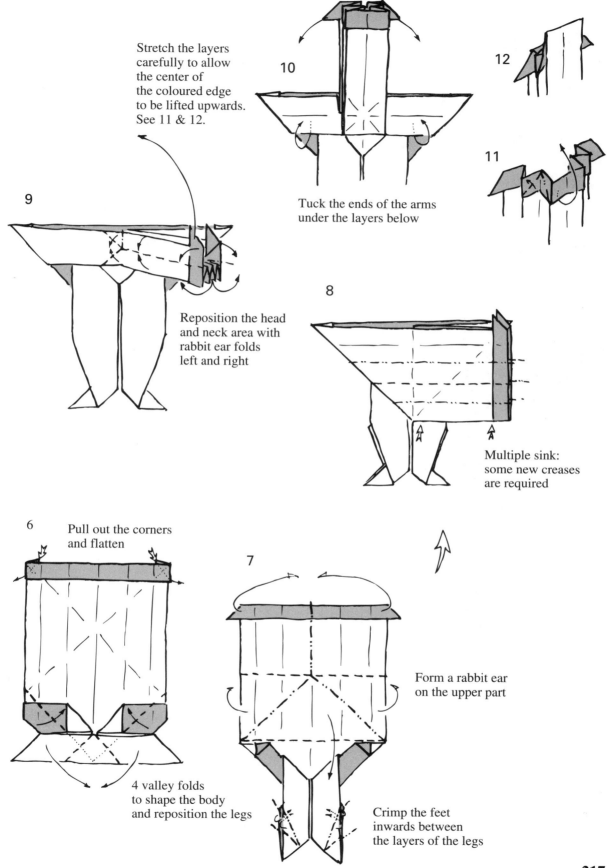

Stretch the layers
carefully to allow
the center of
the coloured edge
to be lifted upwards.
See 11 & 12.

10

12

11

Tuck the ends of the arms
under the layers below

9

Reposition the head
and neck area with
rabbit ear folds
left and right

8

Multiple sink:
some new creases
are required

6   Pull out the corners
and flatten

7

Form a rabbit ear
on the upper part

4 valley folds
to shape the body
and reposition the legs

Crimp the feet
inwards between
the layers of the legs

217

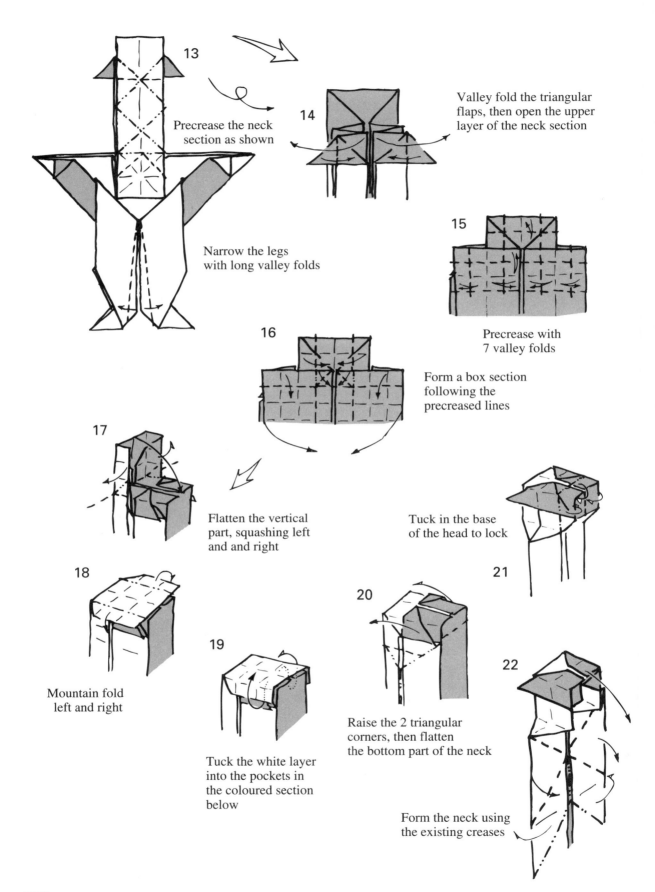

13 Precrease the neck section as shown

Narrow the legs with long valley folds

14 Valley fold the triangular flaps, then open the upper layer of the neck section

15 Precrease with 7 valley folds

16 Form a box section following the precreased lines

17 Flatten the vertical part, squashing left and and right

18 Mountain fold left and right

19 Tuck the white layer into the pockets in the coloured section below

20 Raise the 2 triangular corners, then flatten the bottom part of the neck

21 Tuck in the base of the head to lock

22 Form the neck using the existing creases

218

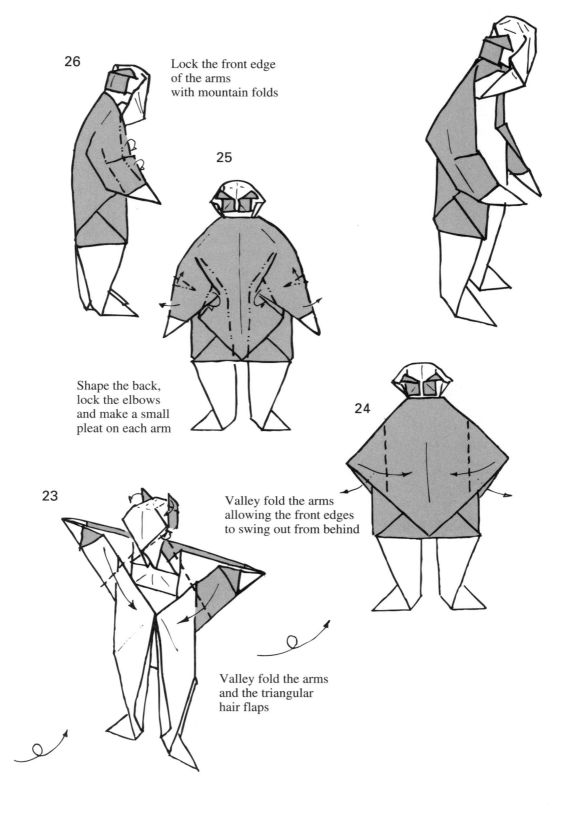

26 Lock the front edge
of the arms
with mountain folds

25

Shape the back,
lock the elbows
and make a small
pleat on each arm

24

Valley fold the arms
allowing the front edges
to swing out from behind

23

Valley fold the arms
and the triangular
hair flaps

Pinocchio

1

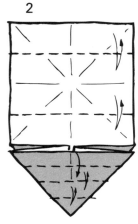

Start with a 2x1 rectangle
3/4 of the size used for
Geppetto

Precrease as shown,
then form a waterbomb
base at one end
of the rectangle

The figures of Geppetto and Pinocchio
were designed as entries for a competition
organised by the Gentro Diffusione Origami
in Florence, to celebrate the centenary of
the Pinocchio story, written by Collodi in
1883.

The scene, completed by the Spelling Book
(p.224), is taken from the beginning of the story.
Geppetto, returns home in the snow, having
sold his overcoat to buy a spelling book for
Pinocchio. His excuse to the enquiring puppet
is that he sold his coat because he was too hot.

My entry won the second prize in the Scene
category of the competition.
See p.14 for a photograph of the scene.

2

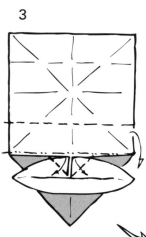

Precrease as shown
then fold down the
upper edge of the
waterbomb base

5

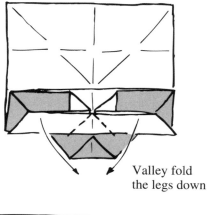

Valley fold
the legs down

3

Pleat behind
and valley fold
the corners

4

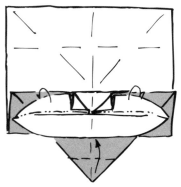

Mountain fold
the upper edge
of the waterbomb base
and turn up the lower
corner

220

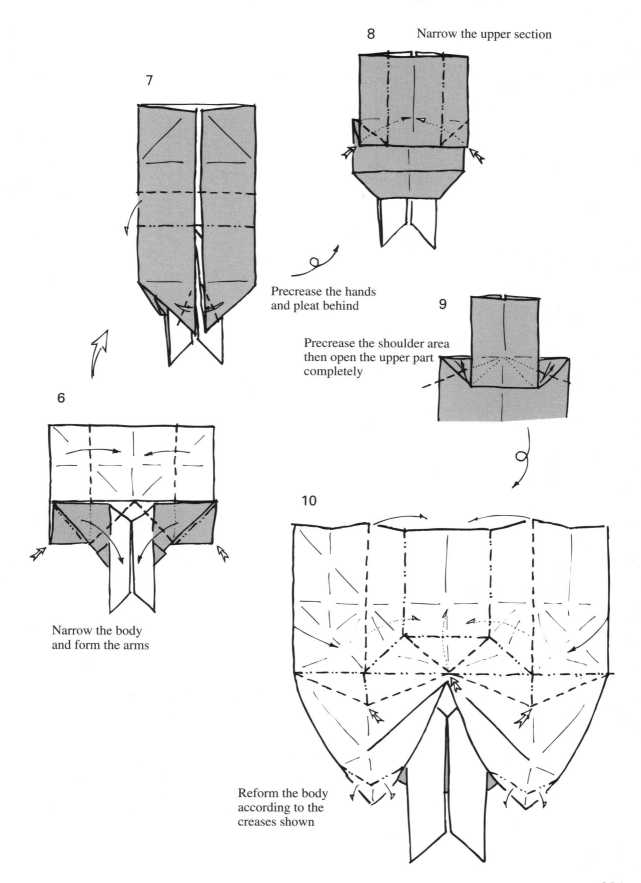

7

8 Narrow the upper section

Precrease the hands
and pleat behind

9

Precrease the shoulder area
then open the upper part
completely

6

Narrow the body
and form the arms

10

Reform the body
according to the
creases shown

Precrease the inside edges
of the arms, and form the
head and neck area as shown

Formation of the nose:
Make a rabbit-ear, then
narrow it as shown

13

14

12

Swing the nose through
the split in the face

Narrow the neck
and valley fold
the head forward

15

Continue to collapse the body
then form the feet with crimps

11

16

Tuck this corner behind

Insert one side
of the chin
into the other

17

18

19

Lock by folding
underneath

Pleat the arms

Pleat the ears

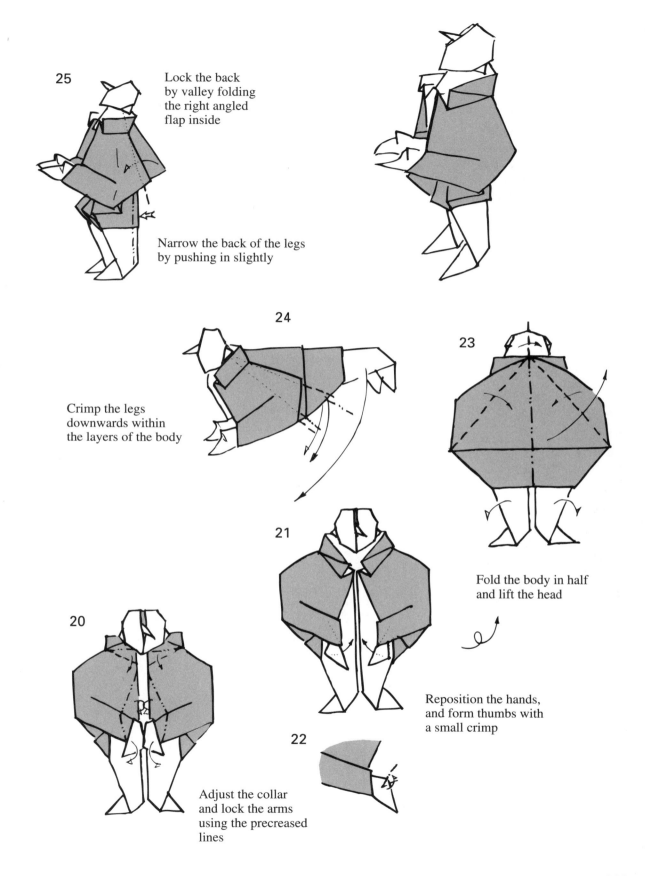

25

Lock the back
by valley folding
the right angled
flap inside

Narrow the back of the legs
by pushing in slightly

24

Crimp the legs
downwards within
the layers of the body

23

Fold the body in half
and lift the head

21

20

Reposition the hands,
and form thumbs with
a small crimp

22

Adjust the collar
and lock the arms
using the precreased
lines

10

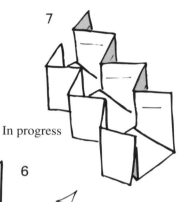

Tuck in
the top edge,
then swing the covers
over the pages

9

Reverse fold
the covers inside

Spelling Book

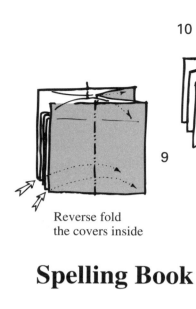

1

Precrease ...

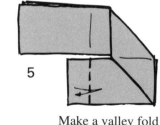

8

Valley fold
front and rear

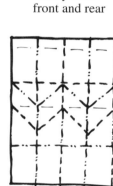

7

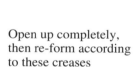

6

Open up completely,
then re-form according
to these creases

2

.. then pleat into 1/6ths

3

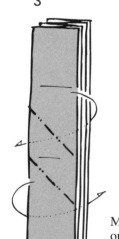

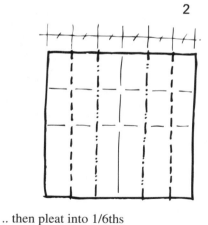

Mountain fold
on either side
of the centre line

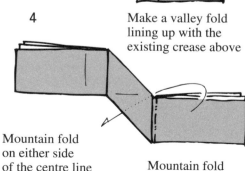

5

Make a valley fold
lining up with the
existing crease above

4

Mountain fold

224

Groups and Scenes

In this final chapter, I wanted to illustrate examples of collections of models grouped together to form a scene. Since my early attempts at origami, I have enjoyed combining my work collectively in this way. Sometimes the design has been intended to go together with a related fold, other times I have realized that some of the things I had already made complement each other well.

There is a danger in putting designs together, however. It is easy to cover up weaknesses of an individual model by linking it with some logical accompanying model, as if answering a question of identity of either of them: individually they may not be acceptable as completed designs, but collectively they may be. I have tried in these groups never to compromise the strength of the individual design, and my aim has been that it should stand up equally as a completed model in its own right.

Folding dosen't damage your health...
Cigarette Packet (p. 58), Matchbox (p. 62) and Ashtray (p. 226)

Ashtray

Precrease into quarters
in both directions
1   then add 4 more valley folds

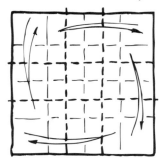

2

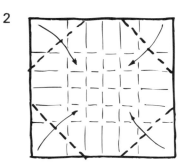

3

Precrease, then open completely

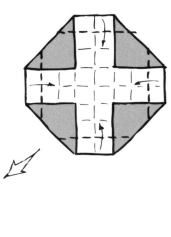

4

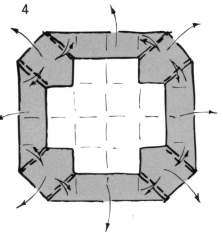

Use this ashtray to add to the
cigarette packet (p.58) and
the matchbox (p.62) to complete
the group which I call "Folding
doesn't damage your health".
Add an origami cigarette too:
I leave the design of this to
your imagination!

Precrease 4 valley folds
in the centre, then form
4 box-like structures at
each corner

5

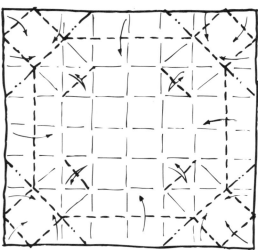

6

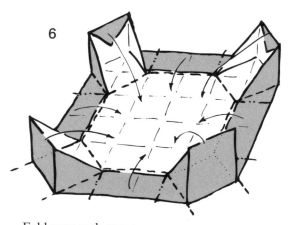

Fold over each corner
and the sides as shown

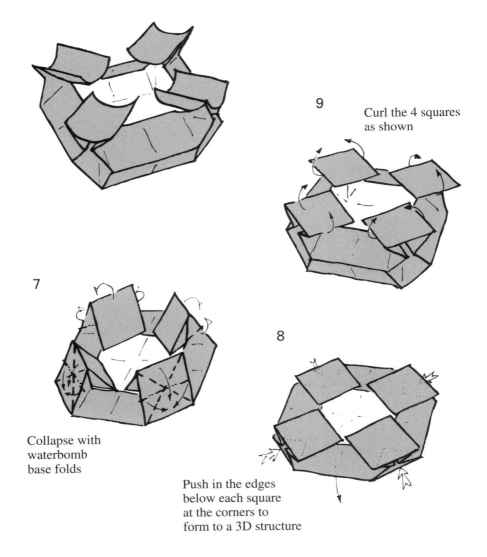

9

Curl the 4 squares
as shown

7

Collapse with
waterbomb
base folds

8

Push in the edges
below each square
at the corners to
form to a 3D structure

Reindeer

The Reindeer and the Sleigh on the following pages will complete the Christmas Eve scene of Father Christmas on his rounds. Make some box-like shapes such as traditional waterbombs for the packages on the sleigh.

Start with step 12 of the Fox (p.125)

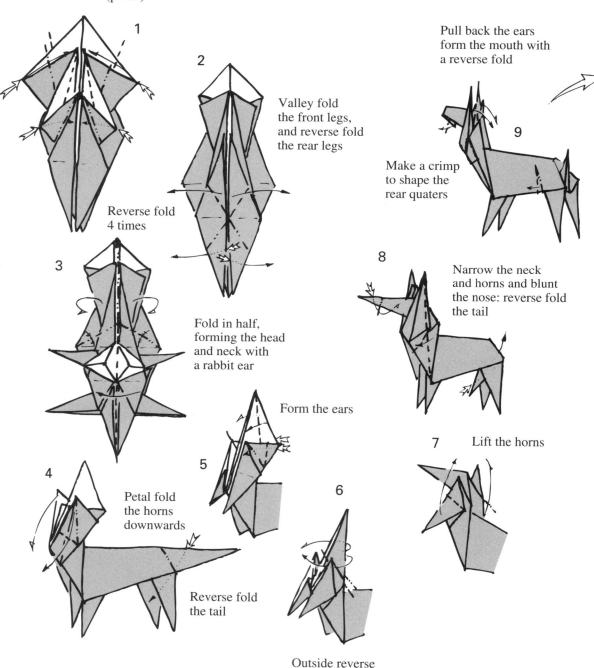

1

2

Valley fold the front legs, and reverse fold the rear legs

Reverse fold 4 times

3

Fold in half, forming the head and neck with a rabbit ear

Form the ears

Pull back the ears form the mouth with a reverse fold

9

Make a crimp to shape the rear quaters

8

Narrow the neck and horns and blunt the nose: reverse fold the tail

7   Lift the horns

4

Petal fold the horns downwards

5

6

Reverse fold the tail

Outside reverse fold the head

Crimp the head downwards

10

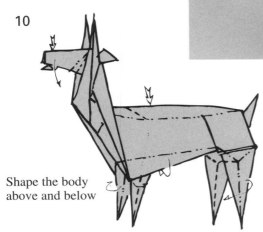

Shape the body
above and below

Narrow the legs
by forming rabbit ears

11

Soften the head
by pushing down
as indicated

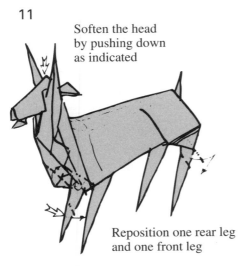

Reposition one rear leg
and one front leg

Tuck the front edges
of the body in
and around the legs

Sleigh

Use a 2x1 rectangle
the same size as for
Father Christmas

Precrease 2 diagonals
at one end of the strip
then valley fold in half

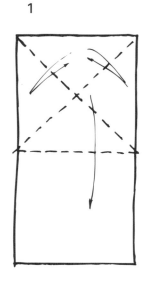

1

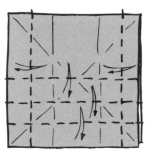

2

Precrease into 1/3rds
with mountain folds

3

Precrease with valley folds:
the horizontal creases are
on the upper layer only

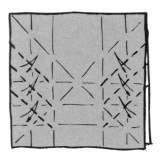

4

Add 6 diagonals on
the upper layer only

5

Now form into a 3D
structure, lifting away
the upper layer using
the indicated creases

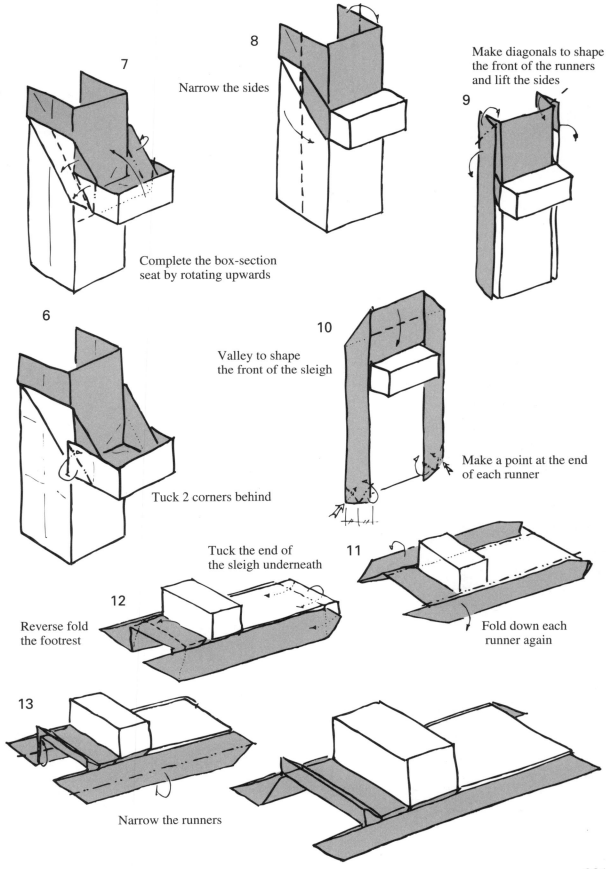

7

Complete the box-section
seat by rotating upwards

8

Narrow the sides

Make diagonals to shape
the front of the runners
and lift the sides

9

6

Tuck 2 corners behind

10

Valley to shape
the front of the sleigh

Make a point at the end
of each runner

Tuck the end of
the sleigh underneath

11

Fold down each
runner again

12

Reverse fold
the footrest

13

Narrow the runners

231

1

Valley fold twice

2

Connect opposite corners with a valley fold allowing the right angled corner behind to swing out

3

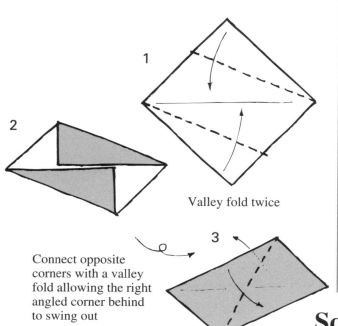

Square Silver Star

This modular star is the centre of attention of the Three Wise Men on pp.204-209.

Connect 4 units to begin the construction

Narrow the points

4

5

Precrease

6

7

Add 8 more units to finish the star: the points of the star form a cubic shape

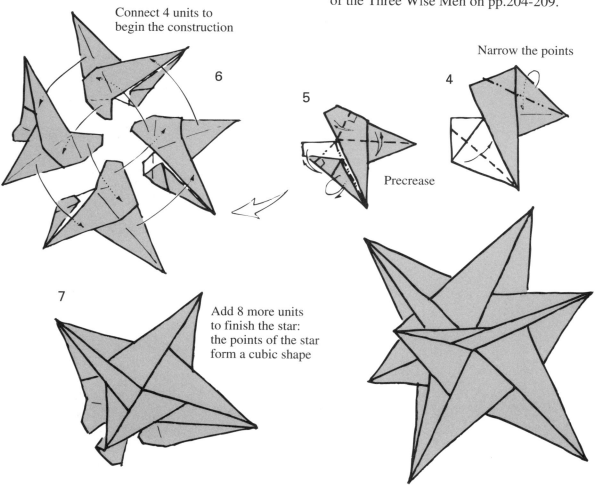

Rotating Double Cube Series

It is possible to adjust the positions of the two cubes of the Venetian Double Cube design by adjusting the size of the starting rectangle. The following drawings give a method of preparing the necessary rectangles for a series of three double cube variations.

You need to cut along one of the creases **a, b,** or **c** shown in diagram **3** to obtain each rectangle, and the subsequent drawings correspond with step **4** and **iv** in the folding sequence for the Venetian Double Cube.
Follow the remaining steps for the basic design to produce the three new double cube variations.

The drawings of the single cube shown on p.234 will enable you to complete a series of double cubes, in which one of the cubes emeres, and then appears to rotate progressively around the other.

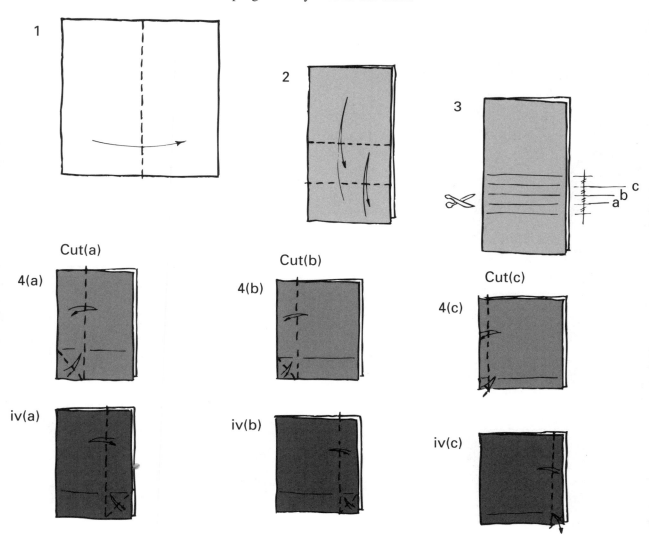

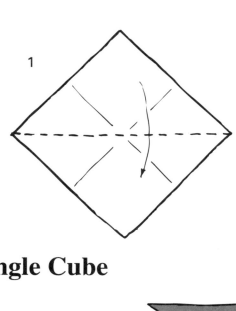

1

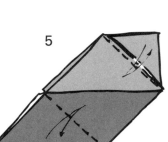

2

Reverse fold
the left hand point
Mountain fold one corner

Single Cube

3

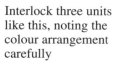

Interlock three units
like this, noting the
colour arrangement
carefully

4

Make a mirror-image
version of 2, turn over
and interlock the 2 pieces
so they are symmetrical

6

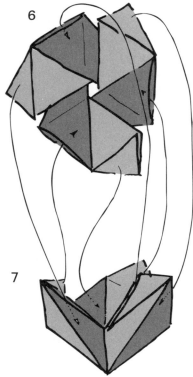

Make another three
unit combination,
this time having made
mountain folds in step 5,
and connect the two
halves of the cube
paying attention
to the colours as shown

5

Make 6 two-piece units
as above, then precrease

7

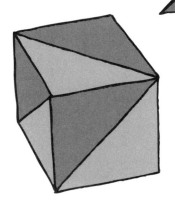

234

Ideas for Creative Approach

Many origami enthusiasts dismiss the possibility of their being able to originate new designs. I confess that before I made contact with the British Origami Society, I found myself unable to comprehend the method of creating. It seemed to me that in all the designs which I particularly admired there was no relation in the folded stages, or the process, to the finished model, and the paper never semed to show any likeness to the final stage until the last few steps. The creative process remained very much a mystery, and any success that I thought that I had had was usually an accident.

Meeting my contemporary creators, Max Hulme and Martin Wall, opened many doors for me. I was shown by them that folding a new design was quite a logical process, and analytical thinking was very much a part of creation. When I had folded from books, this was never obvious. Max and Martin rarely folded as I had done, doodling with the paper to see what possibilities could be identified, but had usually started with an idea for a subject, then analyzed its shape. Then they had tried to unfold it in the mind, or to apply a well-known personal formula to describe in folded form the characteristics of the subject which they wanted to portray. Max in particular seemed to have an uncanny ability to fold quite complicated subjects in his mind, then to achieve the result he wanted at the first folding attempt!

For me things were not so easy: I have always had to work long and hard at satisfying my aims. But I think there are ways in which a potential creator can prepare himself. Firstly, it is necessary to build up as wide a vocabulary of folding techniques as possible. This can itself be intensely enjoyable: folding everything one can find from books, and, in my case, from the rich resources of the British Origami Society's library.

I feel it helps to explore traditional techniques, working through all their possibilities, then to store them away in the mind. Maybe at some future date these can be extracted to be used in some new and original way. The inherent geometries of the paper should be respected, and where possible logical and direct folding sequences should be employed. I find it helps to fold quite carelessly at first until a logical result appears, at which time the design can be tidied up and economies employed. Sometimes it helps also to unfold the design in progress, and examine the crease pattern to see if there is a simpler approach or if unnecessary layers can be eliminated. Maybe also a different starting shape can yield a better proportion.

Keep a track on what is going on in the origami world: communicate with your contemporaries or rivals who will no doubt be willing to share ideas or pass comment on what you have done. You should listen to this criticism even if you don't agree with if: sleep on your ideas and your origami problems, and frequently the solution will arrive in the morning (or sometimes even in your dreams!) .

As I have already said it doesn't pay to force the paper to do what is unnatural to it and you should not impose yourself on the paper too much. Try cultivate the touch and respect for the medium in the way that the best folders do: avoid the mangled finished result. Sometimes it helps to be given a subject to fold with a tight deadline to meet: "Can you make me a bulldozer with a working shovel by a week next Thursday?!"

The creative aspect of origami is without doubt the most exciting and stimulating one: usually first your creations will make you very proud. It is only with the passage of time as your standards are raised that you may realize that your pride may have been a little misguided. In any case I do hope that the work I have shown you in this book may give you a little inspiration to try to work out some ideas for yourself: I hope that in this way you will receive as much pleasure and fulfillment from origami as I have done.

Contacts

The following English language associations exist to promote the knowledge of origami worldwide, and to put enthusiasts in touch with each other. Periodicals, origami literature and supplies are available from both. I strongly recommend that you make contact, and join. Write to either address for details of the many other origami groups in other countries.

British Origami Society
Penny Groom, Membership Secretary
2a The Chestnuts
Countesthorpe
Leicester
LE8 5TL
England

Origami USA
15 West 77 Street
New York
NY
10024-5192
USA

Bibliography

The following list is a collection of books about origami which I have, over the years, found inspiring. Generally I can recommend any the authors' work as being stimulating and enjoyable. Unfortunately not all these books may still be in print.

Luisa Canovi, Giovanni Ravesi and Dario Uri:
IL LIBRO DEI ROMPICAPO
(The book of Puzzles) Italian   Published by Sansoni Editore 1984
  Contains a section on modular origami by former CDO president Luisa Canovi.

Peter Engel:
FOLDING THE UNIVERSE   ISBN 0-394-75751-3
English   Published by Vintage Books New York 1989
  Detailed essays by the author on origami theories, creativity, as well as folding instructions for his own origami designs.

Shuzo Fujimoto:
CREATIVE INVITATION TO ORIGAMI PLAY
Japanese   Published privately 1982
  Many black and white photographs of geometric folds, boxes, molecular structures and translucent patterns.

Tomoko Fuse:
UNIT ORIGAMI
Japanese   Published by Chikuma Shobo, Tokyo 1983
UNIT ORIGAMI: Multi dimensional Transformations   ISBN 0-87040-852-6
English   Published by Japan Publications, Tokyo 1990
SINGLE SHEET BOXES   ISBN 0-480-87203-5
Japanese   Published by Chikuma Shobo, Tokyo 1992
  These three books give examples of the author's styles in modular solids, stars, and boxes in both units and single sheets.

Paul Jackson:
CLASSIC ORIGAMI   ISBN 0-792-45346-8
English   Published by Quintet Publishing Ltd 1992
  A collection of memorable designs, both traditional and contemporary.
THE ENCYCLOPAEDIA OF ORIGAMI AND PAPERCRAFT TECHNIQUES
                          ISBN 0-7472-0416-0
English   Published by Headline Books 1991
  A gallery of photographs of works of art made in a wide cross-section of paper techniques: details of how to make some of these are included.

Kunihiko Kasahara:
VIVA ORIGAMI   ISBN 0-376-83008-2831
Japanese   Published by Sanrio, Tokyo 1982
  A detailed collection of the technically-based work of Jun Maekawa
ORIGAMI OMNIBUS   ISBN 0-87040-699-4
English   Published by Japan Publications 1988
  A huge book describing the best of the author's origami

Kunihiko Kasahara and Toshie Takahama:
TOP ORIGAMI   ISBN 4-387-85096-5
Japanese   Published by Sanrio, Tokyo 1985
republished in English as:
ORIGAMI FOR THE CONOISSEUR   Published by Japan Publications 1988
                                          ISBN 0-87040-670-1
  Modern stimulating designs from around the world

Eric Kenneway:
FOLDING FACES   ISBN 0-448-22557-3
English   Published by Paddington Press 1988
  Includes explanations of Kenneway's "rogues gallery" of caricature famous faces.
COMPLETE ORIGAMI
English   Published by Ebury Press 1987
  Not only a book of instructions, but also an encyclopaedia of origami history
and interesting facts.

Yoshihide Momotani:
ORIGAMI TALES OF OLD JAPAN
Japanese   Published by Seibundo Shinko Sha 1979
  How to fold scenes to illustrate traditional Japanese stories.
ORIGAMI IMAGE AND CREATION   ISBN 2072-500202-4202
Japanese   Published by Shogen Sha 1975
  The author's origami style thoroughly illustrated.

Samuel Randlett:
THE BEST OF ORIGAMI
English   Published by Faber and Faber 1964
A fine collection of designs from the creative period of the 1960's.

Toshie Takahama:
CREATIVE LIFE WITH CREATIVE ORIGAMI Vol II   ISBN 0372-07510-7911
Japanese   Published by Mako Sha 1975
  Shows the author's most decorative work, including animal families, Japanese
playing cards, and Noshi

Akira Yoshizawa:
ORIGAMI DOKUHON I   ISBN 1072-0030-0952
Japanese   Published by Kamakura Shobo 1969
  A classic early book by Yoshizawa explaining his principles for folding animals
and natural forms.
CREATIVE ORIGAMI   ISBN 4-14-031028-6
Japanese   Published by NHK 1984
  The author's largest book full of superb photographs of his extraordinary work,
and many well-described folding instructions.

INDEX